DORSET'S
1939-4

RODNEY LEGG

THE WINCANTON PRESS
OLD NATIONAL SCHOOL, NORTH STREET
WINCANTON, SOMERSET BA9 9AT

DORSET'S WAR

INTERNATIONAL STANDARD BOOK NUMBER 0 948699 02 7

First published 1986. Copyright Rodney Legg © 1986.
All rights reserved. No part of this publication may be reproduced, stored in a retrieval system, or transmitted in any form or by any means, electronic, computerised, mechanical, photocopying, recording or otherwise without prior permission in writing from the copyright owner.

Typeset in 11/12 pt ITC Clearface, by Ian R. Pratt at PCS Typesetting, Stoke House, Christchurch Street West, Frome, Somerset.
Layout and design by the author at The Wincanton Press.
Negatives assembled by Andrew Johnstone and Jonathan Bristow at Wincanton Litho, Wincanton, Somerset, where the book was printed on 115 grams/m^2 Ski-Blade Matt cartridge paper by Steve Taylor, for binding at the Castle Cary Press.

*'I vow to thee, my country—
all earthly things above—
entire and whole and perfect
the service of my love...
And her ways are ways of
gentleness, and all her
paths are peace.'*
—Sir Cecil Spring-Rice

Note about ranks.
Ranks, titles, commands and decorations are as they were at the relevant date — rather than those which were attained later in careers.

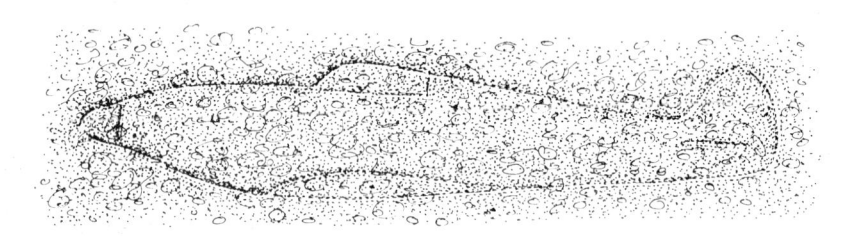

1944. Warmwell Spitfire etched in wet cement by Bere Regis boy Fred Pitfield who is mentioned opposite.

Also by Rodney Legg

Purbeck Island
Ghosts of Dorset, Devon and Somerset
Editor *Steep Holm—a case history in the study of ecology*
Annotator *Monumenta Britannica* with John Fowles
Exploring Ancient Wiltshire with George Osborn
Old Portland with Jean M. Edwards
Romans in Britain
Purbeck Walks
Old Swanage
The Dorset Walk with Ron Dacombe, Colin Graham
The Stonehenge Antiquaries
Guide to Purbeck Coast and Shipwreck
Hardy Country Walks
The Steep Holm Guide
Lulworth and Tyneham Revisited
Walks in West Dorset
The Blandford Forum Guide
National Trust Dorset with Colin Graham
Purbeck's Heath and Brownsea Island
Exploring the Heartland of Purbeck

About the Foreword:

*Written on the northern slope of
Black Hill at Bere Regis, whilst watching
fox cubs play. There it became possible
to piece together reflections on the war
whilst having an open love affair with
the illusion of nature at peace.*

Foreword

I HAVE no qualifications for writing this book; I was not alive at the time. Even when I came along in the post-war baby boom it was as a probable mistake to an almost middle aged Bournemouth ex-ARP warden rather than one of those infantrymen who was commemorating his first home leave from the Dorsetshire Regiment in six years.

As I grew up the physical signs of war were part of daily life. There was the air-raid shelter beneath the garden shed at 21 Easter Road in Moordown. Its timbers came from Bournemouth Pier, breached as was Boscombe Pier to prevent utilisation by invading Germans. A stirrup pump and bucket provided the fun way to water the plants and anyone venturing out of the house.

Opposite Alma Road Schools was a gaping bomb site with rose-bay willow herb seeding from the basement brickwork. There were similar holes in the central townscape around the Square, in Richmond Hill, Exeter Road, Old Christchurch Road and the Lansdowne.

My first lengthy free-choice writing at school was about the war, chronologically like this except we knew next to nothing then of local events and thought of everything interesting as belonging to distant places. It appalled Miss Thomas, my second teacher. Left-handed writing was enough to do that in itself; she would not have us writing about the war, and certainly not with a left-hand. The other thing I remember from her is the promise that we shall be reunited with our pets when we go to heaven. I would like that.

In those days I could draw a passable Spitfire that no one then would mistake for a Hurricane, though I had seen neither. We envied those who had. Nine-year-old Fred Pitfield of Bere Regis had watched the Warmwell pilots winning the Battle of Britain and in 1944 shown his future double destiny as a draughtsman and historian by etching a Spitfire for posterity in the wet cement of a wall by the watercress beds.

Twenty-five years later and his left-handed son, John, at a similar age would be making his streaks directly in the sky with practical rocketry. It was friendship with John Pitfield that made this book possible because he alone among the younger people I know does not share the fashionable view that war is somehow vulgar and unmentionable. Perhaps that's because he also has brown eyes. He pointed out that war is a human failing but it can bring out the best in people. It was enough encouragement, not that I needed much as I feel at ease with active history and find lively doing minds much more stimulating than the lumpish proletariat who have come to be regarded as the true meat of history.

To write another book was to resume a self-imposed exile from life and it was somehow reassuring to know that John was also lying on his bed scribbling away in private. His research, in rocket propulsion, has the discipline of precision that I now try to bring to local history. Having listened for years to a general muddle of folktales I decided that with this book I would curtail the material to hard information. There could still be anecdotes, but they would be ones to which someone could put a date and a place.

Disappointingly, I found that upon the slightest degree of questioning the majority of informants became vague and inconsistent. Worse were those who implied they had information of a higher quality but cultivated a reluctance to reveal anything at all. One West Howe worker who had made airborne H2S radar apparatus determindly took his non-secrets to the grave. In 1966 he refused even to admit the apparatus was a radar set—though the Commander-in-Chief of Bomber Command, Sir Arthur Harris, had published pages on it in 1947. In 1966 I never knew the right reply: "Their lipstick stinks!" For airborne radar was codenamed H2S, a chemical notable for its smell, and by that time the wartime factory was producing cosmetics for Max Factor.

My other reservation about selective memories is that a scientific survey has shown how faulty they can become after four decades. War records of semi-prominent people, some of the good and locally great who are the mainstay of parochial society, were compared with what they now remembered having done during the war. Not only had major decisions, which were preserved above their signatures, been purged from their minds but a high proportion had forgotten the titles or even the existence of posts they had held and committees on which they served. Separate incidents had been merged, condensed and transposed to produce a rounded story. It is the stuff of a Viking saga; but we no longer live in imaginative times.

That said, I am nonetheless hoping that some readers will write to me via the publishers with experiences or documents to which they can provide a date so that these can be incorporated in a future reprint. There is also scope for detailed recollections that can flesh-out some of my terseness.

One of my little satisfactions has been to learn something about the occasional quiet hero of my chance acquaintanceship. "I'd like to see it in print before I go," Eric Wilson told me about a manuscript of his. "Why," I replied, "won't you get a third chance?" To his surprise I knew that he had returned from the dead in British Somaliland to find he had been awarded a posthumous VC.

As for my opinions about the war there are none in the body of the book. Anything that sounds like comment is contemporary and therefore pre-dates me. I shall, however, inflict a few thoughts here that are entirely hindsight.

To grossly over-simplify the whole thing I believe that the British won the Second World War by cheating and the Russians with blood. Our secret game was deciphering the enemy's coded communications, enabling strategic anticipation and giving Churchill the smug satisfaction of knowing his opponents' minds. The other great contribution, under-estimated from our Atlantic viewpoint, was the practical one of the Soviet Union in clogging two-thirds of the German war-machine with their contribution of seven million dead and fourteen million wounded. That's not to belittle the Americans and their 290,000 dead and armaments on a scale that only they can produce. It is to think that all else in reality was a sideshow; though if there is another life George Patton will have fitted out Saint Michael with the finest tank division of the celestial skies.

Even with defeat the Second World War would make this Hitler's century. His visions have prevailed. Poland was no more free on VE Day than it had been when Britain declared war on its behalf. A barrier on political thought came down across the centre of Europe and communism could no longer expand—as we so often delude ourselves—but was henceforth under siege. Likewise imperialism. The Victorian dream of a British Empire was sadly shown to be a monumental bluff. The Jews, converted by Hitler into Zionists, gained their own state in the Holy Land. The successors to the V2 rocket would let men walk on the moon. Hitler's Germans would be rewarded by the highest living standards in Europe and out of anger could come reconciliation, to the extent that Swanage families such as Bob and Merle Chacksfield would twin their town with Rüdesheim-am-Rhein.

Western technology, if you want me to acknowledge an American contribution, provided a couple of atomic bangs but by then the other war in the Far East was already ending. I will not, however, condemn those bombs with our specious current morality. For if you send fighting men thousands of miles to risk death on your behalf there is an obligation to do anything in your power that may help to bring them back alive.

The descendants of those weapons are set to give us fifty years of peace in Europe and the North Atlantic. They were perfected in time to remove the threat that was hanging over my childhood: "Wait till your call-up papers come. National Service is going to sort you out!" I cannot claim that we have become the generation that renounced war, but by conscious decision or otherwise we make it in other ways and in other continents.

R.L.

Avro Anson: flying from Warmwell.

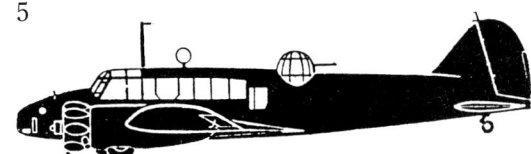

1939

January Hawks and doves.

The politicians have split into the hawks and the doves. Viscount Cranborne, South Dorset's MP, cautions Wyke Regis Women's Institute about the threat posed by Hitler and Mussolini: "These dictators have tasted blood and have applied a policy of force and had considerable effect with it. We must make England an impregnable fortress."

Clement Attlee, the leader of the Labour opposition, was a little less specific when he addressed farm workers in the Corn Exchange, Dorchester: "People may ask what I would have done at Munich. Suppose you had a man who was driving a heavy lorry. He drove it mile after mile on the wrong side of the road, and after narrowly missing other vehicles, came to a position where a collision seemed inevitable, swerved and ran over a child. You might ask me what I would have done had I been driving. I would not have driven on the wrong side of the road. The trouble is that the government has been driving on the wrong side. I would remind you that the right side for an Englishman to drive on is the left." It is not, however, a time when Europe is keeping to the left.

18 March Dorchester Evacuation Committee prepared for 4,612.

A survey of parishes in the Dorchester Rural District, in which Abbotsbury and Maiden Newton are the only significant places that have failed to respond, shows that a total of 4,612 evacuees could be accommodated in the area. Dorchester Evacuation Committee has reservations, however, and will tell the Ministry of Health that water supplies and sanitary facilities are inadequate.

2 June Reception Areas prepare for evacuees.

Billeting Officers met with local government officials for a conference at Dorchester today to discuss how the Reception Areas would handle their expected influx of children evacuated from London. The local reception centre is Maud Road School in Dorchester, which will provide light refreshments and disperse the youngsters with a bag of food each that is sufficient for forty-eight hours.

It was agreed to send 1,600 children into the borough of Dorchester, 1,900 to the surrounding rural district, and 1,300 into the Beaminster area.

June Anti-aircraft guns issued at Poole.

The 310th Anti-Aircraft Battery, which has 130 recruits training at the Mount Street drill hall in Poole, has been issued with the new 3.7 inch AA guns.

June Territorial gunners reorganised.

The 375th and 376th Queen's Own Dorset Yeomanry Batteries, with recruits from Shaftesbury, Blandford and Sherborne, have been amalgamated. The new Territorial Army unit will retain the historic name, as the 141st (Queen's Own Dorset Yeomanry) Field Regiment, Royal Artillery.

Likewise the 218th Field Battery, based in the Drill Hall at the Lansdowne, Bournemouth, has merged with the Dorchester and Bridport 224th (Dorset) Field Battery to form the 94th (Dorset and Hants) Field Regiment, Royal Artillery.

June 1st Dorsets garrison Malta.

The 1st Battalion of the Dorsetshire Regiment have arrived in the Grand Harbour, Valetta, aboard the troopship *Neuralia* from Bombay. They had been serving in India since 1936. These Regular Army soldiers are to man the south-eastern sector of the island's defences.

July Huge tented camp sprouts across Blandford downland.

Race Down, to the east of Blandford, is smothered with more than a hundred marquees and five hundred smaller tents concentrated across the former hutted lines around Cuckoo Clump that were used in the Great War to train the Royal Naval Division who landed at Gallipoli in the Dardanelles.

It was here, it is said, that Sub Lieutenant Rupert Brooke wrote those immortal lines: "If I should die, think only this of me: That there's some corner of a foreign field that is for ever England."

The mobilisation this time is for a Militia Camp to provide volunteers with basic physical and weapons training in a gentler introduction to the military life.

1 August 5th Dorsets reformed.

The 5th Battalion of the Dorsetshire Regiment, a Territorial unit many of whose volunteers are from Poole, has been reformed under the command of Colonel Sir John Lees. It is part of the 43rd (Wessex) Division.

3 August 'War today . . . is unlikely'—Defence Minister.

"War today is not only not inevitable but is unlikely. The Government have good reason for saying that."—Sir Thomas Inskip, the Minister of Defence.

9 August The King at Weymouth—'It's raining everywhere.'

Thousands of visitors pack Weymouth to see King George VI visit the town for a review of the Reserve Fleet which is being mobilised in Portland Harbour. For most in the Royal Navy Volunteer Reserve the last summer of the Thirties has already ended, but on shore the holidaymakers are having their last fling. An estimated 45,000 converged on the station and the situation was worsened by the delay to trains that the royal visit caused. Many fainted in the crush and the St John Ambulance Brigade commandeered the waiting room and parcels office as a field hospital for casualties.

As for the King, he failed to see the ships off Bincleaves because of mist and drizzle. The Mayor expressed regrets about the rain. "Don't worry, Mr Mayor," the King replied, "it's raining everywhere."

13 August Blackout, sirens and Portland mock battle.

Air raid sirens have sounded across south Dorset at 00.15 hours this Sunday and a blackout is being enforced. The lights have gone out on the ships of the Reserve Fleet at anchor in Portland Harbour and there is the drone of air activity. Destroyers are being deployed as 'enemy' vessels to test the defences at the entrance to the harbour. In the villages the death-bells tolled and bewildered country people staggered out of bed to find out what was happening. In Weymouth the news had already got around, or at least among those who had been out on the town, dancing and drinking or laughing with Elsie and Doris Waters. There was a noticeable absence of sailors about last night.

1939. Chickerell Camp. 4th Battalion Dorsetshire Regiment queue for the cookhouse.

1939. Bovington Camp. Toast from the tank crews.

1939. Radipole. Weymouth boys carry gas-masks.

DORSET'S WAR

30 August **Dorchester councillors consider 'war imminent'.**

Dorchester Rural District Council has decided that "in view of the imminent outbreak of war, that the whole power of the council so far as allowed by law, be delegated to an Emergency Committee until further orders".

August **Imperial Airways becomes BOAC and moves to Poole.**

The amalgamated Imperial and British Airlines are to be known from the beginning of next year as the British Overseas Airways Corporation, which will operate under the chairmanship of Lord Reith, the founder of the BBC. Its fleet of Short C-class 'Empire' flying boats is being moved with their support facilities from Hythe on Southampton Water to Poole Harbour.

Here Salterns Pier and its club rooms have been requisitioned from the Poole Harbour Yacht Club and water runways, or 'trots' as they are called, are being marked out by lines of tyres in the Wareham Channel off Hamworthy and the Main Channel between Salterns and Brownsea Island. The yacht club is now the Marine Terminal.

Footnote Airways House was opened in a Poole shop, 4 High Street, and the showrooms at Poole Pottery became the reception area and customs clearance point for incoming passengers. Harbour Heights Hotel was to become the rest centre for those due to embark from Salterns Pier on early morning flights.

August **Ansons bomb Warmwell 'factory'.**

217 Squadron, flying Avro Ansons, is now operational for coast patrols at the aerodrome to the east of Dorchester near Warmwell, where the Royal Air Force set up its school for air firing in May 1937. Their last public display as the Warmwell Armament Training Squadron was a bombing exercise for a 10,000 crowd at the open day. Five Ansons came in and a bomb was dropped on a make-believe factory, a building on the other side of the grass airfield, as the attacking planes were buzzed by three Hurricanes. One of the Ansons was 'disabled' and forced to land. Forty planes took part in the day, including a squadron of Singapore reconnaissance flying boats from Southampton Water.

There will be more practice bombs heard in Dorset as the Air Ministry has announced that sixteen square miles of Lyme Bay, lying six miles off Lyme Regis, will be designated as a bombing range for daylight use. A limit of 120 lb has been imposed on the live bombs that can be dropped.

An inland bombing range is being established on Crichel Down, in the parish of Long Crichel, on the foothills of Cranborne Chase.

August **Christchurch 'death-rays' zap the newspapers.**

Sensational stories are appearing in the national newspapers that the Air Defence Research and Development Establishment at Somerford, Christchurch, has perfected the "death ray". This is an intensely strong electromagnetic wave which, it is said, can heat up anything in its path— including living tissue—to the point at which it explodes.

Footnote This was no precurser of the laser or star-wars. As long ago as 1935, Skip Wilkins had demonstrated at the Radio Research Establishment, at Slough, that the energy need for death rays was way beyond current technology. It was, on the other hand, a convenient cover story for the development of radar systems.

August **Horse-drawn wagons bring out Blandford spoil.**

Contractors with convoys of horse-drawn wagons are removing thousands of tons of earth and chalk from the site of the military encampment that is to be constructed across Race Down to the east of Blandford.

1 September **The lights go out.**

A full blackout will be enforced from today. All street lighting and illuminated advertisements are being turned off and curtaining must be made light-tight to prevent any seepage through windows. Regulation masks are to be fitted to car headlights and sidelight lenses must also be dimmed with double sheets of paper.

3 September **War is declared at 11.15.**

This Sunday morning war hums through military communication lines from 10.00 hours as all units are informed that unless Germany pledges to remove her troops from Poland, war is to be declared by Great Britain. At 11.15 the Prime Minister, Neville Chamberlain, broadcasts to the nation on the wireless from the Cabinet Room in Number Ten Downing Street:

"This morning the British Ambassador in Berlin handed the German Government a final Note stating that unless we heard from them by eleven o'clock that they were prepared at once to withdraw their troops from Poland a state of war would exist between us.

"I have to tell you now that no such undertaking has been received, and that consequently this country is at war with Germany.

"You can imagine what a bitter blow it is to me that all my long struggle to win peace has failed . . ."

4 September **Dorset's first 4,000 evacuees.**

There are already four thousand evacuees in Dorset, mainly children from London, and the number is increasing by every train. Billeting allowances are 8s 6d a head to the host families. Many schools are so overcrowded that shift systems are being introduced, the local children coming for the mornings and evacuees in the afternoon.

13 September **Dorchester girls deliver 14,000 gas masks.**

Volunteers at Dorchester are distributing 14,000 gas-masks and twenty-four men came to the council's depot in Poundbury Road and offered to fill sandbags. By the end of the day they had stacked five thousand.

The ladies are helping too, particularly the staff and pupils of the Dorset County School for Girls who are cycling the district delivering gas-masks. Many have been assembled by the inmates of Dorchester Prison.

16 September **Belgian steamer blown up off Portland.**

The 6,000 ton Belgian passenger liner *Alex van Opstal*, empty and homeward bound to Antwerp from New York, was blown up today by a German mine south of the Shambles, Portland. All forty-nine crew and eight passengers were saved though six have been detained in hospital in Weymouth. They were rescued by a Greek steamer.

The explosions, heard in Weymouth, are the first to be experienced in Dorset from the current hostilities.

23 September **2nd Dorsets on their way to France.**

The 2nd Battalion of the Dorsetshire Regiment today left Aldershot on their way to join the British Expeditionary Force in France.

24 September **Prayer is the best weapon.**

It is three Sundays on from the declaration of war upon Germany. Adela Curtis, the Christian mystic writer, has told her sisters of the Christian Contemplatives' Charity at St Bride's Farm, Burton Bradstock, that she abhors pacificism and regards "the most effective of all weapons in our warfare" as "faithful prayer".

September **Training for AA duties (without a gun).**

A Royal Artillery anti-aircraft regiment is giving basic training to recruits at Blandford Camp; very basic training, in fact, as it lacks any operational gun with which to put them through their paces.

1 October **Hitler's coffee beans impounded at Weymouth.**

In the first four weeks of war a thousand tons of contraband cargo that was intended for Germany has been confiscated, mainly from neutral vessels, and impounded at Weymouth. A total of 513,000 tons had been searched in seventy-four ships that were bound for European ports.

The prize must go to ten bags of fine coffee beans from a Danish vessel. They are labelled: "Adolf Hitler." The little dictator is teetotal.

7 October **Dutch freighter sinks off Portland.**

Another ship has been sunk by a German mine off the Shambles lightship, Portland. She was Dutch steamship *Binnendyk*, returning to Rotterdam from New York.

The forty-two crew were able to abandon the blazing wreck and watched her gradually sink from the bows, from the rescue vessel that was taking them into Weymouth.

12 October **More survivors brought into Weymouth.**

The *Alex Andrea*, a Belgian oil tanker, has docked at Weymouth to bring home the crew of a Whitby Steamer, the *Sneaton*, that was torpedoed by a German U-boat in the South Western Approaches. She was carrying coal, to the Argentine. A stoker was killed.

The U-boat commander surfaced his boat to watch the men abandoning ship and called to them in English: "So long, boys. Sorry I had to do it, but it was my duty."

14 October **Dorset sailors die in the 'Royal Oak'.**

A German submarine [U-47] has slipped into the naval anchorage of Scapa Flow in the Orkney Isles and torpedoed the 29,000 ton battleship HMS *Royal Oak*. She turned over and went down into the cold, grey waters with 810 men inside her. The whole country is stunned and there is hardly a town in the land that doesn't have a wife or a mother who is not suffering personal grief.

In Weymouth, Petty Officer William Helmore left a widow in Hillcrest Road with three children, the youngest of whom he had never seen. Seventeen-year-old Billy Savage came from Holton Heath, near Wareham. Petty Officer Charles Beeling's parents live at Plush, near Piddletrenthide. Twenty-year-old John Hocking had been living with his grandfather at Martinstown. East Dorset's losses include Dennis Brown of Broadstone and Vernon Fay of Branksome Park.

For others, however, the knock on the door that night brought relief after a day of despair. Able Seaman Victor Ayles and Stoker Cecil Lucking, both with Weymouth parents, had survived. So too had Ronald Kenny of Ackerman Road, Dorchester, though the news was not brought to his mother until 2 am the following morning. A call in the early hours of Sunday was also made to St Helens Road, Broadwey, where police were able to tell Mrs Barrett that she still had a husband, Petty Officer W. Barrett.

Footnote Leutnant Prien and his U-boat crew were feted as heroes on their return to Berlin.

1939. Corfe Castle (above) and Bere Regis (below). War games became serious stuff, drawing a Territorial Army unit to Corfe and the 76th Heavy Field Regiment, Royal Artillery, to Bere. In both cases the enemy turned out to be the wet weather.

October **Swimming hero distributes Poole's gas-masks.**

Harry Davis, who in his sixty-six years has saved numerous people who were drowning, is taking an active part in Poole's Air Raid Precautions and has made himself responsible for the distribution of 7,500 gas-masks to local residents.

11 November **The Armistice service takes on a new meaning.**

This Armistice is different. Throughout the decade the November services marking the end of the Great War have been expressions of pacifism. They were a communal revulsion at the memory of the carnage in the trenches. Now however they are having a military flavour as the country once more steps back into uniform.

"Once war seems inevitable again, a million martyrs will have died again," Ramsay MacDonald said at the Cenotaph in 1934.

Few will have experienced similar thoughts during this minute's silence. The picture houses concentrate on newsreel coverage for civilian air-raid precautions. The public is being reintroduced to warfare. Joining the armed services had also been out of fashion. Even with high unemployment the level of Army recruitment remained inadequate.

22 November **Portland mines claim another ship.**

The German mines floating off the Shambles, to the south-east of Portland, have claimed yet another vessel, the Greek steamship *Elena R*.

Footnote The British destroyer HMS *Kittiwake* also hit a mine in the Channel but though listing she was able to make it back to Portland. Five of her crew had been lost.

31 December **Year in perspective (and Dorset girl weds a Churchill).**

The song of the year on both sides of the Atlantic is *There'll Always Be an England* by Ross Parker and Hughie Charles: "There'll always be an England/While there's a country lane/Wherever there's a cottage small/Beside a field of grain."

In Germany the Luftwaffe test the world's first turbojet aircraft, Hans von Ohain's Heinkel 178. German physicists split the uranium nucleus with neutron bombardment, causing Albert Einstein to write to President Roosevelt that a "nuclear chain reaction in a large mass of uranium" would "lead to the construction of bombs". Britain and Germany hoard food. The Germans have 8½ million tons of grain in store, with the promise of a million tons from Russia in 1940.

Britain is the largest global buyer of food—taking forty per cent of world trade. Rationing is planned and state intervention extends to the enrichment of bread and margarine with vitamins and trace elements; though only in that is Britain ahead of American food fads.

The Birds Eye label of General Foods introduce precooked frozen foods. Nylon becomes a commercial product. In Connecticut the Warner Brothers Company introduce cup-sizes for bras. Igor Sikorsky flies the first American helicopter. Al Capone leaves prison, a vegetable from syphilis. German physician F.H. Muller publishes *Tabakmissbrauch und Lungencarcinom*; the world has been told smoking causes lung cancer. Another Muller, Paul, develops DDT for the Geigy Company and saves the Swiss potato crop from Colorado beetles. Batman and Robin join the comic strips.

"This is London," Ed Murrow says nightly to most of the 27½ million US families who listen to the radio. His closing line is always the same: "Goodnight and good luck."

Ten per cent of Britons own 88 per cent of the nation's wealth.

The wedding of the year for Dorset's social set came after Mr Churchill had stepped back into Whitehall as First Lord of the Admiralty; his son, Randolph, married the Hon. Pamela Digby, daughter of Lord and Lady Digby of Minterne Magna.

Supermarine Spitfire: Warmwell pilots fight the Battle of Britain.

1940

7 February Bournemouth ARP now have 11 fire stations.

Bournemouth's Air Raid Precautions are organised from the basement of the Town Hall, telephone 7220. All reports of damage of whatever character are to be made to there. The town has been split into eleven zones, each with its own fire station. Some such as the Central Fire Station and Pokesdown Fire Station are regular fire service establishments but most are auxiliary depots set-up in buildings such as the San Remo Towers at Boscombe and Lee Motor Works in Winton.

2 March Luftwaffe attack Channel shipping.

Cherbourg-based aircraft from Kampf Gruppe 26 today attacked shipping in the English Channel east of Portland Bill. The steamship *Domala* was set on fire.

20 March Steamship 'Barnhill' sunk off Purbeck.

Shipping in the Channel has again been attacked by bombers from Kampf Gruppe 26. The 5,439 ton freighter SS *Barnhill* sank off the Isle of Purbeck.

31 March Paper into shells at Holton Heath.

Paper is being consumed by the Royal Naval Cordite Factory at Holton Heath and made into nitro cellulose. This guncotton pulp is mixed with nitroglycerine; the basis of cordite SC which is the propellant for the Navy's shells.

The factory has used 4,279,141 lb of paper in the past year.

12 April Narvik wreath at Hardy Monument.

A laurel wreath hangs on the door of the Hardy Monument, the memorial to Nelson's flag captain on the hills above Portesham—the village known to Thomas Hardy as 'Possum'—in memory of the men of the Royal Navy who lost their lives two days ago in Narvik fjord, Norway.

A card reads: "To the unfading memory of Captain Warburton-Lee, RN, HMS *Hardy*, and the gallant men who died at Narvik. Nelson's Hardy and Hardy's Possum salute you."

24 April Holton Heath munitions factory hit.

An oil incendiary bomb exploded at 22.10 hours tonight beside the wash-water settling house of the nitroglycerine complex at the Royal Naval Cordite Factory, Holton Heath. The wooden settling house began burning but Walt Dominey and his fire-fighting team brought the fire under control and averted a major disaster.

4 May Two Poole flying boats destroyed in Norway.

Two Short Sunderland 'Empire' flying boats, the *Cabot* and *Caribou*, which had been seconded to 119 Squadron at Invergordon, have been attacked at anchor by a Heinkel floatplane in Bodo fjord. They had arrived today to bring radar equipment to the beleagured British troops at Harstadt in northern Norway.

Footnote The equipment was lost in the attack though the injured crews were rescued and brought home by a British destroyer. A further raid, the following morning, sank the planes. They had been scheduled to operate BOAC's peacetime Atlantic service in 1940.

5 May Telecommunications Research moves to Worth Matravers.

The Telecommunications Research Establishment, an Air Ministry section, who have pioneered the development of early warning radio-direction finding equipment known as radar, have been evacuated from Dundee to Renscombe, a farm a short distance inland from Chapman's Pool at Worth Matravers in the Isle of Purbeck.

10 May 2nd Dorsets in the Belgian front-line.

The 2nd Battalion of the Dorsetshire Regiment, in the Belgian front-line to the east of Genval, awoke this morning to the drone of enemy aeroplanes and have been told to prepare for battle.

10 May Attlee recalled to London from Bournemouth.

Labour leaders Clement Attlee and Arthur Greenwood have been recalled to London today from their party conference in Bournemouth, as the Chamberlain government is in crisis following the invasion of the Low Countries. Chamberlain has offered them posts in a new national government.

They have accepted the posts (Attlee as Lord Privy Seal; Greenwood as Minister without Portfolio) but rejected Chamberlain's continued leadership—which with Parliament's present mood will cause the Premier's instant resignation and a call to Winston Churchill to form the new government.

10 May Churchill's Dorset ancestry.

With the fall today of Neville Chamberlain's government and Mr Churchill's appointment as Premier it is noted with approval in Dorset that his most distinguished ancestor, John Churchill, the first Duke of Marlborough, was the son of Winston Churchill of Glanvilles Wootton, "of a good Dorset family". Winston Spencer Churchill is the grandson of the seventh Duke of Marlborough.

Last year his son, Randolph, married the Hon. Pamela Digby of Minterne Magna.

14 May Three thousand Dutch refugees camp on Brownsea.

Following the sudden Nazi invasion into the Low Countries, which also delivered the coup de grâce to the Chamberlain government, an armada of dozens of overloaded Dutch vessels is being shepherded by the Royal Navy into Poole Harbour. The refugees will be temporarily camped on Brownsea Island where they can be properly screened by doctors, police and the security services before being admitted into the country.

An estimated three thousand are on their way.

16 May 2nd Dorsets withdraw towards France.

"Où est la route pour France?" a Dorsetman heard as Algerian troops were beaten back by the German advance and the 2nd Battalion of the Dorsetshire Regiment found itself under further orders to withdraw in the face of overwhelming odds.

19 May 2nd Dorsets see civilians bombed and strafed.

For the first time the Dorset soldiers serving in Belgium, now pulled back to Tournai near the French border, have seen the bodies of civilians who were bombed and strafed by German aircraft. The town is on fire.

1939–40. Images from six months of war. Neville Chamberlain; black-outs; evacuees; gas-masks; Lord Gort (below, second from right) leading the British Expeditionary Force in France.

DORSET'S WAR

24 May 2nd Dorsets invited to desert.

With German radio announcing that the ring around the French, Belgian and British armies has "definitely closed" the 2nd Battalion of the Dorsetshire Regiment—now withdrawn to La Bassee, south-west of Lille—has been showered from the air with leaflets: "You are surrounded—why fight on? We treat our prisoners well."

29 May Army told not to fraternize with Local Defence Volunteers.

Too much fraternization is taking place with civilians, local sector commander of the Observer Corps, Wing Commander Stewart, has told his men: "Head observers must consult their officers before making any commitments with the Local Defence Volunteers. No instruction has been received with regard to co-operation and any tendency to mingle at posts should be discouraged."

31 May 2nd Dorsets evacuated from Dunkirk.

After five days and nights of marching and fighting as they made their way north towards the Channel coast, the main contingent of the 2nd Battalion of the Dorsetshire Regiment last night completed an orderly withdrawal, under fire, to the Mole at Dunkirk where they boarded a Thames dredger. They were appalled to see that she seemed to be half full of water but heard that dredgers are always like that.

May Local Defence Volunteers: six Dorset units.

Major General Harry Marriot-Smith is organising the Local Defence Volunteers under instructions from the War Office. Dorset is being covered by six battalions.

Footnote Churchill would have them renamed—the Home Guard. The 3rd Dorset Battalion was later split to create another, the 7th (Wareham) Battalion, and a Motor Transport Company was also formed as part of the Hants and Dorset Transport Column.

1939. Portland Harbour. The destroyer HMS 'Brazen' : quite a short war—the Germans sank her in the Channel in July 1940.

1 June Fleeing French troops arrive in Weymouth.

The first train carrying Free French soldiers into Weymouth arrived at 05.00 hours. They are being taken to the former Christ Church, opposite the station, which has been converted into a refugee Welcome Club. There they are being issued with their first rations, half a loaf and a tin of bully-beef, and dispersed to various schools, halls and private accommodation.

2 June Hardy and love of England.

Thomas Hardy was a patriot, speakers emphasised at the ceremony in Dorchester to mark the centenary of the author's birth. It was held beside his memorial statute in Colliton Walks. Earl Baldwin of Bewdley, the former Conservative prime minister, laid a wreath and commented that

Opposite—May/June 1940. The British Expeditionary Force, including the 2nd Battalion of the Dorsetshire Regiment, is evacuated from Dunkirk.

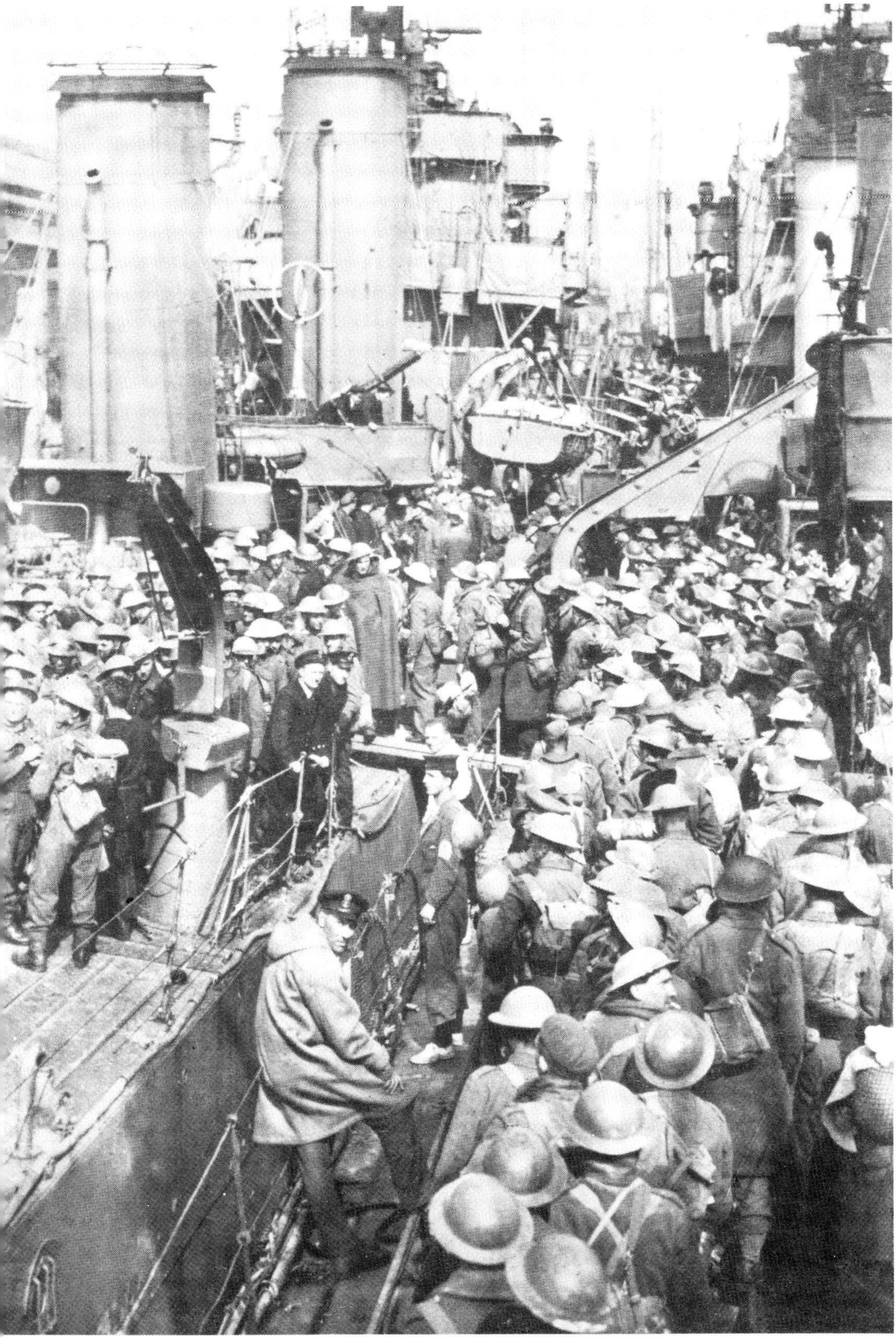

he felt reservations during the week that the celebration should be postponed.

On further consideration, however, he considered there was nothing unseemly even at a moment like the present for English people to gather together in the part of England made famous by a very great Englishman to express their sense of what they owed to him. He had for many increased their knowledge and love of England, for which her sons today were laying down their lives.

4 June   Poole and Weymouth craft help evacuate Dunkirk.

Pleasure craft from Poole and Weymouth are in the armada of Operation Dynamo that today completed the evacuation of the British Expeditionary Force from the beaches of Dunkirk.

Among the craft taken to Dover from Poole were Harvey's *Ferry Nymph* and *Southern Queen*; Davis's *Felicity* and *Island Queen*; Bolson's *Skylarks VI, VIII* and *IX*; and *Thomas Kirk-Wright*, the harbour's inshore lifeboat. These craft were comandeered by the navy and the lifeboat, with its shallow draught, has the distinction of being used to go into the beaches. She has survived shore-fire from Germans positioned less than forty yards away.

The pleasure craft have proved ideal for taking aboard soldiers by the dozen but Poole's fishing fleet, which had also loyally turned up in response to the Admiralty's appeal, was summarily rejected by the navy. Its boatmen, who consider themselves to be the port's only true seamen, were sent home by train and their vessels impounded for possible reserve uses. They are unsuitable for this kind of mass transit.

A third of the 330,000 soldiers who have been brought out are French and 6,000 of these, from Flanders, have been sent to Weymouth. At Dorchester, however, the concern has been of a civilian influx, with news of a further 2,300 evacuees earmarked for the district. Only now are air-raid shelters being constructed in the town.

Footnote   Of the local boats, the *Island Queen* and *Southern Queen* were sunk off Dunkirk, and *Skylark VI* abandoned with bomb damage. She was later salvaged, towed back to Bolson's shipyard at Poole and refitted with a larger engine as an Air-Sea Rescue craft. The fishermen returned by train for their boats a few days later.

9 June   Germans mine the channel into Poole.

Last night the Germans mined the Swash Channel that leads into the entrance to Poole Harbour, in anticipation of its use in some relief operation to bring out the beleaguered units of the British Army struggling in Normandy.

12 June   Poole boats rescue troops from St Valery.

Overall, Operation Cycle failed to live up the Admiralty's expectations of a second mini-Dunkirk, but for some of the small Poole boats taking part it was a triumph. They last night played a key role in bringing 3,321 soldiers, a third of them British, from the salient at St Valery-en-Caux.

This time the Germans were ready for a maritime rescue mission, though it was the fog that disrupted the efforts of the early hours of the 11th and sent six thousand Scottish troops into prisoner-of-war camps. As part of their counter-measures the Germans mined the Swash Channel into Poole Harbour. It has been rendered at least partly clear by navy divers from Portland.

Not completely, however, as the *Princess Juliana*, found. She was sailing out of Poole last night when she hit a mine off the Training Bank and was lifted clear of the water. George Brown, the pilot, was rescued together with three of the Dutch crewmen.

Footnote   Ivor Holland, instrumental in the rescue of *Princess Juliana's* survivors, was to be awarded the Order of the Red Lion by the Netherlands.

13 June 'Abel Tasman' blown up off Poole.

Three of fifteen craft returning from St Valery with remnants of the British and French armies ran the gauntlet of the Swash Channel into Poole Harbour today. The fourth and unlucky craft was the *Abel Tasman*, fortunately returning empty. She hit a mine and was blown to pieces, killing all eleven of her complement from the Royal Navy Volunteer Reserve.

An order was flashed to the remaining ships to turn and they sailed to Southampton.

13 June 'British Inventor' mined off St Alban's Head.

The steam tanker *British Inventor* struck a mine off St Alban's Head. Although she stayed afloat long enough to be put under tow the line had to be released as the stricken vessel began to go under.

Channels into the ports of Weymouth and Poole are being kept open through the efforts of two Portland-based minesweepers, HMS *Kindred Star* and HMS *Thrifty*.

15 June Swash Channel has first magnetic mines.

The mines that have claimed two ships in recent days in the Swash Channel at the outer entrance to Poole Harbour include some, at least, of a new magnetic type that explode when they come close to a steel ship. These C-type mines have not yet been retrieved intact for examination and today the first attempt burst into a spectacular failure on Studland beach.

Harold Cartridge with the Poole fishing boat *Smiling Through*, under navy orders, managed to tow one on a seven hundred foot line from the Bar Buoy to the shallows of Studland beach—where for some unknown reason it decided to explode, though without more than a shock and a wake for Cartridge and his craft.

Footnote The Germans were slow in deploying this potentially devastating weapon. The first to be dismantled by the British would be recovered from Shoeburyness, Essex, on 22 November; the Germans had been lax in not incorporating an anti-handling device.

19 June Highcliffe sighting of French refugees.

Two boats, apparently carrying French troops fleeing from Cherbourg, have been spotted by the Local Defence Volunteers from their Highcliffe lookout, the Cliff Top Café. The craft are heading for Steamer Point, Christchurch.

20 June First air raid warning.

Condition Red: this is the first air-raid warning at Christchurch, though there have been earlier alerts for Condition Yellow, the precautionary message from Fighter Command that enemy air activity is to be expected. With Condition Red the activity has been monitored and appears to be coming our way—it is a warning to take to the shelters, given as a two-minute warbling blast on the sirens.

Later there was a continuous two-minute wail from the siren to declare that it was All Clear. Nothing, thank God, happened in the interim.

Footnote Christchurch would experience 956 air raid warnings, the vast majority of them being of as little consequence. The last would be on 15 July 1944.

20 June Weymouth tears as the French leave.

Tearful farewells marked Weymouth's parting with the French soldiers, the last of whom have now left to resume the war with fighting units. They were taken to heart, in a way that perhaps the Londoners and others weren't—but the town has experienced an influx unprecedented for anywhere in England. John Murphy has recorded one sad incident where a Catholic priest tried to say something kind to an unhappy Belgian woman but utterly failed.

"Are they all yours?" joked Father Jules Ketele when he saw she had three children with her. A good Catholic should have known better!

She burst into tears and sobbed that she had seven children when she left home eight days ago; those were all she had left.

The total number of arrivals for the past week has been 27,400 refugees, of which the bulk—23,743 of them—have come from the Channel Islands which faces impending German invasion.

Footnote The Germans took over the Channel Islands at the end of the month, on 30 June and 1 July.

21 June **Christchurch Ansons fly in search of the 'beam'.**

The Telecommunications Research Establishment, Worth Matravers, has organised a flight tonight of three Anson aeroplanes, formerly based at Christchurch. They will try, in poor weather, to use American radar receivers, to track the course of a German radio direction signal, intended to aid the navigation of bombers, that appears to lead from Spalding, Lincolnshire, and cross with another similar 'beam' above the Rolls-Royce aeroengine factory at Derby. The Anson tracking this signal is flown by Flight Lieutenant H.E. Bufton with Corporal Mackie as radio operator.

Footnote The Special Counter Measures Unit was to function as part of 109 Squadron.

23 June **Wooden glider blips on Worth's radar.**

A British Avro 504N biplane today took off from Christchurch Aerodrome to tow a German Minimoa glider into the middle of the English Channel and released the wooden craft at 10,000 feet for it to glide back towards Purbeck. The glider pilot, Philip Wills, returned below cliff level at St Alban's Head and prepared for impact but was saved by the phenomenon of currents rising beside vertical surfaces.

The object of the exercise was for the Telecommunications Research Establishment at Renscombe, Worth Matravers, to establish with its radio direction finding aerials [RDF, now known as radar] whether short-wave radiation that bounced off metal bombers would also reflect from wooden gliders. Worth houses the country's principal radio research unit.

The answer was affirmative; to the relief of the scientists as the country is in fear of a mass invasion of German gliders.

25 June **69th Infantry Brigade takes over.**

The 69th Infantry Brigade, late of France and the Dunkirk beaches, is now back in the front-line at Poole and east Dorset where it has taken over the anti-invasion defences from the Queen's Bays. The Officer Commanding, Brigadier Barstow, is at Bovington Camp.

The Brigade comprises the 7th Battalion of the Green Howards, the 5th Battalion of the East Yorkshire Regiment and the 6th Battalion of the Green Howards, who are dispersed into the countryside. The Adjutant of the Green Howards has found that the unit no longer possesses a duplicator—and is to ask Poole Corporation if he may borrow theirs.

June **Anti-ship guns emplaced around Poole Bay.**

The 554th Coast Regiment of the Royal Artillery, with its headquarters at the Conningtower,

1940. The invasion coast: barbed wire and soldier at Seatown, with Golden Cap beyond. The 6-inch gun is on Brownsea Island, manned by 347 Battery.

**June 1940. England alone—
the Dorset beaches are now the front line.**

West Road, Canford Cliffs, has sited naval guns, taken from warships and armed merchantmen at the end of the Great War and put into store, as the teeth of the anti-ship defences in Poole Bay. The positions are:

        Two × 6-inch guns, Battery Hill, Brownsea Island—347th Battery.
        Two × 5.5-inch guns, Hengistbury Head—172nd Battery.
        Two × 6-inch guns, Mudeford—175th Battery.
        Two × 4-inch guns, Swanage—386th Battery.

Each set of emplacements has a complement of about a hundred men.

1940 (photographed, after some subsidence, by Colin Graham in 1983). Dragon's teeth anti-tank obstacles and pillbox, across the Chesil Beach at Abbotsbury. The concrete cubes are 3½ feet high and four feet apart, in double rows. The western flank of the proposed German invasion, Operation Sealion, was earmarked for the Wehrmacht's Army Group B, under Field Marshal Feodor von Bock—victors of Poland and the dash to the Channel.

June Ship and boom defence for Poole Harbour entrance.

An Examination Ship is positioned in the Swash Channel at the entrance to Poole Harbour. The duty is being undertaken by the ex-Belgian trawler *Rosa Arthur*, now His Majesty's Trawler XVI, with her sister craft HMT XVII (*Roger Robert*) and HMT XVIII (*Marguerita Marie Louisa*). The alert code for the sighting of enemy forces is "Blackbird". That for a landing of troops is "Gallipoli". For a landing of tanks it is "Caterpillars".

Once a warning of invasion had been radioed and received on the mainland the craft's duty is to suspend the watching brief with a final signal—"Finish"—and head to sea to intercept enemy vessels.

As for the harbour entrance, it has a steel boom with suspended torpedo heads that have been provided by the Royal Naval Cordite Factory at Holton Heath. There is a passage open at the centre in daytime but in the evening this is closed by boatman George Mitchell.

Inside the harbour six pleasure craft have been requisitioned by the Royal Navy and armed with machine guns. They are H1 to H6; the boats of the Poole Harbour Patrol.

In the Main Channel of Poole Harbour an old steamship, the *Empire Sentinel*, has been packed with explosives and in the event of invasion the harbour patrol will sink her to block the approaches to the port. Their prime duty is to ensure the closure of this channel.

Footnote Only one of the pleasure boats, *Etrillita* in civilian days, was retained as a patrol craft. The others were phased out and replaced.

June **British mines laid in Poole Harbour.**

The Naval Officer-in-Command, Poole, is completing the laying of a minefield between Sandbanks and Brownsea Island to prevent the intrusion of German submarines or surface vessels. Anti-tank "islands" of urban coastal areas impregnable to tank attack have been established behind concrete obstacles, minefields and flame traps at the Old Town in Poole and at Christchurch. The Garrison Headquarters is also strongly defended in the centre of Bournemouth.

The whole of the area from Upton to Mudeford is under the control of the Garrison Commander at Bournemouth.

June **Royal Naval Air Station Sandbanks.**

Seaplane training for Fleet Air Arm pilots is now based at Poole, from the middle of this month, with the removal from Calshot on Southampton Water to Sandbanks of 765 Squadron, the Royal Navy Seaplane School. At Calshot they had been heavily bombed.

The squadron trains its pilots on the air-sea rescue Walrus, which is distinctive with a chugging sound and three-decker wings. It is known as the 'Shagbat'. They also have the Swordfish torpedo-reconnaissance biplane (known as the 'Stringbag') and Kingfisher and Seafox floatplanes.

The base is known as Royal Naval Air Station Sandbanks.

Footnote But to Poole people it was HMS Tadpole—because it handled beginners with seaplanes that were dwarfed by the Short Sunderlands operating from the harbour with BOAC and Coastal Command. The name was later adopted by the Navy for real, in 1943, for a pre-invasion landing craft training establishment.

June **Bovington's tank collection scrapped or used as pillboxes.**

The collection of the world's first tanks at the Armoured Fighting Vehicles School, Bovington Camp, has been dispersed to help the war effort. Many have been taken away for scrap and others are in strategic positions as stationary pill-boxes.

The vehicles had been put in a shed after Rudyard Kipling visited Bovington in 1923 and expressed disappointment that nothing was being done to preserve them.

June **Four hundred French soldiers rest in Bournemouth.**

As the exhausted armies are dispersed from the reception ports a detachment of four hundred French soldiers is told to go to Bournemouth for a short recuperation whilst billets are found. Canon Hedley Burrows found they had been sent to St Peter's Hall in the centre of the town.

He phoned up the Town Clerk to ask who was in charge of these men. "You are!" he was told. Canon Burrows is arranging their accommodation.

1 July **Ration books and identify cards.**

Ration books for food came into force today, with green coupons for meat, yellow for butter and margarine and orange for cooking fat.

Identity cards are being issued to all those living in the Military Control areas, which in Dorset include the entire coast and its towns and stretch twenty miles inland. The Commissioner responsible for the control of civilians in the South-west Region is Sir Geoffrey Peto but the National Registration Identity Cards, each carrying the individual's photograph, are issued locally. In the case of Sandbanks, for instance, they will be signed by the Officer Commanding

Description

Age 47
Colour of Hair GREY
Height 5 7
Build SLIGHT
Any Distinguishing Marks

MILITARY CONTROL

SANDBANKS AREA POOLE

RENEWED
FROM
TO
O.C. POOLE DEFENCES.

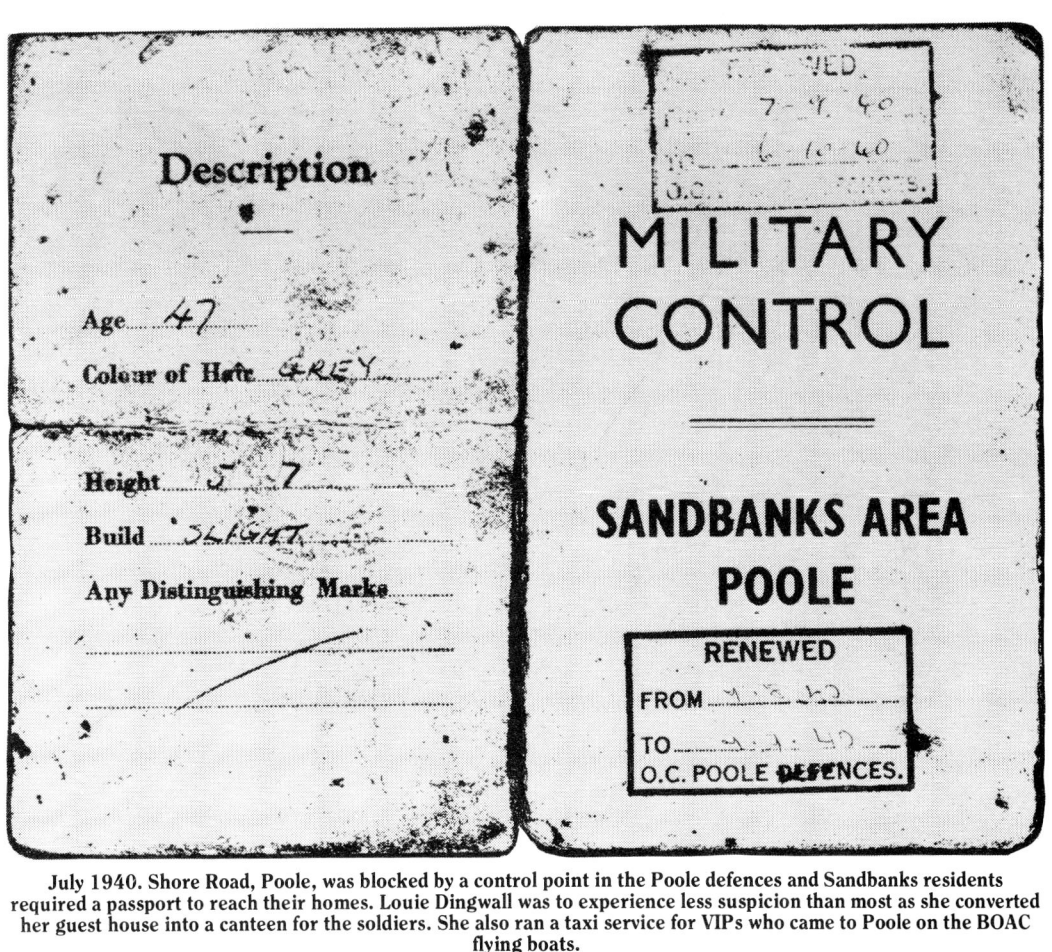

July 1940. Shore Road, Poole, was blocked by a control point in the Poole defences and Sandbanks residents required a passport to reach their homes. Louie Dingwall was to experience less suspicion than most as she converted her guest house into a canteen for the soldiers. She also ran a taxi service for VIPs who came to Poole on the BOAC flying boats.

Serial No. 61
National Registration Identity Card N. WKEF 32 2
Issued to Mrs. Dingwall
SURNAME
Louisa Eileen
CHRISTIAN NAME(S)
Address
Occupation Garage Proprietress
Nationality British
Available From July 2nd 1940
To August 5th 1940
Issued by
O.C. Troops Poole Defence Area.
On 6.7.40
Signature of Holder L. Dingwall

Troops, Poole Defence Area.

Those without cards have to give reasons for entry into the Military Control areas when they encounter vehicle check points and police also carry out spot-checks inside the zone on bus passengers and in public places.

2 July Green Howards wiring up the Bournemouth beaches.

All beach chalets and huts are to be removed from the beaches of Bournemouth and Poole, having been considered to have been requisitioned by the military. Their clearance has been demanded to ensure a proper field of fire across the sands. Wire barriers are to be erected by the Green Howards along the low-tide line and emplacements built along the coast and in particular at the Haven Hotel and Sandbanks Pavilion. Sandbanks is to be sealed-off.

4 July Control points surround Sandbanks.

Effectively, from today, Sandbanks is sealed with military control points in operation at Shore Road and the Haven Hotel crossing point—and on the Studland Road at Shell Bay. From the 6th the position will be regularised by the issue of permits to the 544 inhabitants who will have to gather at the Haven Hotel to have their photographs taken and undergo an interview before they are accredited with official clearance documents.

4 July Portland hero keeps firing as he dies.

Ninety Junkers 87 'Stukas' today attacked Convoy OA 178 between Portland and Hengistbury Head, sinking the steamship *Elmcrest* and three other vessels. A further nine ships were damaged.

The dive-bombers then attacked Portland Harbour where they sank two ships, including the anti-aircraft auxiliary HMS *Foylebank*. A dozen 'Stukas' came at her and one of the first casualties was 23-year-old Leading Seaman Jack Mantle from Southampton. Despite having his legs shattered as bombs tore the ship apart, causing loss of electrical power, he stayed at his pom-pom and continued firing even as he suffered further wounds, and must have known he was mortally injured.

Fifty-nine of his comrades were also killed and a total of sixty were injured—the other sixty somehow came out of it unscathed.

Perhaps the unluckiest people on Portland that day were nine contractors from McAlpine's, who had been digging a tunnel. They sheltered inside it during the raid and came out when it was thought to be over; to be killed by a last bomb from a single German plane that turned back from the sea. Four of those workers were boys.

Footnote There were repercussions. The Admiralty closed the English Channel to ocean-going merchant vessels, though coastal convoys would continue.

Jack Mantle was gazetted with the first Victoria Cross that the Royal Navy had won inside territorial waters. He is buried in Portland's Naval Cemetery on the Verne Common hillside.

Open air gatherings were henceforth restricted. Only family mourners could attend the funerals that resulted from the day's events. At one the Fortuneswell Methodist minister, Rev F. Jowett, said: "We owe a tribute of gratitude and affection to the one who has departed. He has given his life for his King and country, and those things for which we Englishmen stand."

5 July 'Hartlepool' sinks in Weymouth Harbour.

SS *Hartlepool*, a British steamship, has sunk at the entrance to Weymouth Harbour as a result of enemy action.

1940

5 July **E-boats maul Convoy OA 178.**

The remnants of Convoy OA 178, which suffered considerably from a Junkers 87 'Stukas' onslaught yesterday, were harassed last night by E-boats off Poole Bay. One ship has sunk and two more are damaged.

6 July **Warmwell taken over by Fighter Command.**

Warmwell has become a front-line defensive aerodrome with the arrival of the Spitfires of 609 (West Riding) Squadron under Squadron Leader H.S. (George) Darley. The Squadron code letters are "PR". Control of the airfield has been transferred to No. 10 Group of Fighter Command, the headquarters of which is at Box, near Bath, and its sector base and home aerodrome is Middle Wallop, near Andover, Hampshire. The pilots return there in the evening and come back to Dorset the following morning.

Scramble time is fifteen minutes and the accommodation tented.

Footnote There was an inflexible meals timetable that often caused friction and Darley would damn Dorset for its treatment of his men. Once he started the day with a row with the cooks and had to prepare his own breakfast, breaking off to take to the sky to fight off some 'Stukas'. Back on the ground he rang the Station Commander to say he wished to be spared any thanks "for saving the hangars, personnel, and planes, not to mention the officers' mess and kitchens".

Lance Corporal Tony Hollister, later of Swanage, witnessed a gratuitous insult from an ex-Indian Army major to a couple of Warmwell pilots: "Take your bloody hands out of your pockets and salute a senior officer." They deflated him with unprintable public school drawl. There used to be a simple phrase for causing apoplexy amongst such persons: "I always regarded the terrorists as the cream of Bengal."

1940. Squadron Leaders of the Warmwell Spitfires—George Darley of 609 Squadron and Peter Devitt (far right) of 152 Squadron.

1940. About to become a legend—the Supermarine Spitfire in its Mark IX version. There were 187 in squadron service in Britain when war was declared. A month later 4,000 were on order.

9 July Warmwell pilot killed over Portland.

Pilot Officer Drummond-Hay was killed this evening in action against enemy raiders above Portland. He had intercepted them with 609 Squadron from Warmwell.

9 July Poole now a sealed-off town.

Poole is now part of the Defence Area, with access restricted to those with reason for entering the town, under a regulation signed by Regional Controller Harold Butler.

10 July Poole flying boat arrives in Sydney.

The British Empire's air link resumed today with the arrival in Sydney of a BOAC flying boat from Poole. Another has reached Durban. They have flown a horseshoe-shaped route to Lisbon and across the southern Sahara.

The Australian plane then travelled northwards via Khartoum and Cairo on to the usual peacetime flight path across Palestine, the Persian Gulf, India and Malaya.

The South African route is via Lagos and Leopoldville.

11 July Anti-glider precautions erected at Poole.

Among the various anti-landing traps being laid to discourage enemy glider forces are rows of telegraph poles which are being cut into sections and dug into the fairways of Parkstone golf links and across Branksome playing fields. The poles are ten feet apart and form rows every hundred yards.

11 July Two more Warmwell losses.

Two more Spitfires from Warmwell's 609 Squadron have been lost in action over the English Channel, whilst fighting off a 'Stuka' bombardment of a convoy of British merchant ships.

The attacks were in Lyme Bay, by fifty enemy aircraft, and 609 Squadron had gone to the aid of the hard-pressed Hurricanes from Exeter which had battled alone against an attack earlier in the day by twenty bombers and forty fighters. The steam yacht *Warrior II* was sunk in the first attack and another ship damaged in the second raid.

12 July More Spitfires for Warmwell.

An unblooded support squadron, 152 (Hyderabad) Squadron, has flown into Warmwell Aerodrome, led by Squadron Leader Peter Devitt who learnt to fly at the age of nineteen in 1930.

Their markings are "UM". The squadron is equipped with Spitfires and has had its practice flights in the north of England.

12 July   Northumberland Fusiliers to smash Bournemouth's piers.

Veterans of Dunkirk, the 4th Battalion of the Royal Northumberland Fusiliers have arrived in Bournemouth after a short stay at Yeovil followed by a few days in tents at Piddlehinton. Here in the seaside resort they are taking over the coast defences from the Royal Artillery and will lay mines and erect wood, steel and concrete anti-invasion obstacles.

It is going to shock anyone who cherishes memories of the Victorian bathchairs, for the battalion's first task is to wreck both Bournemouth Pier and Boscombe Pier by taking out the central supports and leaving the seaward ends as islands, to deny their use to the Jerry invaders.

13 July   'Stay-put if the Germans invade'—mayors order.

Learning from the chaos brought to France and Belgium by refugees blocking the roads in the hours that preceded the arrival of the Germans, the mayors of the Bournemouth conurbation have emphasised that there is to be no civilian evacuation if the enemy invades. All major roads would be sealed off for the use of the Army and if the enemy comes he will in the Bournemouth area take on the burden of an army of occupation with a quarter of a million population to control and support. Resistance will continue from the 'fighting boxes' garrisoned by upwards of fifty armed men, and in some cases two hundred or more. These, it is said, are "fortified, supplied and organised to withstand siege without outside assistance".

An Australian volunteer with RAF Warmwell, Flight Lieutenant J. C. Kennedy, lost his life today at the age of twenty-three.

16 July   'I have decided to prepare a landing against England' — Hitler.

Luftwaffe Enigma machine-coded radio messages have today carried a directive from Hitler. The translation of the deciphered intercept, passed to Churchill by the Government's Code and Cipher School at Bletchley Park, reads: "I have decided to prepare a landing operation against England and if necessary to carry it out."

17 July   Churchill visits the Dorset invasion coast.

Winston Churchill today saw the invasion precautions along the most vulnerable beaches of the South Coast when he inspected units at Branksome Chine and Sandbanks. At Branksome he showed his skill as a bricklayer by making a practical contribution to the defences that are taking shape.

He recalled to General Alan Brooke, the chief of Southern Command who had driven with him from Gosport, that it was from the rustic bridge at Alum Chine that he had fallen twenty feet as a young child—very nearly plunging to his death.

They dined at the Armoured Fighting Vehicles School, Bovington, and were at Wool Station at 20.00 hours for Churchill's train back to London. Brooke is less than confident with what he has seen, he confides to his diary: "What has been going on in this country since the war started . . . The ghastly part is that I feel certain that we can only have a few more weeks before the Boche attacks." For all that, he admitted, he realised it was imperative to "maintain a confident exterior".

Footnote   Brooke was unimpressed by his men's equipment and means but Churchill realised he had a considerable asset in Brooke—two days later he was promoted Commander-in-Chief Home Forces; on Christmas Day 1941 he became Chief of the Imperial General Staff.

DORSET'S WAR

17 July 1940. Below and opposite—Winston Churchill sees the invasion coast at Sandbanks. It is the day after Hitler issued his directive ordering preparations for landings in England.

These photographs sum up the national spirit of resistance, as expressed by Churchill to Parliament on 4 June 1940 in the best war leader's speech this side of Shakespeare: 'We shall defend our island, whatever the cost may be, we shall fight on the beaches, we shall fight on the landing grounds, we shall fight in the fields and in the streets, we shall fight in the hills; we shall never surrender.'

18 July **Warmwell celebrates revenge.**

Warmwell's Spitfire pilots have returned with their first kills. Two enemy aircraft have been shot down by 609 Squadron, which has done much to restore morale after their own recent losses.

One of the kills, a Dornier bomber which crash-landed close to Fleet church, became the first German aircraft to be brought down in Dorset. It had been attacking shipping in Lyme Bay. The pilot, who was the only survivor, passed looted Players cigarettes to his captors.

20 July **Warmwell pilot killed.**

Pilot Officer Posner, a young South African volunteer flying a Spitfire from Warmwell with 152 Squadron, has been lost in an engagement with enemy planes off the Isle of Wight. Only yesterday the squadron flew its first operational sortie from Warmwell Aerodrome.

24 July **Liner torpedoed off Portland.**

The *Meknes*, a French liner, has sunk after being torpedoed off Portland.

25 July **Two German planes and two Spitfires shot down.**

Squadron Leader Peter Devitt today led the Spitfires of 152 Squadron from Warmwell in their first successful interception. Calling "Tally ho!" and hearing an "Achtung, Spitfire" response his fighters attacked a Dornier with Junkers 87 'Stuka' dive-bombers over Portland.

The Dornier crashed near Weymouth, killing one of the crew, and a 'Stuka' was seen plunging burning into the sea. Both kills were claimed by Ralph ('Bob') Wolton flying UM-F for Freddie with the coup de grâce being delivered to the Dornier by 'Jumbo' Deanesley who then went after a 'Stuka' but ended up baling out wounded as his Spitfire crashed into the sea.

Another pilot failed to return at all to Warmwell; Sergeant S.R.E. Wakeling, aged twenty-one.

DORSET'S WAR

26 July E-boats sink three ships off Dorset.

An E-boat Flotilla, comprising three German motor torpedo boats—Schnellboote S19, S20 and S27—have sunk three merchant vessels in attacks in the Channel between Portland and the Isle of Wight.

29 July Destroyer loss shock—Germans have radar.

HMS *Delight*, a 1,375 ton destroyer of the 'Defender' class was today dive-bombed by Junkers 87 'Stukas' and sank twenty miles south of Portland Bill.

Footnote Shortly after she had gone down an intercepted German radio message in the 'Enigma' code was deciphered by the British Code and Cipher School at Bletchley Park. It stated that the warship "had been sunk with the aid of Freya reports".

'Freya' was the codename for some device. Her name was plucked from Norse mythology and Dr Reg Jones, head of scientific intelligence at the Air Ministry, had already heard of "Freya Gerät" (Freya apparatus).

Jones writes in *Most Secret War* that seeing a mention of "Freya-Meldung" on 5 July (Freya reporting) he had bought a book on myths from Foyle's and found that "Freya was the Nordic Venus who had not merely sacrificed, but massacred her honour to gain possession of a magic necklace, Brisinga-men. The necklace was guarded by Heimdall, the watchman of the Gods, who could see a hundred miles by day or night."

The last phrase is the crucial one—making Heimdall a wholly appropriate code for radar, though rather too obvious. Freya was chosen, by association, in its place.

Twelve days before the loss of *Delight*, Jones had used this reasoning to predict the existence "of a coastal chain and detecting system with a range of a hundred miles". The sinking of the destroyer removed any possibility that Freya was detecting associated objects in the sky—for *Delight* had neither balloon protection nor a fighter escort.

"The apparatus must have been able to detect her directly," Jones concluded. "It appeared to be sited near the village of Auderville on the Hague peninsula north-west of Cherbourg, but it had to be very different from our own coastal chain stations, since it was completely undetectable on the best air photographs that we possessed of the area.

"This confirmed the idea that Freya was a fairly small apparatus, which had already been suggested by the fact that it had been set up so quickly after the Germans had occupied the Channel coast."

The story would resume on 24 February 1941.

29 July Admiralty bans Channel convoys and destroyers.

The English Channel has been placed off-limits to destroyers in daytime as a result of today's loss of HMS *Delight*. It brings to four the losses of destroyers in the mid-Channel area this month—the others being HMS *Brazen*, *Codrington* and *Wren*.

Thirty-six merchant ships have also been sunk, five of them when Convoy CW8 was mauled by Junkers 87 'Stuka' dive-bombers. As a result of these awful losses the Admiralty suspended coastal convoys in the English Channel, as from two days ago.

Southern Command had its Camouflage School at Poole and practised with the defences at Canford Cliffs. Meanwhile the townspeople wanted their principal buildings to be disguised . . .

July **Poole camouflage requests rejected.**

The Air Ministry has turned down requests from Dorset County Council for the camouflaging of prominent buildings in Poole, saying that this would make attacks more likely: "Low flying aircraft would easily see these buildings even if they were camouflaged, and, if they were seen to be camouflaged they would be taken to be more important targets than they really were. Thus camouflaging them would attract attack rather than avoid it."

July **'British Resistance' guerrilla hideouts in Dorset.**

Thirty-two underground hideouts have been established secretly by the Royal Engineers in woods and commons scattered through the Dorset countryside to conceal the weapons, explosives and food necessary for Auxiliary Units of British Resistance to operate behind German lines in the event of an invasion.

This is considered most likely to take place on the sandy beaches between Studland and Hurst Castle, with secondary landings perhaps in Lyme Bay. The plan is that these élite units of the Home Guard should have the local knowledge and connections to sustain a campaign of harassment against the occupying forces. Each unit is under the control of regular Army officers to ensure the necessary level of expertise and professionalism.

July **Fascist Dorset landowner interned.**

A major Dorset landowner has been arrested and imprisoned with the round-up of pre-war members and supporters of Sir Oswald Mosley's British Union of Fascists. He is Captain George Henry Lane Fox Pitt-Rivers of Hinton St Mary, who was last in the news when he opposed the billeting of city children in rural Dorset. Pitt-Rivers is being held under Defence Regulation 18b.

Footnote By August there were 1,600 detained in prison without trial; three out of four of them were Mosley's members. All but four hundred would be released during the winter of 1940–41. Pitt-Rivers was among those who were still held.

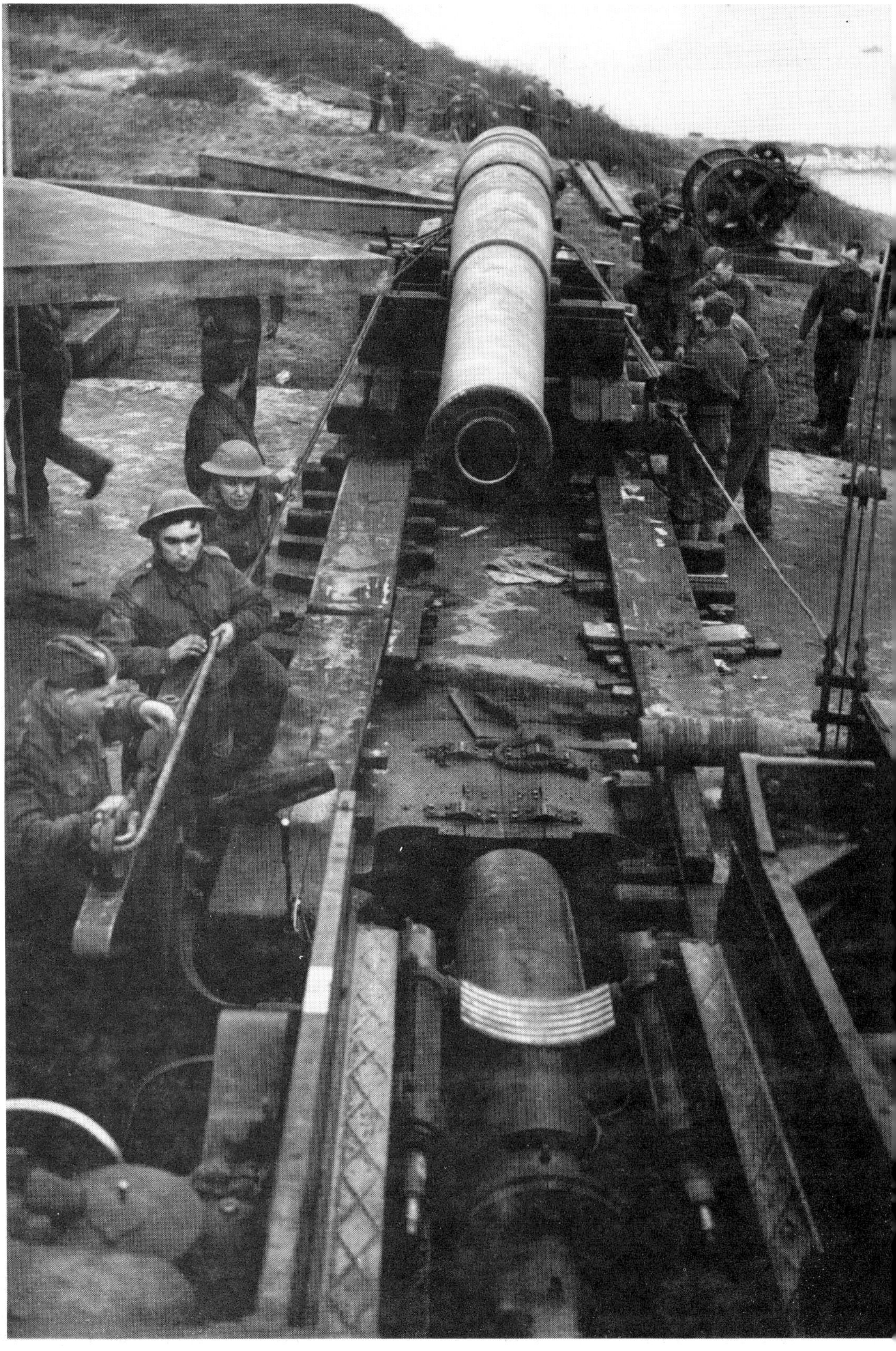

1940

July **Dorset Heavy Regiment redesignated.**

The Dorset Heavy Regiment of the Royal Artillery, which includes the gunners responsible for the defence of the naval anchorage at Portland, has been reformed as the 522nd (Dorset) Coast Regiment. They have 9.2 inch guns in the batteries at East Weares, four hundred feet up on the Portland cliffs, and on the other side of Weymouth Bay at Upton Fort, to the east of Osmington Mills.

1940. Opposite and below. 9.2 inch anti-ship gun being emplaced and loaded at East Weares, Portland, by 102 Coast Defence Battery of the 522nd (Dorset) Coast Regiment. 'Ever ready,' ran the original captioning. 'Men on duty keep watch as a searchlight sweeps the sea.' The gun then opened fire across the night.

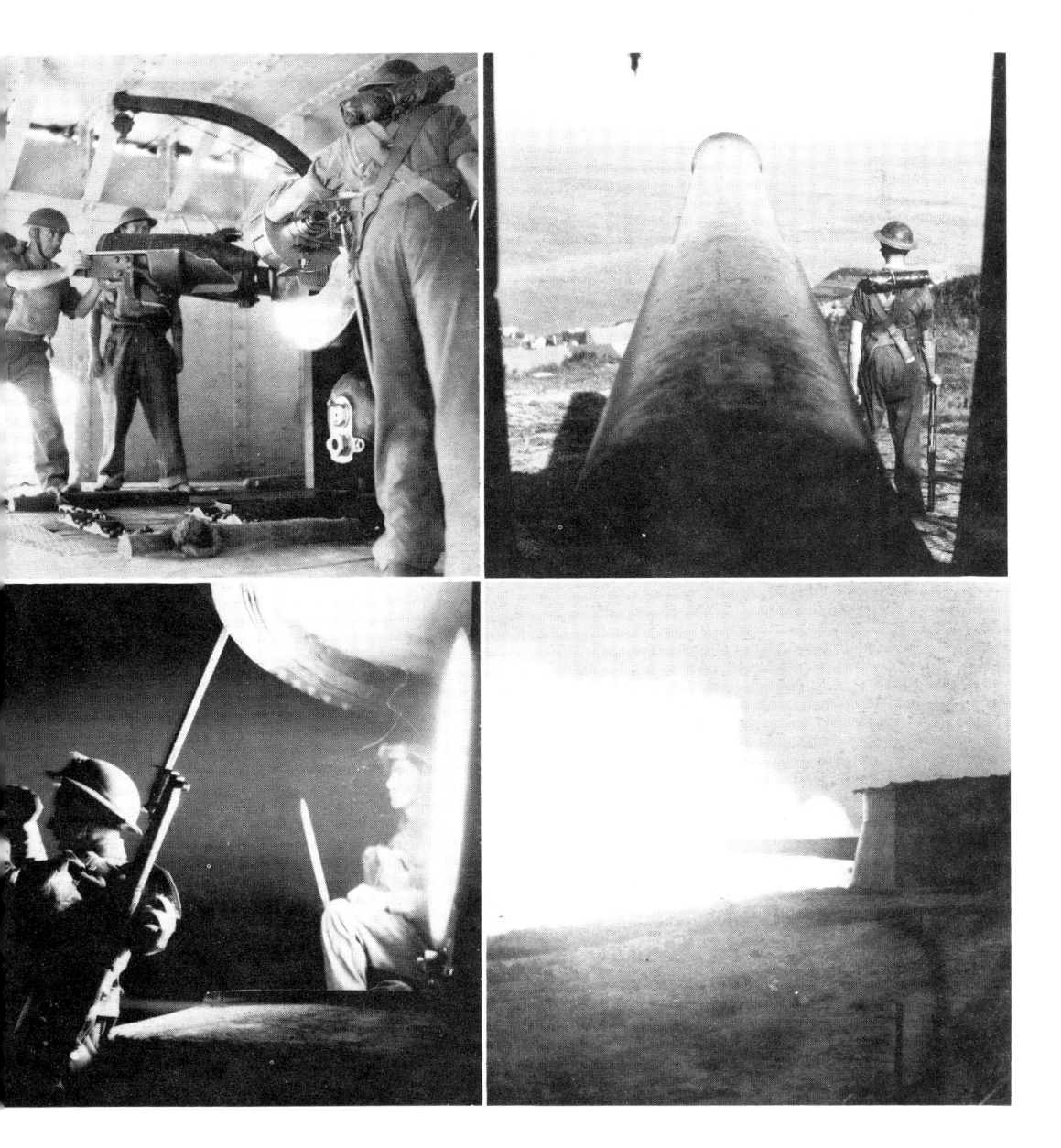

DORSET'S WAR 36

1940. Portland's Home Guard, in Easton Drill Hall.

1940–44. Bere Regis Air Raid Precautions wardens, in their later uniforms of the Wareham and Purbeck Civil Defence Corps, photographed beside the pavilion on the village recreation ground in North Street. They are (front row) Ken Woolfies, Charles Kellaway, Evelyn Lys, Jock Strang, Gertrude Miller, Fred Lys, Edward Hewitt, (centre row) Frank Applin, Henry Hann, Charles Davis, Jack Legg, Louis Joyce, 'Nobby' Bartlett, Harry Pitfield, (back row) Denis Skinner, Leslie Barnes, Percival Pitfield and Michael Miller.
Kellaway would give the air raid warning on his whistle from an ancient Morris Minor. He used a handbell for the all-clear.

14 August 1940. Flying boat 'Clare' on her return to Poole from the first wartime transatlantic air crossing. She had flown out on the 4th.

4 August Poole flying boat crosses the Atlantic.

The Short Sunderland 'Empire' flying boat *Clare*, which took off early yesterday from the 'trots' in Poole Harbour as the water runways are known, today landed on the east coast of the United States and thereby resumed the transatlantic service. She carried three American government VIPs and will return with ferry pilots.

The flying boat's pilots are Captains J.C. Kelly Rogers and G.R.B. Wilcockson, with crewmen White, Burgess and Rotherham.

5 August French general leaves Poole to arrange a coup.

General Edgard de Larminat, the high commissioner of Free French Africa, has flown from Poole in the 'Empire' flying boat *Clyde* to arrange a coup d'état in the Vichy controlled French colonies in the Congo basin. They are flying via Lagos to Leopoldville in the Belgian Congo from where the general and his staff officers will begin their programme for the repossession of French Equitorial Africa.

Footnote The Free French army, led by General Carretier, walked back to power after taking Brazzaville by complete surprise.

8 August More mines laid off Dorset.

The Channel shipping lanes have been subject to further German minelaying in the past thirty-six hours. The Raumboote of the enemy's 3rd Mine Laying Flotilla have been active off Dorset, protected by Schnellboote of the 5th E-boat Flotilla.

8 August More losses as another convoy tries to get through.

Convoy CW9 has broken through the enemy's blockade of the English Channel, but with severe losses. Three ships were sunk and one damaged by E-boat attacks off the Isle of Wight and two destroyers were called out from Portsmouth to give help. An air attack by sixty planes was intercepted and driven off but the convoy then fell victim to a second wave of more than 130 enemy aircraft off Bournemouth.

Here three more ships were lost and thirteen damaged. The Germans lost fourteen aircraft.

11 August **Air raids at Weymouth and Portland.**

Portland Harbour and Weymouth again came under enemy air attack today.

13 August **Warmwell's Spitfires have four Dorset kills.**

Eagle Day: the Luftwaffe's Adler Tag attack of nearly three hundred aircraft against military targets in central southern England has been routed. One of the twenty-seven Junkers 87 'Stukas' of II Group Stukageschwader 2 that had been targeted on Middle Wallop airfield, Hampshire, was shot down between Portesham and Rodden at 16.00 hours, killing its two crewmen. [Feldwebel Linderschmid and Gefr. Eisold]. The kill was claimed by Flight Lieutenant Boitel-Gill of 152 Squadron. At the same time Pilot Officer Crook of 609 Squadron sent an Me109 smoking into the cloud and descended to see the debris of a crash near the Hardy Monument. This, however, was another 'Stuka', which came down two hundred yards from the railway station at Grimstone [killing both crew, Feldwebel Erich Haack; second man unidentified]. The two crew and the discovery of an unexploded 250 kilogram bomb in the wreckage confirm that it was a 'Stuka'.

The others deployed today never reached their targets.

As for the Messerschmitt Bf 109 E1 escort fighters being chased by 609 Squadron, as they turned for the coast short of fuel, Crook's kill ended up in Poole Harbour [the pilot, Unteroffizier Wilhelm Hohenseldt, was rescued and made prisoner of war]. Another was shot down into the sea off Weymouth [its pilot, Leutnant Heinz Pfannschmidt, was also saved and taken prisoner]. This kill was claimed by Pilot Officer Nowierski.

Footnote Eyewitness E.G. Read of Stratton recalled the Grimstone crash for me in 1981: "My neighbours and I had been watching an aerial battle and machine gun ammunition clips had fluttered down around us. Suddenly there was a bloodcurdling banshee wail. It was heart stopping as it approached us.

"Right over our heads came the stricken plane. There was dense black smoke pouring from its starboard engine, and the two young airmen were clearly visible. They had just seconds to live. Later came the news that a German plane had crashed behind Grimstone viaduct. We went there immediately on our bikes, but a sentry was there on guard with fixed bayonet. Beneath two white parachutes were the crumpled bodies of the airmen.

"The next day the sentry was gone and we went souvenir hunting. I pulled off a small electrical bakelite plug that was stamped 'Made in England'. The two young fliers were interred in a green unploughed curve at the side of the field. Later two ornately carved and inscribed wooden crosses appeared at the spot. The bodies remained there from that sunny afternoon in 1940 until the late 1960s when they were reburied in Germany.

"I found their crosses in a dilapidated shed at Frampton churchyard in 1964. The galvanised roof was holed and they were covered in wet lichen. Since then both shed and crosses have disappeared. So, too, has my souvenir component, which I inadvertently threw out with an unwanted box of oddments before moving house in 1978."

1940. Opposite, top. Junkers 87s, the dive-bombers generally known as 'Stukas'—short for 'Stukageschwader'. On 4 July 1940 they sank the 'Foylebank' anti-aircraft gunship in Portland Harbour and on 13 August were back for the Adler Tag ('Eagle Day') attacks on military targets in central southern England. That day's events were a setback for the fearsome reputation they had gained, which pre-dated the Second World War and had been established by cinema newsreels of its preview, the Spanish Civil War.

13 August 1940. Opposite. Wreckage of a 'Stuka' shot down near Grimstone railway station, four miles north-west of Dorchester, by Flight Lieutenant Boitel-Gill of 152 Squadron from Warmwell. The two crewmen were killed. E. Read describes the crash in the footnote above and the photograph is courtesy of Len Parsons and John Norman.

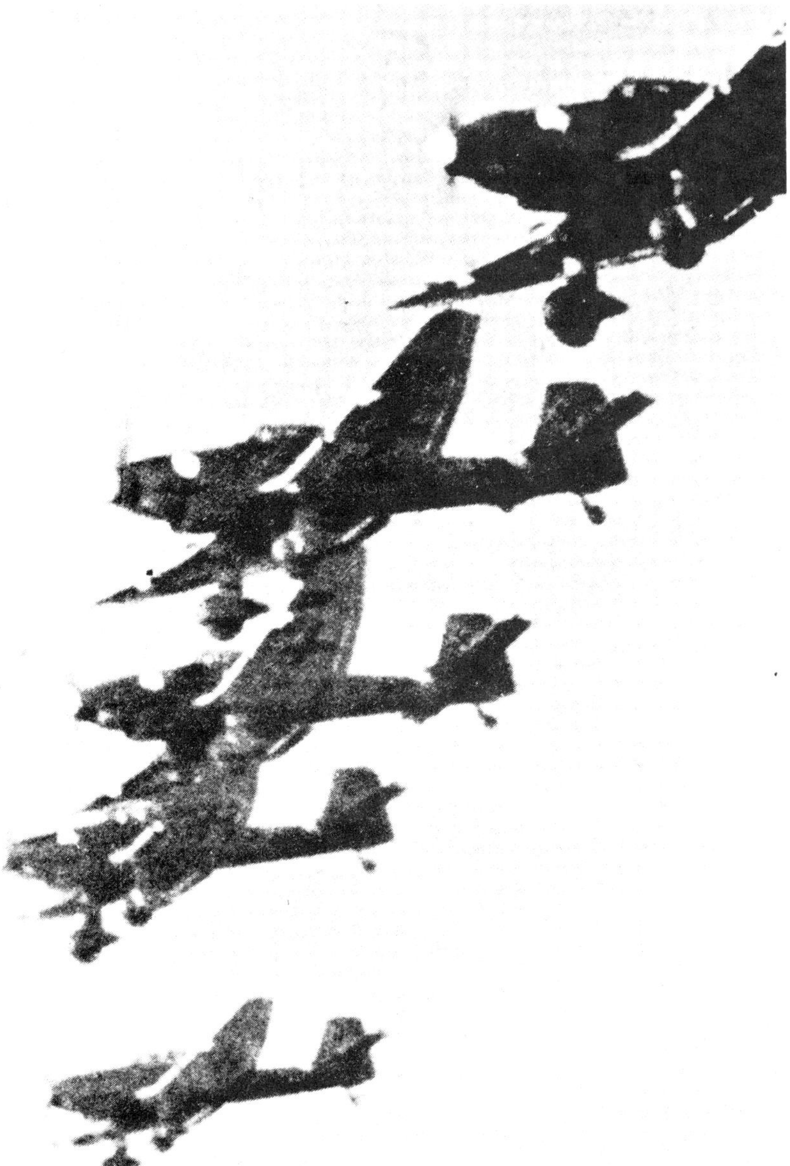

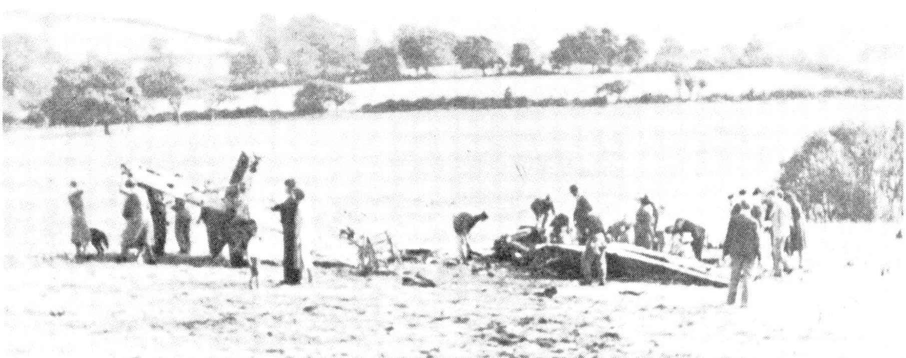

1940. One of ours. A Warmwell Spitfire approaches the Observer Corps post at Poundbury Camp, on the edge of Dorchester.

13 August An entry in the Dorchester Observer Corps log.

Time: 16.35. Location: Poundbury Camp, north-west of the town. Area of activity: South of sector R4, Dorchester. Report: "Confirmed hostile and friendly pilots approaching the post. Much machine gun and cannon fire. Fierce contest going on. Plane shot down believed Me110, another plane down, much confused sound-plotting and heavy firing for a considerable period. One plane believed friendly, flying low east. Believed forced landing this side of the Maiden Castle House and in neighbourhood of the Fever Hospital."

Footnote John Norman of the Royal Observer Corps remembered that emergency Spitfire touch-down for me in 1980: "It landed in the field at Maiden Castle Farm at the back of the cottages and I cycled over in time to see it take off."

14 August Second transatlantic crossing from Poole.

The Air Ministry Under-secretary, Harold Balfour, is flying today from Poole to the United States on the second wartime transatlantic flying boat crossing by *Clare*.

Footnote The flying boat was back in Poole on the 18th. Balfour bought three Boeing 314s—'Clipper' flying boats—from the Americans. These long-range boats will be delivered to British Overseas Airways at Poole early next year.

1940. Spitfire trails in the sky over Dorchester, photographed from the Observer Corps lookout at Poundbury Camp.

15 August **A pilot dies a hero at Abbotsbury.**

Twenty-seven year old Squadron Leader Terence Lovell-Gregg, flying a crippled Hurricane with 87 Squadron from Exeter, failed in a desperate attempt to make a crash landing in The Fleet lagoon.

He came down at Abbotsbury. Roland Beaumont, one of the Warmwell Spitfire pilots, returned with the story of how Lovell-Gregg had led his squadron into the midst of a mass of German aircraft at 18,000 feet over the English Channel: "We saw the 'Beehive' almost straight ahead at the same height and, with his eight Hurricanes, Lovell-Gregg flew straight at the centre of the formation without hesitation or deviation in any way."

One hundred and twenty enemy aircraft were heading towards Portland. Lovell-Gregg was a quiet pre-war professional, from Marlborough in New Zealand, who had taught many of the emergent generation of fliers. His courage was never in any doubt, though he had only led his squadron for a month, since 12 July.

Footnote William Dunford, then an Abbotsbury schoolboy, described for me how he put out the flames on the pilot's burning body: "Lovell-Gregg's Hurricane was shot down in flames, at about 6.00 to 6.30 pm, but he recovered control to put the plane into a perfect glide and attempted to land in The Fleet lagoon at Abbotsbury Swannery. He came low over a small wood but was not quite high enough. The underside of the Hurricane hit the top of an oak tree, and

DORSET'S WAR 42

Lovell-Gregg was thrown out of the cockpit. The plane went on through the trees and crashed.
 "With another schoolboy I ran to the spot where the pilot had fallen. He was badly shot about and burning. We put out the flames with two buckets of water. About two hours later a truck came from Warmwell and we were then told the flier's identity. Though he had those wounds, I am sure, had he made it into the water, that he would have survived."
 Lovell-Gregg is buried in Warmwell churchyard.

15 August   Spitfire pilot rescued off Chesil Bank.

Ralph ('Bob') Wolton of 152 Squadron was shot down today in an engagement with Junkers 87 'Stuka' dive-bombers off Portland and fell out of his Spitfire seconds before it crashed into the sea. He managed to swim to one of the marker buoys of the Chesil Beach bombing range, from which he was then rescued by an RAF launch from Lyme Regis.

15 August   Spitfire crashes at Bournemouth.

The eastern side of the Middle Wallop Sector also saw action today with a formation of bombers approaching Bournemouth. The Spitfires of 234 Squadron were scrambled at Middle Wallop at 17.05 hours and intercepted the bombers, which were heading homeward, over the town. A sustained air battle took place at 4,000 feet, during which Spitfire R6988 was hit by fire from one of the German rear gunners.
 It spiralled into Leven Avenue, to the west of Meyrick Park golf links, leaving a crater and wreckage across a wide area. One of the wings fell on a hedge in Walford Road. Pilot Officer Cecil Hight fell from the aircraft but his parachute did not open. The New Zealander had been

15 August 1940. Left. Squadron Leader Terence Lovell-Gregg—killed in his Hurricane at Abbotsbury.

15 August 1940. Below. Pilot Officer Cecil Hight—killed in his Spitfire at Bournemouth. Both fliers came from New Zealand.

seriously wounded and apparently passed out before he could pull the rip-cord. His body was found in Mr and Mrs Hoare's garden.

Footnote The town has named Pilot Hight Road in his memory. Cecil Hight was the only allied airman to die over Bournemouth. He is buried at Boscombe and a memorial tablet was unveiled at St Peter's church in the town centre on 7 April 1943.

Mr and Mrs Hoare's house was again to be visited by the war. Ian McQueen records in *Bournemouth St Peter's* that it was hit by a German bomb. Canon Hedley Burrows recalled that it was the house where Hight's Spitfire had crashed.

"The dear old man, Mr Hoare died," Canon Burrows said, but then they heard Mrs Hoare. "Who is that," she asked. "I am Canon Burrows; keep still; they are going to get you out."

"Canon Burrows," she replied, "how kind of you to come and see me today."

16 August 152 Squadron's two firsts.

Pilot Officer Roland Beaumont, flying a Spitfire with 152 Squadron from Warmwell, has scored his squadron's first kills with two Me109s brought down over the Isle of Wight.

8 December 1940, the drawing is dated. The subject is Pilot Officer Eric 'Boy' Marrs of 152 Squadron, who flew a Spitfire from Warmwell. He would become the station's hero and win the Distinguished Flying Cross—which would save his life by taking him to London for the day. But there is a saying about those 'whom the gods love'.

18 August Warmwell's 'Boy' Marrs has his first kill.

Formations of more than a hundred Junkers 87 'Stuka' dive-bombers, escorted by Messerschmitt 109 fighters, crossed the Channel to attack the radar station at Poling and aerodromes at Ford, Thorney Island and Gosport. Eleven Spitfires of 152 Squadron were scrambled from Warmwell.

The Spitfires dived from 4,000 feet on the Stukas as they swept back to sea after dropping their bombs. Pilot Officer Eric 'Boy' Marrs claimed a kill:

"We dived after them and they went down to about a hundred feet above the water. Then followed a running chase out to sea. The evasive action they took was to throttle back and do steep turns to right and left so that we would not be able to follow them and would overshoot. There were, however, so many of them that if one was shaken off the tail of one there was always another to sit on. I fired at about six and shot down one. It caught fire in the port wing petrol tank and then went into the sea about three hundred yards further on."

DORSET'S WAR 44

1940. German air reconnaissance photograph of the northern part of Portland Harbour. The coastal features (bottom to top) are the Chesil Beach, Small Mouth and the Ferrybridge, Wyke Regis, Bincleaves and the Northern Arm of the Breakwater, the Nothe promontory and Weymouth Harbour. Ships are identified by numbers and anti-aircraft gun sites by letters.

The picture also shows a munitions factory—Whitehead Torpedo Works, on the Weymouth side of the Small Mouth opening at the Ferrybridge. It occupies the land nearest the shore, between the road (left bridge) and the railway line (right bridge).

19 August **Enigma decrypt gives warning of Warmwell attack.**

01.52 hours. "From a reliable source, information has been received of an impending attack on Warmwell aerodrome this morning. Aircraft are to be ready to leave at 07.00 hours." [From a German 'Enigma' radio signal decoded by the Government Code and Cipher School, at Bletchley Park.]

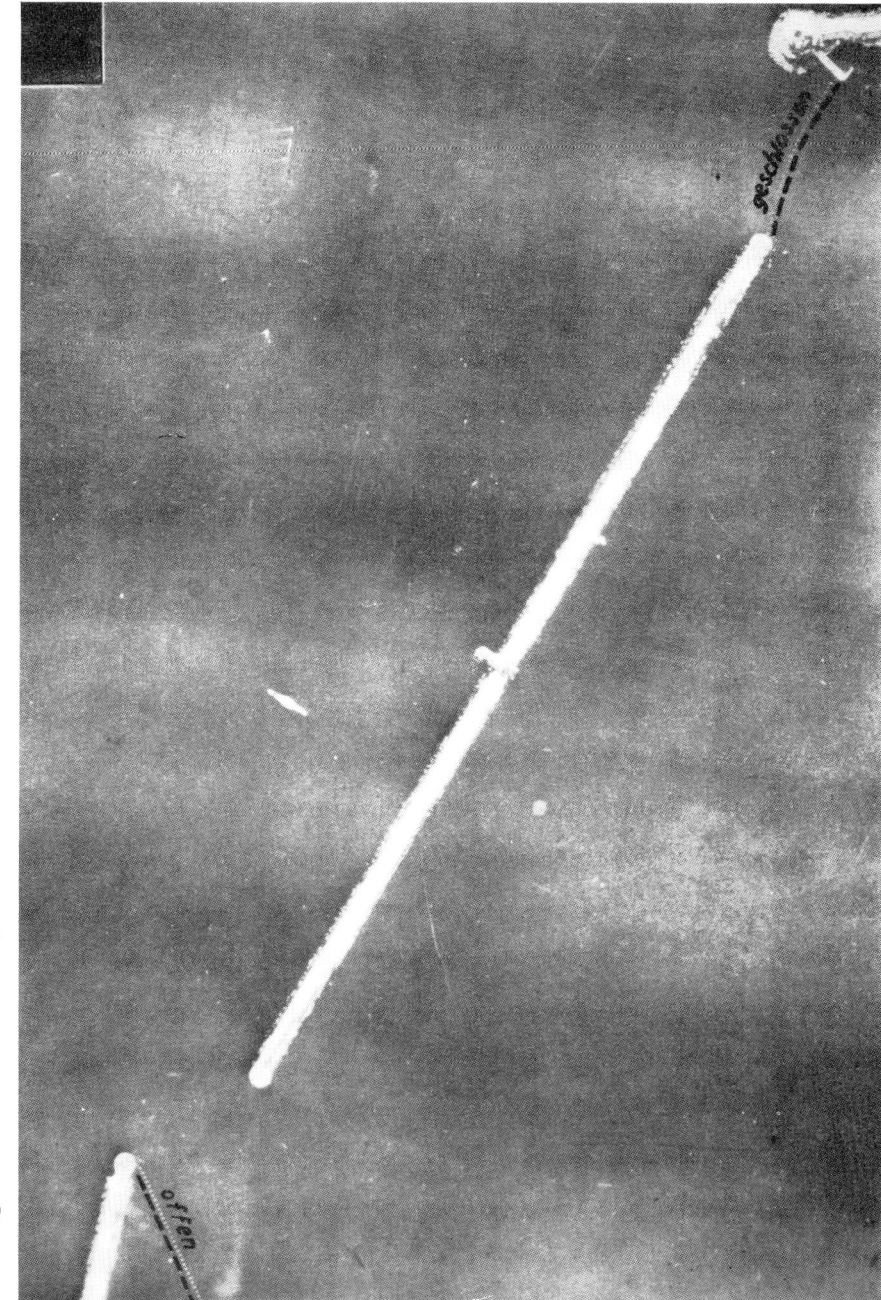

1940. German reconnaissance photograph of 'Netzsperren von Portland'. The central breakwater of Portland Harbour is seen from the north-west. The East Ship Channel (top) is blocked by anti-submarine nets. The North Ship Channel (bottom) is open but also has a line of nets that could be closed.

21 August **Two killed by afternoon bombs at Poole.**

Mrs Pauline Fairbrother of 38 Market Street and Frederick Landrey of 18 South Road were killed this afternoon when a single German raider, a Junkers 88, came in low over the Old Town area of central Poole from Sandbanks. It dropped six bombs. The one that killed Mr Landrey destroyed the National School air-raid shelter, thankfully unoccupied, and the others hit shops and timber stores.

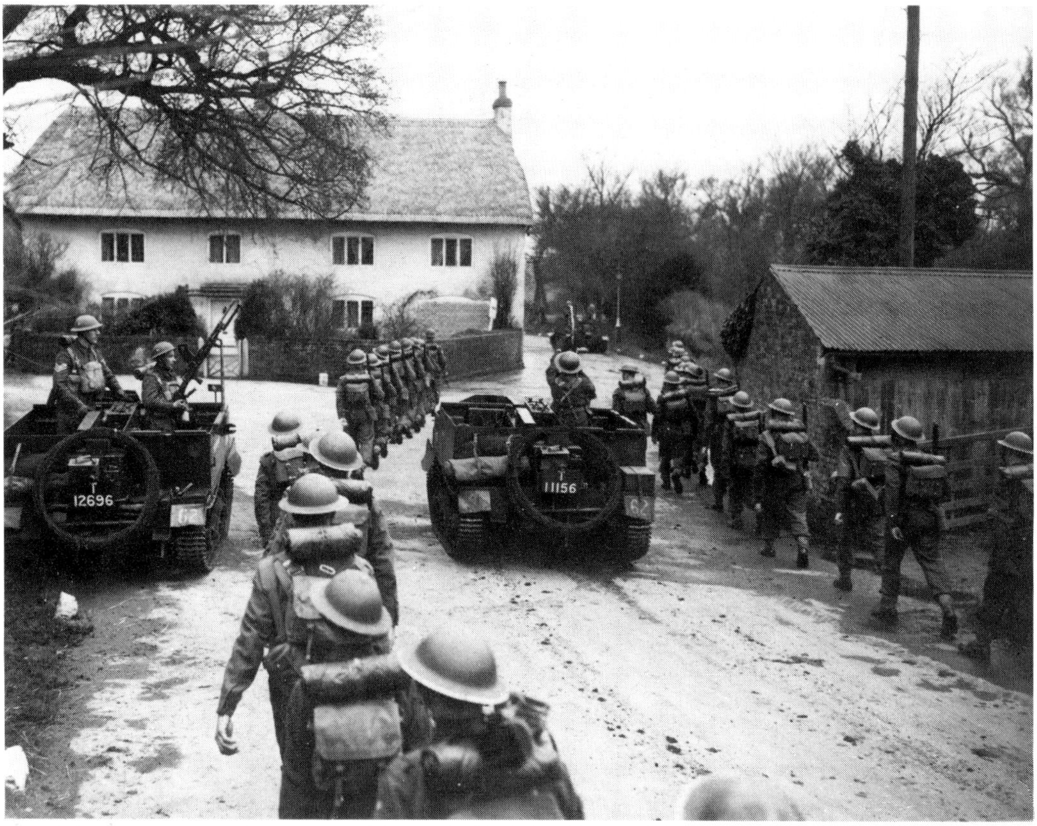
12696
11156

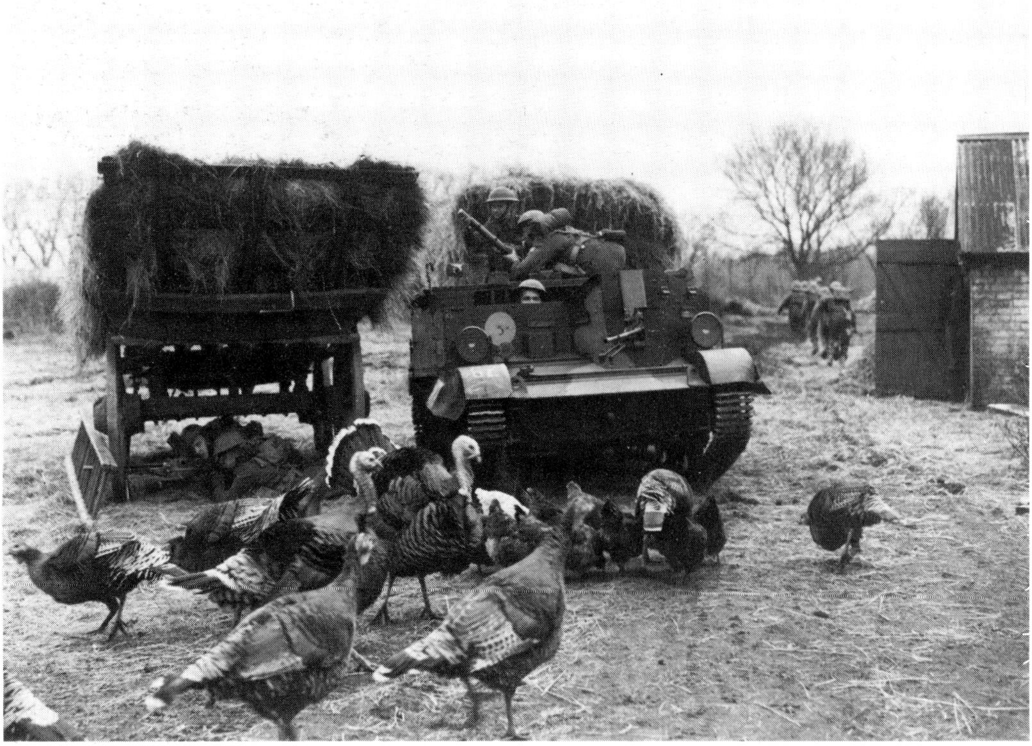

1940. 5th Battalion of the Northants Regiment put the Bren gun carrier amongst the turkeys during a little mock warfare in the Christchurch countryside.

1940. School for Junior Leaders with unarmed combat practice in the car park of a Bournemouth clifftop hotel (name removed in accordance with Defence Regulations). They used dummies for the finer points of bayonet training.

1940. 12th Battalion of the Hampshire Regiment in cliff exercises at Hengistbury Head, Bournemouth.

25 August Shops bombed at Poole.

Early this morning a single German bomber attacked the Ashley Road and Contitution Hill area of Upper Parkstone, Poole, destroying three shops and a house. Two people were injured.

25 August Decoded signals warn of another Warmwell bombing.

07.40 hours. "It is reliably reported that air attacks are to be expected during the course of today 25th August 1940 at Warmwell, Little Rissington and Abingdon aerodromes and reconnaissances by a single aircraft in the area Southampton-Aldershot-Brighton." [From German 'Enigma' machine-coded radio signals deciphered by the Government Code and Cipher School at Bletchley Park.]

By 17.00 the twelve Warmwell Spitfires of 152 Squadron were airborne. Half an hour later the station was rocked by twenty bombs, destroying the sick quarters and damaging hangars. Delayed action bombs went off over the next couple of days. The Spitfires had met Luftflotte 3 over Portland but despite the advance warning it was a more or less even match. Three enemy planes were claimed but two pilots never returned to Warmwell that evening.

29 August Extensive bomb damage at Poole.

04.00 hours. Though no one has been injured, high explosive and incendiary bombs have caused considerable damage to buildings in the Longfleet, Oakdale and Parkstone suburbs of Poole.

29 August Bombs miss Christchurch.

Early this morning incendiary bombs landed near the Priory, Millhams Street and at Queens Avenue in Christchurch. One was on the roof of the air-compressing station. There were also the thuds of high explosive bombs but daylight revealed they had dropped on the north side of the town into heathland and woods at St Catherine's hill. Ten had gone off and one had failed to explode.

August Burton Bradstock call for Hitler prayers.

Writing in *The Two Edged Sword*, Adela Curtis, leader of the Christian Contemplatives' Charity at St Bride's Farm, Burton Bradstock, advises on methods of furthering the war effort through positive prayer: "We are to summon each enemy leader by name. For cumulative effect the message should be spoken three times—Adolf Hitler! Adolf Hitler! Adolf Hitler! Hear the Truth!"

August Cranborne Chase motor-cycle exercises.

The 4th Battalion of the Royal Northumberland Fusiliers have been reorganised as a motor-cycle reconnaissance column and are based at Blandford Camp. Their sidecar patrols are seemingly everywhere in the Cranborne Chase villages.

The 2nd and 8th Battalions of the Fusiliers are also in Dorset, dispersed through the Blackmore Vale.

August–October 1940. Opposite. 4th Battalion of the Northumberland Fusiliers—veterans of the British Expeditionary Force, Dunkirk and defending Bournemouth beach—fitted out with motor-cycles and sidecars as a reconnaissance column and training across the rolling downlands of Cranborne Chase.

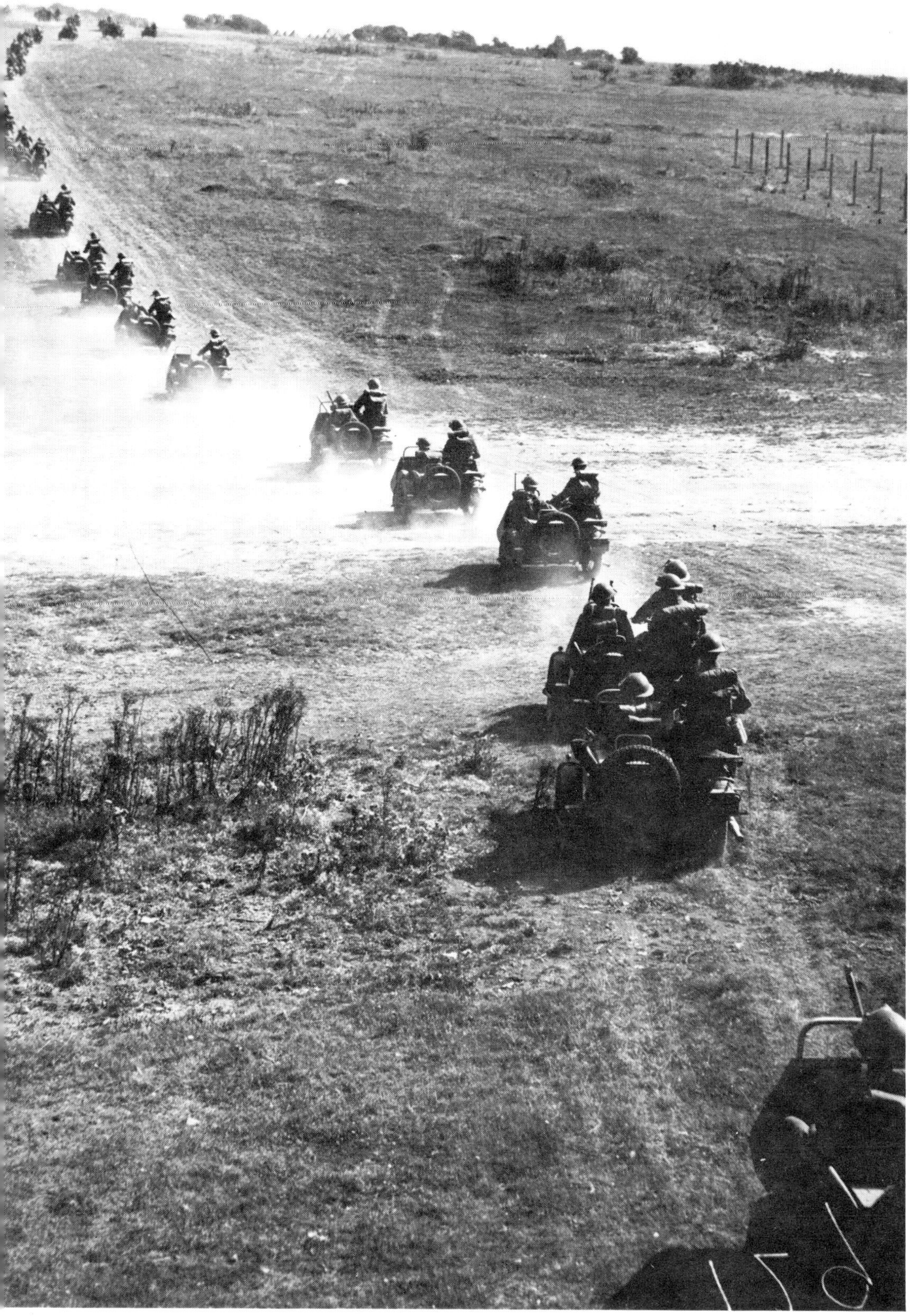

August–October 1940. From Blandford Camp the 4th Battalion of the Northumberland Fusiliers rode out into the Dorset countryside, with frequent stops to manhandle their Nortons across ditches, trenches and other obstacles.

4 September   **Another Warmwell pilot killed.**

Spitfire pilot John Barker failed to return to Warmwell Aerodrome today after 152 Squadron had been scrambled for an operational sortie.

5 September   **Bomb hits Druitt's House, Christchurch.**

Druitt's House, the solicitors' offices and former residence of one of the town's leading families—which produced Montagu James Druitt who was a suspect for Jack the Ripper, the Whitechapel murderer—was destroyed by a German bomb at 01.30 hours this morning. Just after midnight a bomb had dropped on Iford golf course but that one failed to explode.

7 September   **Spitfire crashes near Dorchester.**

Ralph ('Bob') Wolton, flying at the rear of a flight of Spitfires with 152 Squadron from Warmwell, today lost control of his fighter whilst attempting a sudden dive. He jumped from the falling plane at 13,000 feet though he estimates that it was not until nearly a thousand feet from the ground when he managed to sort out the cords and activate the chute. The Spitfire crashed near Dorchester.

No enemy plane was involved.

7 September   **The great invasion scare.**

The German invasion appears to have started. Reports have been received of a seven-mile convoy heading towards the Dorset coast and there is a general flap on that Operation Sealion is taking place and Field Marshal Feodor von Bock is on his way with the victors of Poland, the Wehrmacht's Army Group B. The fuel tanks are to be fired to set the beaches ablaze and an aircraft from Gosport is dropping incendiaries to start them off.

Troops at Bournemouth have manned the cliffs and keep emphasising that this is not an exercise.

The Home Guard at the Supermarine aircraft factory in Southampton has been alerted to enemy landings at Portsmouth.

7 September   **Invasion expected tonight.**

20.07 hours. A national alert has been issued by the War Office: 'Condition Cromwell'. An invasion is regarded as imminent and probable within twelve hours.

Footnote   Nothing happened! One set of 'Fougasse' tanks ignited a beach but the plane was recalled to Gosport before it set alight to any more. There was no landing in Dorset or anywhere else.

10 September   **Fourteen bombs at Christchurch.**

Fourteen bombs landed in the Christchurch area last night, at about midnight, fracturing water mains and bringing down telephone wires. There was serious blast damage to Hoburne Farm. Six of the bombs fortunately exploded harmlessly on Chewton Common.

14 September   **Another Warmwell pilot killed.**

A further fatal casualty has been inflicted upon RAF Warmwell, taking the life of Flying Officer C.O. Hinks.

15 September   Warmwell's Spitfires defend London.

The Spitfires of 609 Squadron from Warmwell were drawn into the air defence of London today as the Battle of Britain reached its climax. Total claims for the day were 186 enemy aircraft shot down.

Footnote   The Air Ministry was warned by its own intelligence department that 'kill' claims were being overstated and that no more than 76 planes could have been destroyed on 15 September. Post-war examination of German records showed that even this was exaggerated; the real figure was 62.

For all that it was a victory. Air Chief Marshal Sir Hugh Dowding had handled his forces with precision and economy. They had not been wasted on pointless patrols. A combination of radar and decoded German radio traffic meant that the sectors that were going to have a quiet day—as with Middle Wallop and Warmwell on the 15th—could provide planes for an area where the resident defenders would be outnumbered. Dowding's achievement was to deny the Luftwaffe its one prerequisite for winning the Battle of Britain. This was done by ensuring there were always planes in reserve and that something could be done about the following day's attack.

Göring was frustrated by this and had ordered his commanders: "You must bring the RAF up to battle."

15 September   Cattistock carillon destroyed by fire.

14.30 hours. The tall 1873-built tower of Cattistock church has been gutted by fire, destroying its famous carillon of thirty-five bells. The village will miss the tunes. Officially the cause is not known, but locally it has been blamed on a cigarette discarded by a member of the Home Guard who was in the tower for fire-watching.

17 September   Marrs loses his 'Old Faithful'.

Pilot Officer Eric 'Boy' Marrs from Warmwell today intercepted a Junkers 88 near Bath and sent it streaming glycol from its radiator with the first burst of fire from his Spitfire. The bomber descended into thick cloud and crashed near Imber, only three miles from his old school, Dauntsey's, in Wiltshire.

Marrs, however, then suffered engine failure. 'Old Faithful', in which the young pilot had flown 130 hours, was coaxed down from 12,000 feet on to the concrete runways of a disused aerodrome that had been partly obstructed to prevent German landings.

A bullet had smashed the air cooler and caused the Merlin engine to lose its oil. A maintenance squad removed the Spitfire by road and Marrs will never fly it again; probably it will go back into service with a training unit.

17 September   Operation Sealion postponed indefinitely.

Hitler today postponed Operation Seelöwe [Sealion], the planned invasion of England, which should give the country's nerves a reprieve until next spring. Winston Churchill has read out a deciphered German Enigma machine-coded radio message to the Chiefs of Defence Staff—a minor order of huge significance, for the dismantling of loading equipment on Dutch airfields. Churchill refers to Sealion as Operation Smith, to lessen the risk of compromising the Enigma intercepts that revealed its name.

19 September   Bournemouth Garrison stood down.

With the abandonment of Operation Sealion any immediate prospect of a German invasion has receded and accordingly the Bournemouth Garrison has stood down. The Garrison Commander has been replaced by a new posting, that of Officer Commanding Troops, Bournemouth.

20 September **Steamship sinks in Lyme Bay.**

SS *Trito*, a British steam freighter, has sunk after being bombed by German aircraft in Lyme Bay.

25 September **Heinkels shot down at Poole and Studland.**

A German mass bombing force of 220 attacking planes and their escorts passed over Portland and flew to the Bristol Channel coast where they turned between the islands Steep Holm and Flat Holm and made an approach across the water towards the Bristol Aeroplane Company's works at Filton. This was devastated by 350 bombs and from 15,000 feet the aerodrome rippled with flashes.

On the way home, however, the raiders were harried by the RAF. Five aircraft were brought down and a further three had to crash-land in France. The two shot down in Dorset were both claimed by Hurricanes of 238 Squadron from Middle Wallop. One Heinkel 111 (markings G1+LR) ploughed into 'Underwood', a house at Westminster Road, Branksome Park, and all but one of its five crewmen were killed.

The second Heinkel 111 (G1+BH) crash-landed at Westfield Farm, Studland. Josef Attrichter, the flight mechanic, was taken from the wreckage but died half an hour later. The other four crewmen had aching backs from the impact but survived. Wine waiter Theo Janku took them prisoner with the aid of an unloaded Home Guard rifle and relieved them of their Lugers. On seeing there were casualties the Studland villagers then tried to help the Germans and provided cigarettes and tea.

Footnote Later the Heinkel was salvaged and reassembled for Cardiff's war weapons week. Before it was removed from Studland it had been guarded by a detachment of the Suffolk Regiment. "This is war, not a bloody peepshow," one of the sentries snapped at onlookers. It seems to have been from this bomber that a document was found forbidding the use of explosive ammunition against troop concentrations and other human targets.

The burial of the Branksome Park Germans in Parkstone Cemetery, next to graves of British seamen, enraged the Poole Herald which protested that "Nazi murderers and British heroes" were "placed side by side" and a week later felt utterly let down by one of its readers: "Someone has put flowers on the grave!"

25 September 1940. Wreckage of 'Underwood' and the Branksome Park Heinkel.

DORSET'S WAR 56

26 September **Warmwell pilots in action again.**

Flight Lieutenant Derek Boitel-Gill led a section of 152 Squadron from Warmwell into combat against a formation of Junkers 88s over the sea to the west of the Isle of Wight. One was seen to fall into the water, the kill being the work of Ralph ('Bob') Wolton.

  Footnote Boitel-Gill was no mean shot, having been credited with five kills in a week in August. He became Commanding Officer of 152 Squadron early in 1941 and Wing Commander in June. He then lost his life in a flying accident, in July 1941.

27 September **German planes crash all over Dorset.**

This Friday has been the day when German planes crashed all over Dorset, plus Mick Miller and his Spitfire from 609 Squadron. The full account of the abortive raid on the Parnell Aircraft Company—makers of gun turrets—at Yate, near Chipping Sodbury, was told in 1979 by Kenneth Wakefield in his *Luftwaffe Encore*.

  Ten fighter-bombers of Erprobungsgruppe 210 from Cherbourg, led by Hauptmann Martin Lutz, had the support of eighty-nine fighters. The Gruppe's aircraft have as their crest a red map of the British Isles superimposed with a yellow ring-type gun sight.

  The German bombers, coming in fast over north Bristol on their attacking run at 11,000 feet, were met head on by Murray Frisby in a Hurricane. He scored a hit that damaged Lutz's plane, and the others too were forced to turn. The rest of 504 Squadron, scrambled from Filton, chased after the scattering planes and forced them to jettison their bombs. Escape was now the only

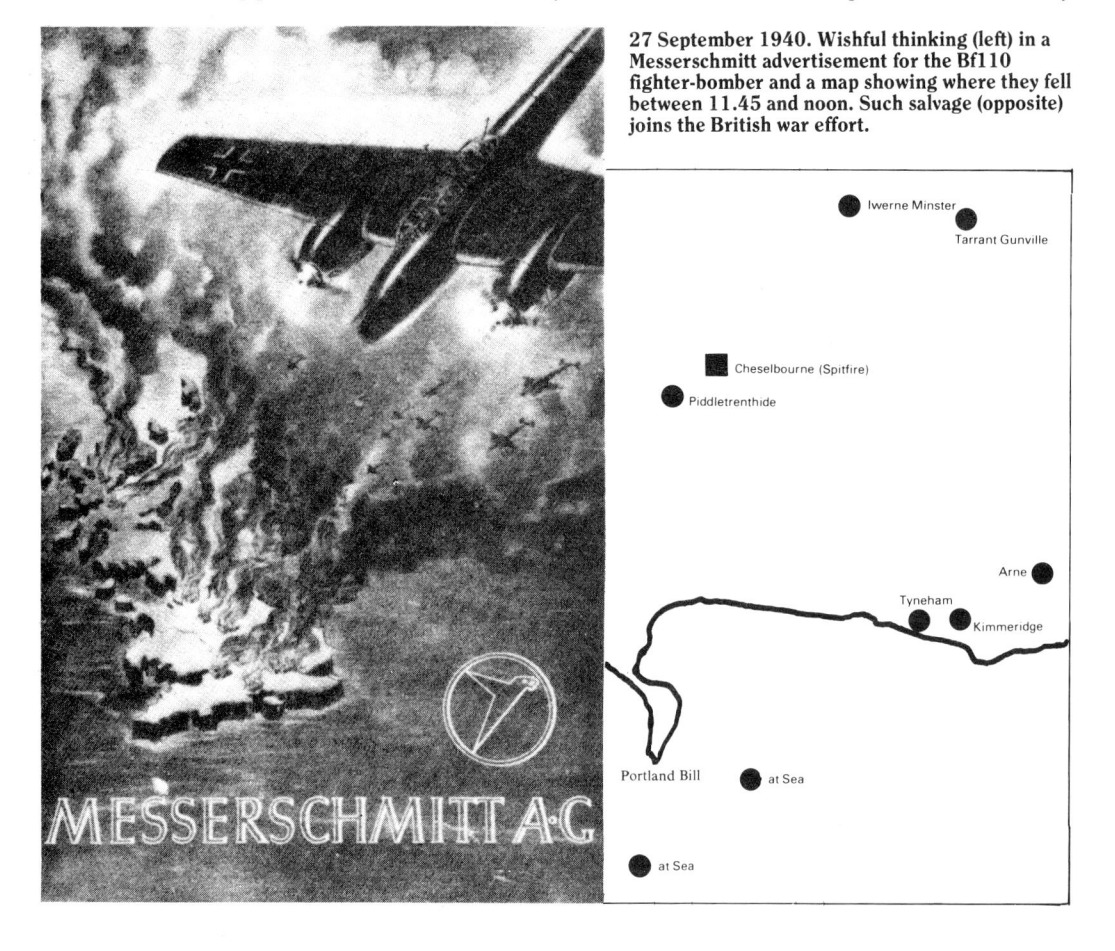

27 September 1940. Wishful thinking (left) in a Messerschmitt advertisement for the Bf110 fighter-bomber and a map showing where they fell between 11.45 and noon. Such salvage (opposite) joins the British war effort.

German objective.

One of the Bf110s was shot down over Fishponds, Bristol. Another came down at Haydon Hill, near Radstock.

That was 11.45 in the morning. At the same moment, over Bellamy's Farm, Piddletrenthide, there was a similar bang as one of the rearguard manoeuvres went wrong. Pilot Officer Mick Miller, in Spitfire X4107 and leading 609 (West Riding) Squadron—scrambled from Warmwell, where they arrived each morning from Middle Wallop—had collided with a Bf110 (number 3U+FT) at 24,000 feet. Miller and the Messerschmitt's wireless operator, Emil Lidtke, were killed instantly. But the German pilot, Georg Jackstedt, was able to free himself and parachuted (minus his boots) into a field. He was given some lemonade and then taken off by police.

His dead comrade was treated with less respect: "Ralph Wightman recalled that when the body was removed from the wreckage it was left in full view for some hours before someone covered it with a sheet. Later a dispute arose over the burial, one report indicating that the local clergy refused to bury the body; apparently the dead airman was eventually buried beside the hedgerow where he fell." That was the boundary between Bellamy's and Dole's Ash Farm. The Spitfire came down to the east, nearer Cheselbourne. Miller was an Australian.

Another Bf110 (3U+IM) was exploding at about 11.45, at 1,000 feet over Salter's Wood, Middlebere, in Purbeck. It had been attacked by a Spitfire of 152 Squadron, Warmwell's second squadron. In the crashed plane were Arthur Niebuhr and Klaus Deissen. Both were killed.

Equally unfortunate, at 11.50, were the crew of another Bf110, between Tyneham and Kimmeridge. It was almost certainly aircraft 3U-BD manned by Hans Carschel and Unteroffizier Klose. Luckier—five-minutes later and only a mile away—were the crew of 3U+DS. Fritz Schupp and Karl Nechwatal had been attacked by Spitfires and their port engine was hit and burning. But Schupp successfully brought his plane to a crash landing near Gaulter Gap. It had three 'kill' bars, which as Wakefield says, denoted "victories over RAF aircraft".

At noon, another Bf110 (S9+DU) made a belly landing. It received engine damage over Iwerne Minster and came down at The Beeches, beside the A350. The pilot was Friedrich Ebner, who was unhurt, but the gunner, Werner Zwick, was taken to Shaftesbury Hospital with major wounds.

Another noon crash was at Bussey Stool Farm, near Tarrant Gunville. It was S9+DH—the Bf110 of the attack's leader, Martin Lutz. It had been damaged at Bristol. The plane was travelling at speed but losing height and hit trees before ploughing into the ground. Both Lutz and his radio operator, Anton Schön, were killed. Lutz was aged 27, and had flown with the Condor Legion in the Spanish Civil War.

Two Bf110s were also shot down at mid-day into the sea off Dorset. One was S9+JH, the crew being Gerhard Schmidt and Gerhard Richeter, whose bodies were later recovered. The crew of the other plane, S9+GK (Wilhelm Rössiger and Hans Marx) were never found. They were brought down twenty-five miles south of Portland Bill.

The attacking Spitfire was flown by Noel le C. Agazarian, from Warmwell.

Footnote Agazarian was killed later in the war but he left one of the most evocative of all memorials. His plane, R6915, survived the war and is now suspended over the displays in the Imperial War Museum, Lambeth Road, London SE1. It dominates the exhibits, as does Dorset's Roman mosaic of Christ in the British Museum.

28 September **Armed trawler mined in Lyme Bay.**

HMT *Recoil*, an armed trawler crewed by the Royal Navy, has hit a mine and sunk in Lyme Bay.

29 September **Christchurch radar establishment hit.**

01.07 hours. Six high explosive bombs and a number of incendiaries dropped on to the Ministry of Supply's Air Defence Experimental Establishment which makes radar components at Somerford, Christchurch. Damage, however, is slight. All the fires were put out by 02.48.

30 September **Sherborne's 300 bombs in three minutes.**

Yeovil's barrage balloons were raised a few minutes before four o'clock on a warm but cloudy afternoon. In Sherborne the air raid sirens wailed. Three hundred bombs would rain on it in three minutes as a disturbed grouping of fifty German bombers—they had been targeted on Bristol—followed the north side of the railway line into the ancient yellow-stone town of clustered terraces and scholastic and ecclesiastical roofs. In those moments the casualties were numerically less than the damage to the buildings: seventeen dead and thirty-two hospital cases, one of whom was to die. Fortunately the schools had just gone home.

1 October 1940. Sherborne. Looking west along Half Moon Street and showing the result of yesterday's bombing.

1 October 1940. Sherborne. Phillips and Son's outfitting department (above, left) and the public bar of the Half Moon Hotel. Below is Foster's Infants School on the east side of Tinney's Lane, Newland.

Footnote This was to be just about Sherborne's only direct sacrifice for the duration of hostilities; only four others went to hospital as a result of the war in the period 1939–45. Despite the damage, in a line across the town from Lenthay Common to Coldharbour, it was of little architectural consequence. The Abbey, Sherborne School, the Almshouse, Sherborne Castle and even the older ruined castle survived with only flecks of superficial damage. For all that it was the worst Dorset air raid of the war.

There was a heroine amongst the debris. Miss Maud Steele, the supervisor of the telephone exchange which was blown apart by a direct hit, stayed calm and ensured that the town's initial calamity reports were sent out by road.

She was to be awarded the George Cross for her pluck; it had been instituted as the "Civilians VC" only a few days previously. The town had 766 damaged buildings, some ten per cent of them devastated, out of a total of 1,700. The sewers as well as the phones were out of action. Blankets had to be brought in by the Red Cross and a council appeal fund, competing with many others, raised £2,200 including contributions from Sherborne in Massachusetts.

For the victims there is a brass plate behind the cross that commemorates the Great War in Half Moon Street, in front of the Abbey precinct:

THOSE WHO DIED IN THE AIR RAID ON SHERBORNE
30 SEPTEMBER 1940

BUTLIN John	LE GALLAIS Albert I.E.
DAWE Leonard J.	LINTERN Arthur J.
GARTELL Albertina B.	MARDEN Elizabeth A.
GOULTER Percy H.D.	MORGAN William S.
HUNT Douglas	REASON A.H.
IRELAND Henry	TRASK Barry A.
JEFFERY William C.	WARREN Ronald K.
KNOBBS Edward D.	WARREN Robert G.
LEGG Horace G.	WARREN Partricia A.

1 October 1940. Sherborne. 'Homemead' on the west side of Acreman Street.

1 October. 1940. Sherborne. 'Stonegarth' (above) was Miss Margaret Billinger's home in Newland, at the south end of The Avenue. 'Sedber' (below, now known as 'Rathgar') is on the east side of The Avenue. Opposite is the centre of Cheap Street, with a crater outside T.E. Gillard's hairdressing salon. 'Have Faith In God' the sign reads above the clearance team.

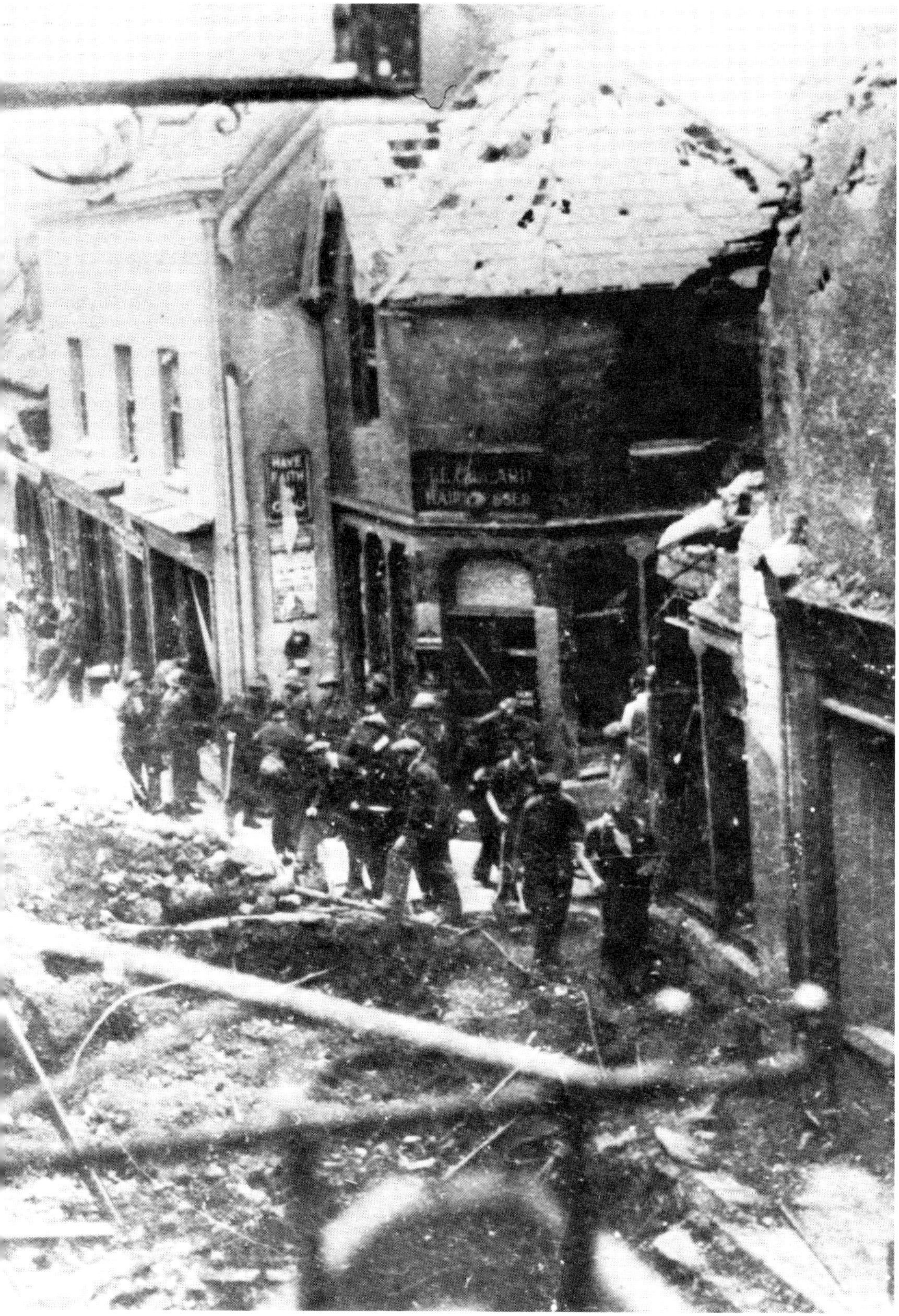
HAVE
FAITH

1 October 1940. Sherborne. Cottages and terraced houses at the Knapp, Acreman Street, left in ruins by yesterday's bombs.

In 1984, for the story of the disaster and the town's resilience and recovery, I interviewed the District Air Raid Precautions Controller, Edward J. Freeman MBE who was also the Clerk to the Sherborne Urban District Council between 1936–74. The account was first published in Harold Osment's *Wartime Sherborne*. In it Mr Osment poignantly recalls that one of the dead was a school chum: "There came the cruel realisation, so cruel as to be almost beautiful, that we should never again see, let alone play with Bobby Warren." This is how Mr Freeman recalled the day and its aftermath, from his bungalow beside the fields at Rimpton, to the north of the town:

"The Sherborne raid is being forgotten. Last year I heard a guide at Sherborne Castle say in answer to a question, about whether any bombs had fallen at Sherborne during the war, that he thought there had been one dropped in the town. I interrupted to say that I had been the town's ARP Controller and there had been 300 bombs that fell in three minutes on 30 September 1940.

"At the time I was on the pavement in Yeovil standing in a queue to see a picture—it was one of the few days in the entire war when I was away from my desk. It was my birthday. The thud of the bombs in the east was followed by a pall of black smoke, which could only be from Sherborne, and I drove straight back. It took me twenty minutes to reach the council offices, picking my way through an unimaginable shambles.

"The theory is that the fifty German planes had been on their way to the Bristol Aeroplane Company at Filton" [seriously damaged by an attack five days earlier, on 25 September] "and were intercepted by a squadron of Hurricanes, two of which were brought down each side of Yeovil. The local people thought one of the pilots was a German as they saw his parachute open. The bombers came to us from the southwest, across Lenthay Common, and then they unloaded. We were underneath.

"There were no longer any services at all. No water, no telephones—the exchange had a direct hit—no gas, no electricity, and the sewers and all roads out of the town were blocked.

"One of the miracles was in Newland where Foster's Infants School received a direct hit and had to be pulled down afterwards. It was hit only a quarter of an hour after the children had left. One story I heard, though I cannot vouch for it, was that in The Avenue Miss Billinger climbed from her bath into the open air. Perhaps the strangest damage was in Horsecastles where bombs landed on both sides of the terrace and the outhouses imploded away from the main buildings, which was caused by a bellows effect. Six or eight delayed action bombs went off twelve hours later. One caught us out as it was hidden under debris. The strangest debris came from the midnight bakery next to the Picture Palace in Newland. They had hoarded silver coins which were thrown on to the cinema roof and retrieved by my ARP warden.

"As I plotted the bombs on to our ARP area map and the number climbed into the hundreds I ran out of red pins. It was quite extraordinary that there hadn't been more casualties.

"The worst thing was a direct hit in the cemetery. The coffin of a friend whom we had buried a week earlier was blown out of the ground. My gravediggers disappeared and we did the best we could to clear up with a firm of undertakers from Yeovil.

"Down Lenthay there was terrible damage and I sent the Billeting Officer down on his bike to see how many I had to rehouse and find accommodation for. Ten of our council houses were completely destroyed, and there was damage to all the remaining 108 of them, mainly on a serious scale. To my astonishment when he came back he said, 'No need to worry—people have come forward and offered shelter. Everyone has been given a home somewhere.' It was quite extraordinary what happened there, and it happened all over the town. If ever I have admired the people of Sherborne as a whole it was after the raid.

"I had told the schools they might have to put people up that night, but in the event it wasn't necessary. One little thing, after that raid there was no all-clear as we had no electricity. From then on we had to use rattles and a whistle for air raid sirens.

"The ministry men thought I was exaggerating and panicking when they heard from me on the only emergency phone line we had left, but when they came down they apologised to me. They had never seen such complete devastation in a small country town.

"I took the Regional Commissioner around in my car. Twelve hours later all my tyres were flat, punctured by the glass.

"Opposite Phillips and Son's store, outside the Westminster Bank, an unexploded bomb had fallen, leaving a hole that the bomb disposal team had covered with sandbags. An officer calmly sat down beside these on a lump of stone and lit a cigarette. I showed some concern that we were sitting down beside a bomb, 'If it goes off, we won't know anything about it,' he said.

"'It's a big one,' he said, 'but I can't touch it for a fortnight. In the meantime you'll have to evacuate everyone around.' The police and army sealed off the area and we got the stretcher cases out as best we could.

"I had to arrange temporary rationing arrangements because we couldn't get into the butcher's shop.

"A fortnight later that officer came back to me laughing, saying: 'You'll never believe this, Mr Freeman, but it was only a small one. The big hole was because it had gone down a disused well shaft!'

"I was flooded with visits from people in London, Bristol, Reading and the cities, and had to explain how we got out of difficulties. It is surprising how the help came that we needed; there was a wonderful spirit everywhere.

"The ministry admitted there were certain things we had to do that might be outside the law, but they said go ahead anyway as legislation was on the way.

"I still wonder how the devil we coped with it all. Twenty or thirty evacuees would come down the day after a London raid and we would have to find homes for them. The evacuation was worked out on paper and by the train timetables, but we would have cases where 600 would come down from one school, bound for Sherborne, and some of ours would get off at Sidmouth. We had to sort that out, have the doctors inspect them, and give out 48-hours rations. You saw how people had been living in London. It was a trying time, particularly as my staff were being called up. We coped by making our minds up at a moment's notice.

"One night I had a red warning that there would be a raid, and suddenly the whole place was lit up by parachute flares, but then nothing happened. We had been told that if the flares dropped they would be followed by bombs. The lights ringed the town and someone phoned to say there was a landmine hanging out of his front door, but it was a flare that had caught in his chimney. He was so excited and frightened he said he couldn't get out of the house—I asked him what had happened to the back door!

"I kept on good terms with most of the town. The only time I upset the school was when I requisitioned its tuck shop as a British Restaurant.

"Later in the war, because of our experiences, we were chosen for bomb instruction exercises, and a special invasion exercise in Newland in May 1943. For that one they had a particularly realistic casualty, with his eye hanging by a thread, provided by the butcher. I think they went too far. One old lady in the crowd fainted.

"My biggest regret is that I didn't keep a diary, but I never had the time. A little regret is that there was a relic of the raid that could have been preserved, three pieces of bomb-case that were embedded out of harm's way in a school wall. I asked General Waller, the bursar, to leave them but he had them hooked out and the stone repaired."

30 September **The boy who just made it back to Warmwell.**

The Heinkel 111s that jettisoned their bombs on Sherborne had been met by 152 Squadron as they flew at 21,000 feet over Portland. They had apparently been intending to raid Filton, at Bristol, or the Westland Aircraft factory at Yeovil which produced the Whirlwind, though with only a hundred produced this was about to turn into a failure. Anyway, the bombers were heading northward.

After his engagement with the formation that was to cause havoc in the abbey town of Sherborne, 19-year-old Eric 'Boy' Marrs (so called from his engagingly youthful looks) limped back to Warmwell in a crippled Spitfire and found that only one of his wheels would come down. It would not then retract, and to attempt a landing on one wheel is much more hazardous than a belly flop. He turned off the engine and glided in to land, touching down on the grass as gently as possible: "I began to slew round and counteracted as much as possible with the brake on the wheel which was down. I ended up going sideways on one wheel, a tail wheel and a wing tip. Luckily the good tyre held out and the only damage to the aeroplane, apart from that done by the bullets, is a wing tip which is easily replaceable.

"I hopped out and went to the MO to get a lot of metal splinters picked out of my leg and wrist. I felt jolly glad to be down on the ground without having caught fire."

Footnote In September 609 Squadron claimed nineteen German aircraft for the loss of two Spitfires. Even allowing for overclaiming, the result was decisive. The confusion over claims was inevitable in that often several fighters had a part in accounting for the same bomber and it was often impossible to follow victims down to the ground. Station morale would have been depressed by continuous inquests over dubious claims. What dropped on to the fields showed the trend, but the sea could anonymously accommodate any amount of further hopes.

1940

1 October **Plane crashes off Hengistbury Head.**

An unidentified aeroplane fell into the sea off Hengistbury Head at 10.55 am. Machine gun fire had been heard. No one baled out.

7 October **More Warmwell kills and losses.**

609 and 152 Squadrons from Warmwell clashed with German aircraft on their doorstep, at times over the aerodrome itself, as an enemy force crossed the Channel at Portland to bomb the Westland Aircraft factory at Yeovil. Four kills were credited to 609 Squadron but for the loss of two Warmwell Spitfires and their pilots, Sergeant A.N. Feary and Pilot Officer H.J. Akroyd.

Eric 'Boy' Marrs claimed a Messerschmitt 110 for 152 Squadron and saw its crew bale out. He circled them as they drifted down from 15,000 feet.

Footnote The two RAF officers are buried in the RAF plot at Warmwell churchyard. "One of the few," Feary's stone reads. He was twenty-eight.

7[?] October **Four die as bomb blasts Weymouth bus depot.**

Four died and many were injured when the Southern National bus depot at Weymouth received a direct hit by a German bomb. Fourteen buses and coaches were badly damaged.

8 October **Bomb wrecks Moreton church.**

21.00 hours. Moreton's eighteenth century parish church has been completely wrecked by a German bomb that fell beside the north wall. This has collapsed and the glass is blown out and fittings destroyed. The building is a ruin.

Footnote The building was restored and re-dedicated, in May 1950, and since 1958 has been enriched by the finest set of modern engraved glass windows in Britain—the creation of Laurence Whistler.

9 October 1940. Moreton church, the morning after, in a snapshot taken by E.W. Pride that was confiscated by the military.

DORSET'S WAR

10 October **Warmwell Czech is killed.**

The latest pilot at RAF Warmwell to lose his life is a Czechoslavakian, Sergeant Jaroslav Hlavac.

11 October **Poole boy killed by bomb.**

Stanley Ricketts, an 11-year-old Poole boy, was fatally injured this evening by a German bomb as he walked home at Kingsbere Road. Incendiaries also landed in the Constitution Hill area and other parts of the town, including the Cornealia Hospital where Stanley died.

14 October **Lyme minefield claims another Navy trawler.**

The British armed trawler HMT *Lord Stamp* has sunk after striking a mine in Lyme Bay.

16 October **Bovington and Poole air raids.**

Cryptanalysts at Bletchley Park, deciphering the German 'Enigma' radio traffic, gave warning of today's bombing raid on east Dorset, which hit Bovington and Poole. The intercepted signal was "Target No. 1 for Y".

Target No. 1 is known to be the Armoured Fighting Vehicles School at Bovington, and 'Y' indicates that Y-beam radio direction signals were being used.

17 October **Further Navy trawler goes down.**

The Royal Navy's losses of armed trawlers to the German minefield off west Dorset continued today when HMT *Kingston Cairngorm* blew up off Portland Bill.

17 October **The 'false invasion'.**

An intended raid on the Dorset and Devon coast to cover the infiltration of fifth columnists, mostly Irish Republicans, has been thwarted by the Royal Navy. Submarine L27, an ex-Danish boat, has shadowed the attack on the German convoy and many of the enemy have drowned, including SS agents. It has been the day of the false invasion.

The German force included the 5th T-boat Flotilla, 1,300 ton vessels the size of a light destroyer, and the destroyers *Karl Galster, Friedrich Ihrs, Hans Lody* and *Erich Steinbrinck*. They are having a running fight to escape from a mixed Allied force of two British cruisers supported by two Free French destroyers, two Norwegian destroyers, and one each from the Dutch and Danish navies.

19 October **Two 12-inch guns en route for Dorset.**

Two 12-inch Mark II railway mounted howitzers, dating from the Great War, have been released to Southern Command from the Ordnance Depot at Chilwell, Nottingham. They have arrived at Ringwood where they will remain in a siding until they can be deployed in the Isle of Purbeck.

22 October **Portland minefield sinks the 'Hickory'.**

The *Hickory*, a diesel-powered civilian vessel, is the latest victim of the German minefield off Portland.

October **Dorset's Somaliland hero returns from the dead to a VC.**

Captain Eric Wilson of Long Crichel, who was seconded to the Somaliland Camel Corps, has been gazetted posthumously for the Victoria Cross as a result of his part in the heroic defence of the British colony in the Horn of Africa during the Italian invasion of 4–19 August. He commanded a series of Bren gun positions that were blown to pieces in a sustained attack over four days and he held out until the end.

The award was cited in the London Gazette but the story does not end there as three days later news reached the British that Captain Wilson had survived and was prisoner-of-war.

Footnote Neither would the story end there. As the war turned against the Italians he was liberated and fought with the Long Range Desert Group. Lieutenant Colonel Wilson retired from the Army in 1949 and became an administrator in Tanganyika, until 1961, before returning to a West Country cottage, at Stowell near Sherborne.

October **Winterbourne Abbas loses last church band.**

The last church band in England is now a memory as William Dunford, its sole surviving player, has taken his bass-viol home from Winterbourne Abbas parish church.

26 October **Bournemouth's Carlton Hotel becomes a rations office.**

The prestigious Carlton Hotel on the East Cliff at Bournemouth has been requisitioned by the Board of Trade for use as a ration-coupon issuing office for the documents that are now needed for the restricted allowances of petrol and clothes.

In recent months it has only had five residents, since visitors were banned from the Defence Area, and one of these, Mrs Myers, has been fined 10 shillings with £1 12s 6d costs for an infringement of the blackout. The hotel felt obliged to pay.

October **Bournemouth's Home Guard totals 8,000.**

Recruitment of civilian volunteers into the Hampshire Regiment (Home Guard) units under the control of the Officer Commanding Troops, Bournemouth—whose area includes the other two towns in the conurbation, Poole and Christchurch—is set to reach eight thousand men. The detachments and their approximate manpower on call are:

> 3rd (Poole) Battalion—2,500 men
> 6th (Bournemouth) Battalion—2,300 men
> 7th (Boscombe) Battalion—2,500 men
> 22nd (Post Office) Battalion—400 men
> B Company (Southern Railway) Battalion—300 men

October **City pets evacuated to Shaftesbury.**

The animal shelter opened by Nina, Duchess of Hamilton, on her estate at Ferne to the east of Shaftesbury has become a refuge for hundreds of city pets, made homeless by the bombings and the general upheavals of war. As far as possible they are being cared for as if they were still at home, with freedom and exercise, rather than being permanently impounded in cages. Larger animals, such as horses, ponies and goats, are also being given refuge.

In reply to criticism that it is a waste of resources to care for animals in wartime, the Duchess quotes a Regional Commissioner of the Ministry of Home Security: "Experience shows that effective arrangements for dealing with animal casualties and for caring for the domestic pets of homeless people plays an important part in the maintaining of public morale after air raids."

November 1940; photographed on 17 May 1941. Opposite. One of the two 12-inch rail-mounted howitzers at Furzebrook, north-west of Corfe Castle. The pines are draped with camouflage netting.

1 November Rail-guns brought to Purbeck.

Two 12-inch Mark II railway mounted howitzers are now in the Isle of Purbeck where the first gun-spur has been made ready near Furzebrook by the 14th Super Heavy Battery of 5th Corps the Royal Artillery. The gunners came down from Catterick, Yorkshire, on 15 October and have now been united with their weapons.

The guns are being pulled by a Drummond K10 class mixed traffic locomotive, a 4-4-0, number 393.

3 November Motor-cycles leave Blandford.

The Blandford Camp Reconnaissance Battalion, the 4th Battalion of the Royal Northumberland Fusiliers, are leaving Dorset today for Amesbury Abbey, Wiltshire.

6 November Heinkel lands at Bridport—thinking it France.

In the early morning a Heinkel 111 of Kampf Gruppe 100, the élite two per cent of German bombers operating from Vannes, Brittany, and acting as pathfinders for the attacking formations, suffered a compass failure. It was confused by the British masking of German radio beacons into thinking it was back over France when in fact it was running out of fuel above Dorset.

The pilot landed on the shingle beach at West Bay, Bridport, and three out of the four crew survived—though they soon had their illusions shattered regarding France and found themselves in captivity.

Soldiers guarded the plane and had some difference of opinion with a naval detachment that came to drag the plane up the beach. The soldiers followed orders not to let anyone touch the bomber and it was engulfed by the tide.

6 November 1940. The Heinkel awash at West Bay—the sequel is on page 72.

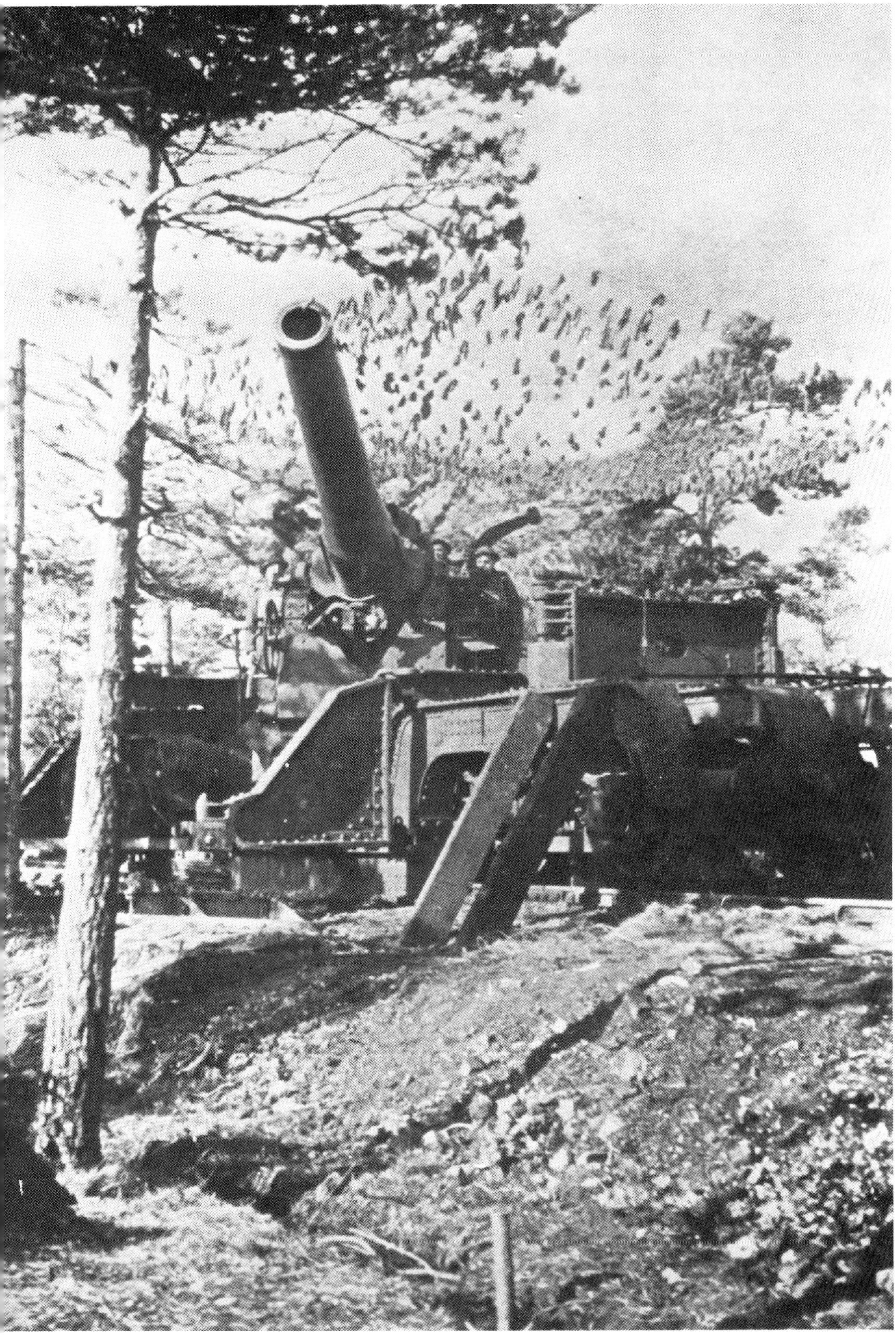

Footnote The aircraft had three vertical aerials and an intact X-Gerät radio direction finding gear. This was soon awash, corroding the light alloy components and leaving the apparatus full of sand. The damage delayed the cracking of its secrets until 21 November.

Then the Royal Aircraft Establishment scientists at Farnborough found it was tuned to 2000 cycles per second (equal to top 'C' on a paino) whereas British jamming had assumed a note of 1500 cycles (corresponding to 'G'). Dr Reg Jones, head of scientific intelligence at the Air Ministry, comments in his *Most Secret War*:

"So the filter could distinguish between the true beam and our jamming, even though we had got the radio frequencies correct. It was one of those instances where enormous trouble is taken to get the difficult parts right and then a slip-up occurs because of the lack of attention to a seemingly trivial detail."

This belated revelation—further delayed by the Army in Dorset failing to understand about the tides — came too late to prevent the Coventry raid but it did ensure that radio countermeasures were perfected in time to save the vital Rolls-Royce aeroengine plant at Derby. On the night of 8 May 1941, in moonlit conditions similar to those of the Coventry raid, Derby's bombs fell on Nottingham—and those intended for Nottingham dropped into open fields.

8 November Both rail-guns now operational in Purbeck.

A second gun-spur has been completed at Furzebrook, on the heath north-west of Corfe Castle, for its railway mounted 12-inch howitzer. It is positioned three hundred yards from the gun that was emplaced on 1 November—after some difficulty as it was brought down the branch line facing the wrong way.

Last night the gun had to be taken to Swanage to go round the turntable there so that it now points towards the coast. Both guns can fire 750 lb. of high explosives at three minute intervals and are controlled by observation posts on Ballard Down to the east, East Man to the south-east and Tyneham Cap to the south-west.

They have a range of eight miles and are targeted on prospective invasion beaches. To protect them from air attack they have been draped with 4,200 yards of Cullacort netting, suspended between the pines on 3,456 feet of scaffolding and 10,400 yards of wire.

14 November Junkers explodes on a Poole cobbler's shed.

In the morning No. 10 Group Fighter Command, at its headquarters near Bath, plotted a single German reconnaissance aircraft crossing into the Middle Wallop sector from France. Pilot Officer Eric Marrs and Sergeant Bill Kearsey, of 152 Squadron, were scrambled from Warmwell to investigate.

Kearsey spotted the intruder, a Junkers 88, on a course for Yeovil or Bristol, near Blandford. Both Spitfires attacked and the plane turned for the Channel. The Warmwell pilots caught up with it over Poole where the smoking German aircraft made desperate efforts, via its rear gunner and the pilot's last struggle with the controls, for a different ending.

Marrs had withdrawn, forced to become an observer by a shattered windshield, and Kearsey found himself out of ammunition, but by this time the Junkers was about to become a ball of fire. One of the four crewmen dropped out but his parachute failed to open and his body fell through the roof of Kinson Potteries.

The pilot, Oblt A. von Kugelgen, may have been making some last attempt to level the plane but it hit the ground near the corner of Ringwood Road and Herbert Avenue, exploding fifty feet from a cobbler's shed. Mr Stainer and his family had narrow escapes, as did their neighbours. One night-time fire watcher was trapped in his bed by roof debris. Part of the fuselage ended up in the roof of Moore's Garage.

15 November   **Coventry bombers pass over Christchurch.**

Last night a massed formation of 499 German planes flew across the Channel along a director radio beam from the Cherbourg peninsula and crossed the coast at Christchurch and New Milton. They then headed up the Avon valley and passed two miles to the east of Salisbury.

    Their code name for the operation was "Moonlight Sonata" and they were aiming for Target 53, which turned out to be Coventry. The city was devastated by 1,500 bombs [503 tons] leaving 554 dead and many more injured, and the cathedral and a third of the factories destroyed. The total of damaged houses is estimated at 60,000.

15 November   **Fifty-three died in Bournemouth raid.**

German bombers attacked Bournemouth this evening and left major destruction in three suburbs. Six parachute mines floated down on Westbourne, Malmesbury Park and Alma Road Schools. Fifty-three people have been killed and 2,321 properties damaged.

16 November   **Four killed in Poole blast.**

Sidney Sherwood and his sons, Fred, Henry and Robert, were killed when a parachute mine landed on their home in Fancy Road, Poole, early this morning.

    There were other blasts in Haskell's Road and Cynthia Road, causing serious injuries. Though she was able to protect her daughter, Molly, Mrs Lillian Kitkat was badly lacerated by flying debris and lost an eye.

16 November   **R.L. Stevenson's house is bombed.**

Last night's Bournemouth air raid badly damaged Skerryvore, Robert Louis Stevenson's home at Westbourne—near the head of Alum Chine—where he lived from 1885 until he left for the Pacific in 1887. Two poems about the house appeared that year in *Underwood*.

    Footnote   Pleas for its restoration were ignored and the remains of the house were demolished in 1941. In 1954 the site became a municipal garden, with the footings of the house being marked in concrete and a model erected of the Skerryvore lighthouse. Perhaps it would have been saved if he had written *Treasure Island* there; probably not.

17 November   **Parachute mine devastates Chapelhay, Weymouth.**

At 21.00 hours, when the Jack Buchanan programme had finished on the wireless, a German raider glided over Weymouth—he is said to have cut his engine—and dropped a parachute mine.

    This caused the town's worst explosion of the war, destroying seventy-seven of the tightly packed terraced houses at Chapelhay and inflicting damage on another 879 properties. Twelve died, including children.

    The device had been intended for the harbour—investigation of its remnants showed it was a sea mine.

18 November   **Poole houses evacuated.**

Houses in Newtown, at Poole were evacuated last night after an unexploded bomb had created a large crater in Gwynne Road. Not that it was anything like as large as the hole left by the bomb that did explode in Grove Road—you could put a house in that one!

18 November   **Poole firm celebrates its silver jubilee.**

Hamworthy Engineering's three hundred employees are marking their firm's silver jubilee with

DORSET'S WAR

a dance at the Woodlands Hall, Parkstone. The company was formed one year into the last war so it does not seem inappropriate to be celebrating the occasion a year into the present war.

28 November **Two Warmwell Spitfires lost in a day.**

Having quietly congratulated itself of an "unusually quiet most of November" the month has been marred for 152 Squadron at Warmwell by the loss of two pilots today. Sergeant Klein's Spitfire fell into the sea, and Pilot Officer A.R. Watson crashed near Wareham, as a result of dogfights with Me109s over Poole Bay and off the Needles. Eric 'Boy' Marrs shot one down; his second kill of the month.

29 November 1940. Where a Spitfire fell: the shattered stump at Field Grove, Durweston Forest. It had a plaque, placed on the tree by Captain Gerald Portman: 'In grateful and respectful memory of Pilot Officer John Frederick Woodward Allen aged 19 years, who gave his life for his country on this spot 29 November 1940.' In 1978 the stump was removed and replaced by a much less evocative granite memorial.

1940. The graceful and reassuring lines of the commonest plane in the Dorset skies.

29 November Spitfire plunges into Durweston Forest.

15.14 hours. A flight from 152 Squadron, including Spitfire R6907 flown by Pilot Officer John Woodward Allen, was scrambled because of a suspected enemy fighter sweep. They were instructed to patrol Warmwell at 25,000 feet.

Allen sent a radio message but it was unintelligible and nothing further was heard from him. His Spitfire was then seen to break away and dive shallowly, though under control. Suddenly it plummetted vertically into the ground and completely disintegrated on impact. The severity of the crash precluded any mechanical examination. It is thought the pilot fainted because of loss of oxygen. He had been flying Spitfires for three weeks.

The plane fell in woods at Durweston, to the north-west of Blandford.

Footnote The crash site was marked by a plaque, replaced in 1978 by a granite memorial. Ernest Day of Okeford Fitzpaine recalled seeing the plane in difficulties: "It was late afternoon, the day that a sixpence fell from the sky, hit my right shoulder and fell in the main road at Thornicombe. The fighter was climbing. Then I saw, very high in the sky, three German bombers returning from Bristol. The fighter made one attack on the bombers, then slowly descended towards me for a while, then it came straight down towards the ground with the throttle open.

"I stood thinking it was going straight into the ground, nose first, about fifty yards from me. Then what seemed like seconds before hitting the ground the throttle closed and the fighter turned out of the dive very sharply, just missing the ground by inches.

"It proceeded on a course towards Blandford, very unsteadily, just missing the telegraph poles on Thornicombe Hill, but slowly gaining height. When it reached Gipsy's Corner it turned left, then it flew over Fairmile where it slowly descended and went out of my view. A few hours later a friend told me that the fighter crashed near Travellers' Rest."

1 December Bournemouth AA gunners claim two planes.

This evening and last night there was bombing at Southampton and the enemy aircraft were harassed by Hurricanes and anti-aircraft fire as they flew over Poole Bay and Bournemouth.

Six German aircraft were shot down—two of them being claimed by anti-aircraft gunners. One of the planes dropped into the sea off Hengistbury Head.

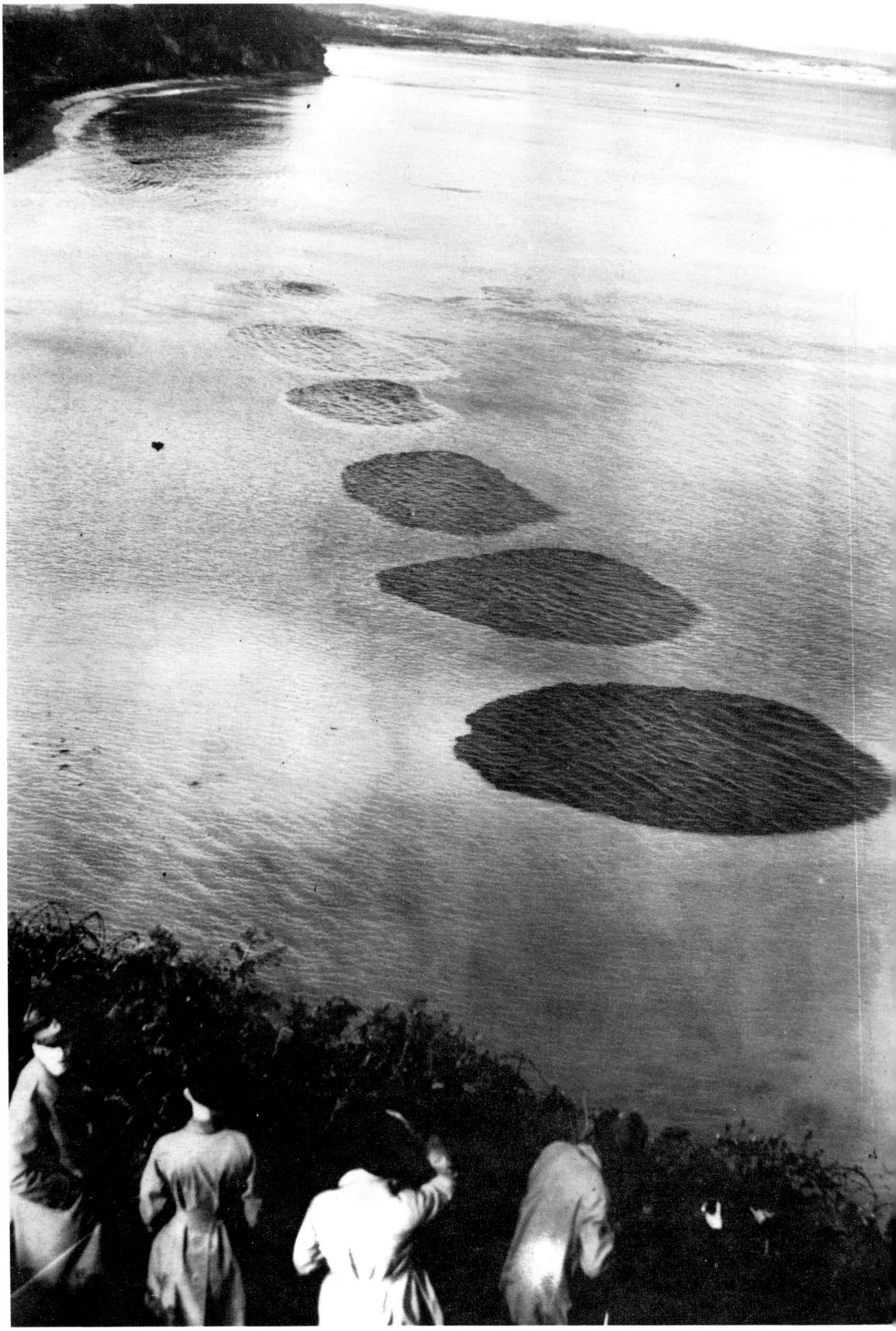

3 December **Hurn Aerodrome bombed.**

The aerodrome being built at Hurn, to the north of Bournemouth, had its first raid today. Five high explosive bombs and a number of incendiaries fell at 18.50 hours.

13 December **Christchurch families evacuated just in time.**

Families between Freda Road and Kings Avenue, Christchurch, were evacuated from their homes just in time this evening. A crater with an unexploded bomb, outside 1 Kings Avenue, had been reported at 09.25 hours but the decision to clear the area was not taken until 17.25. A bomb disposal team had then taken a look and decided to leave the bomb for 96 hours.

At 18.55, however, it went off—damaging three houses and rupturing gas and water pipes.

December **Spitfires now spend the night at Warmwell.**

The daily two-way shuttle of Spitfires from Warmwell to Middle Wallop, where the planes were dispersed at night, has ceased. 609 Squadron is now stationed solely at Warmwell.

20 December **Alexander and Montgomery see Studland sea ablaze.**

General Harold Alexander, Commander of the 1st Division, and Major General Bernard Montgomery of 5th Corps, today stood on the clifftop between Redend Point and Old Harry Rocks, Studland, to watch the sea on fire. Pipes have been laid from the beach in Project Fougasse to release oil in a series of slicks to form a continuous strip that is then ignited. It has been a calm day and the water was burning; waves would disperse the slick, though on the other hand the enemy is likely to choose a day when landing conditions are favourable.

Footnote The intention had been to repeat the exercise in the night, because British intelligence suggested that the German troops feared a conflagration on the beaches, but this was a disappointment due to waves lashed up by a cold on-shore wind.

20 December 1940. Opposite. The sea is to burn—VIPs watch the oil slicks emerging from underwater pipes between Old Harry Rocks and Redend Point (top left) at Studland. General Harold Alexander (left) turns towards the camera. Below—the sands of Studland are ignited in another Project Fougasse experiment. Turn to page 78.

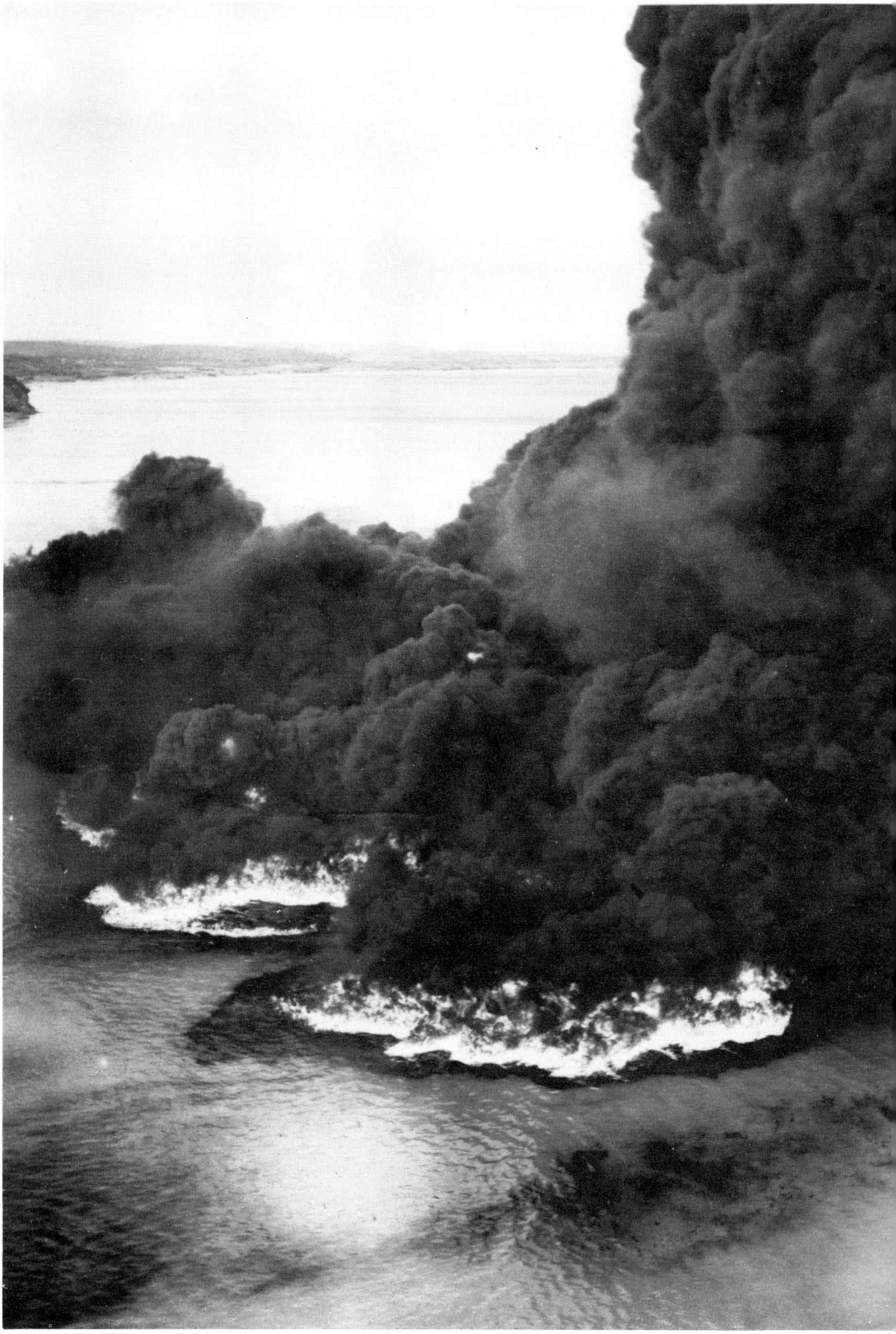

1940

24 December **E-boats sink two ships off Dorset.**

Convoy FN 366, sailing between Portland and the Isle of Wight last night, was attacked by the German 1st Schnellboot Flotilla (of six E-boats, S26, S28, S29, S34, S56 and S59). The enemy torpedo boats sank a Dutch ship, the *Maastricht*, and a Royal Navy armed trawler, HMT *Pelton*.

25 December **Mobile radar goes into the field at Sopley.**

A mobile ground-to-air radar antenna, developed by the Telecommunications Research Establishment at Worth Matravers and built at Somerford, Christchurch, by the Air Defence Experimental Establishment, is being tested for the first time today in the countryside. Known as Type 15 the unit has been placed on a flat part of Lord Manners's estate at Sopley, between the River Avon and the New Forest.

20 December 1940. Opposite. Project Fougasse. The sea burns off Redend Point (towards the top left) at Studland for the benefit of General Harold Alexander and Major General Bernard Montgomery—and to remind any German invaders that they would receive a warm welcome.

25 December 1940. Christmas cheer: the Type 15 ground to air mobile radar antenna that was devised at Worth Matravers, built at Christchurch, and installed at Sopley.

DORSET'S WAR 80

December **Blandford's Battle Training Camp.**

Blandford Camp is now designated a Battle Training Camp and provides a variety of intensive assault courses to simulate combat conditions.

1940. The year of retreat and anti-invasion precautions—a tommy-gunner in a cliff exercise at Bournemouth.

Airspeed Oxford: made at Christchurch.

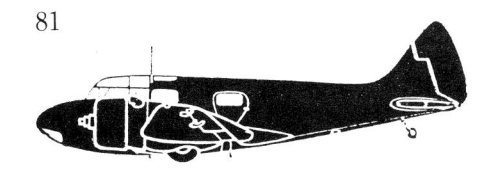

1941

10 January Two Poole men blown up as they leave shelter.

Leaving their garden air raid shelter last night after an incendiary attack, Frank and Henry James of Canford Cliffs Road were blown up by the following wave of German bombers. The town was well alight for a time from numerous incendiaries and there was even a fire at the Fire Station. 248 houses are damaged though only one, a Lilliput bungalow, was completely gutted.

Henry James died yesterday evening and Frank, an auxiliary coastguard, died today in the Cornelia Hospital, Poole.

13 January Observer Corps post machine gunned.

00.38: a Heinkel 111 passed about a hundred yards from the Poundbury Camp observation post, Dorchester, at about 300 feet. 02.45: the post was machine gunned by an enemy aircraft. There was no casualty.

25 January More mines laid off Dorset.

Over the past three days the German destroyer *Richard Britzen*, operating with two T-boats, the *Iltis* and *Seeadler* of about 1,300 tons displacement, have been laying mines off the Dorset coast.

27 January Dorchester burglary ends in murder.

01.30 hours. Private David Jennings, aged twenty, has been charged with the murder last night of Dorchester tailor Albert Farley of The Grove.

What started as a burglary had turned horribly wrong. Jennings was breaking into what he thought was an empty licensed club and did so in the style of the American films. He shot the lock off the door. Unknown to Jennings the building was still occupied and Farley was about to unlock the door from the other side. The tailor was shot dead.

Footnote Jennings was to hang at Dorchester.

Such homicides ceased to be murder under the Homicide Act 1957 and Criminal Justice Act 1967, in that the jury can now decide whether the accused intended or foresaw the results of his action. Clearly here he did not as the object was theft from a building he considered to be locked-up and unoccupied. The present definition would be manslaughter, not that the surviving jurymen have much patience with such niceties. One told me: "We didn't think of things like that, we were at war."

January Airspeed moves to Christchurch Aerodrome.

Christchurch Aerodrome has been selected as a shadow-factory for an aviation company. Airspeed (1934) Limited will move to the grass pre-war club flying ground at Somerford near Christchurch Harbour. The company is best known for the Envoy and the Oxford.

Footnote 550 of the twin-engined Oxfords would be made at Christchurch, mainly for use as trainers.

2 February Fougasse breaks the blackout.

For a time last night there was no blackout over Bournemouth. You could read a newspaper in the Square. The cause was the ignition of the anti-invasion oil slicks of Project Fougasse on the beaches of Studland. It was a test; to remind the enemy that we are ready.

12 February Coast batteries fire on E-boats.

The two six-inch guns at Hengistbury Head coast battery opened fire at 06.50 hours on E-boats in the Channel.

24 February 609 Squadron leaves Warmwell.

The Spitfires of 609 Squadron have lifted off from Warmwell's turf for the last time. They are now stationed at Biggin Hill, Kent. Their replacements at Warmwell are the Mark II Spitfires of 234 Squadron. With 609 went their two odd-job planes, a Puss Moth and a Magister.

24 February German radar signal picked up at Worth Matravers.

Derek Garrard, a scientist from the Air Ministry seconded to the Telecommunications Research Establishment at Worth Matravers, has succeeded in picking up transmissions on a VHF receiver at the 2.5 metre wavelength. Having failed with the official equipment he put a radio set in his car and drove off to St Alban's Head to point it towards the Cherbourg peninsula; for which activity he was arrested as a Fifth Columnist in a 'Defended Area'.

He returned to London today with bearings that suggest a source in the area of Auderville, where coincidentally two square-mesh aerials in a field were photographed by Flight Officer W.K. Manifould two days ago. The twenty-foot turntable apparatus is the 'Freya' unit to which the Germans credited the sinking, off Portland, of HMS *Delight* on 29 July 1940.

Air Marshal Sir Philip Joubert has called a meeting for this afternoon with one item on the agenda: "To discuss the existence of German radar."

Footnote More than fifty Freya units would be located by a combination of listening, intercepted messages and reconnaissance, by the end of 1941.

4 March Sopley radar claims first kill.

The Type 15 mobile radar unit established in a field at Sopley, four miles north of Christchurch, on Christmas Day is fully operational and today celebrates the first kill to result from one of the aerial interceptions that it has stage-managed.

The unit provides combat guidance to 604 Squadron which operates from Middle Wallop.

9 March Another burn-up of the Studland beaches.

Last night the Studland 'Sea Flame' experiment was repeated for the benefit of General Harold Alexander, Commander 1st Division, as the pipes of Project Fougasse ignited the sea with burning oil. A landing craft was towed through the flames to show the effect of the scorching.

Footnote The Petroleum Warfare Department were authorised to instal fifty miles of such barrages but shortages of steel piping would restrict 'Sea Flame' to Deal, Dover and Rye in the prime invasion area of Caesar's coast and Porthcurno at the landfall of the transatlantic cables.

12 March Bombs shatter Winton houses.

Eight houses were destroyed by German bombs at Portland Road and Morley Road, Winton, at 22.09 hours. Bournemouth rescue squads are digging people out of the wreckage.

1941. Blenheim bomber over someone's shipping loss in the Channel—till now it would have been British but by the end of the year the German lake will have open fishing rights.

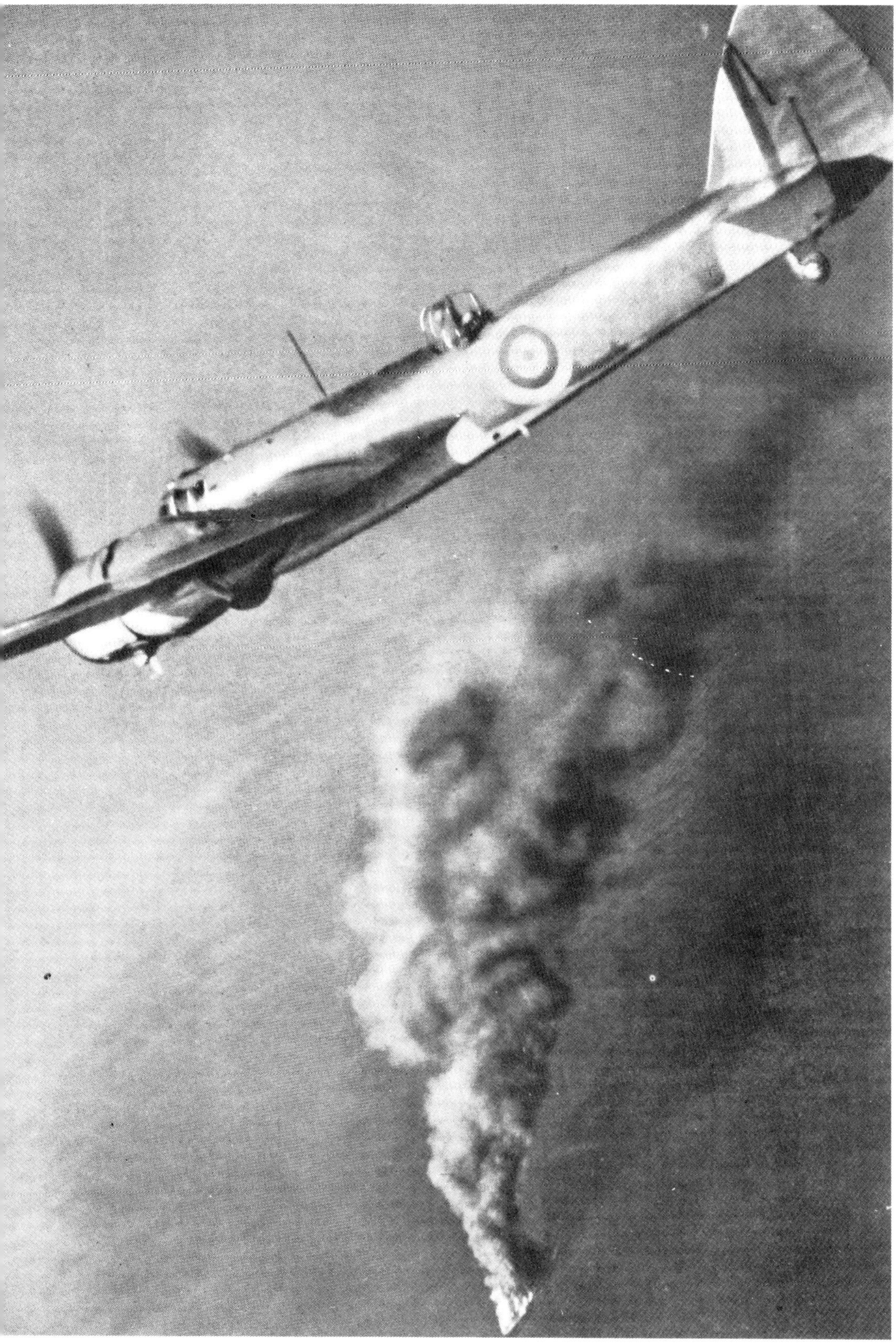

12 March Poole flying boat 'Clio' fitted with gun turrets.

The Poole 'Empire' flying boat *Clio* has today been returned to service after a refit at Belfast to equip her with armour plating, bomb-racks on the wings, four machine guns in each of two Boulton-Paul turrets in the dorsal and tail, and radar, for her new Coastal Command role. She has logged over four thousand miles of civilian flights. Her new number is AX 659 and she will serve with 201 Squadron covering the Iceland Gap from northern Scotland.

Footnote She would be lost on 22 August 1941.

12 March Royal Blue depot hit at Bournemouth.

A bomb has damaged the Royal Blue's coach depot in Bournemouth.

14 March Re-equipped squadron's first combat.

Improved Mark II Spitfires issued to 152 Squadron at Warmwell, replacing their Mark I planes, were scrambled today for their first combat patrol. They intercepted a Junkers 88 reconnaissance plane which was hit but escaped back across the Channel.

21 March 'Glamour Puffer' is shell-shocked.

The 'Glamour Puffer' as she is known—a works train for the Royal Naval Cordite Factory on Holton Heath that brings young ladies from Christchurch, Bournemouth and Poole—attracted the attention of a German raider as it steamed home this evening. It pulled out of Holton Heath station at 17.19 hours.

Just as it crossed Rocklea Bridge towards Hamworthy Junction a stick of six bombs straddled the embankment and blew out all the windows of the ancient non-corridor "birdcage" stock. It kept going to the semi-protected cutting and waited but he plane did not turn back. The train then drew into the platform.

None of the ladies was found to have anything worse than minor cuts; apart that is from quite a fright.

26 March Four bombs hit Warmwell Aerodrome.

A solitary Junkers 88 came across the Channel today and dropped four bombs on the RAF station at Warmwell. There were no casualties and the damage was limited to holes in the grass.

The station did, however, lose a flier today; Pilot Officer L.D. Sandes who held the Distinguished Flying Cross. He was aged twenty-eight.

27 March Thirty-four killed by Branksome Gas Works bomb.

The air raid siren has sounded at Branksome almost every day this month and sometimes more than once; but today has been different. Despite the alarm business continued as usual at the Gas Works and the staff were gathering in the canteen at noon for lunch.   Then a single enemy aircraft dived out of the clouds towards the Bourne Valley viaducts.

Two bombs fell short and landed on the gas works. The first blew up the stores and the second smashed through an upper storey and wedged for a few seconds protruding from the canteen ceiling to the horror of those beneath. There was no time to evacuate the crowded tables before the not-much-delayed fuse activated the bomb with deadly effect. The explosion devastated the hall, killing thirty-four men, including Home Guard members Leonard Bartlett, Archibald Cherrett and Herbert Williams, and injuring twenty-three.

Anxious wives soon thronged the gates as Royal Artillerymen helped the survivors to drag out their dead and wounded collegues.

27 March 1941. The wreckage of the canteen at Branksome Gas Works, in which 34 have been killed by a lunchtime German bomber.

27 March   Unexploded bomb at Winton.

In Bournemouth a high explosive bomb that fell at Lowther Road, Winton, failed to go off.

27 March   Lyme Regis pilot lost in action.

Wing Commander Edward Collis de Virac Lart, who was born in Lyme Regis in 1902 and has served as an RAF pilot since he was twenty-three, has failed to return to his base. He was one of Britain's most experienced fliers. In the 1920s he flew with 60 (Bombing) Squadron in India.

March   Canford Cliffs bomb for the bouncy Air Marshal.

One of the bombs that dropped on Canford Cliffs this month hit the home of Air Marshal Sir Philip Joubert, nominally the commanding officer of Combined Operations which is being set-up at Poole. In fact that job is a blind; since 14 June last year he has been running the RAF's radar and signals intelligence system, right through the Battle of the Beams, and in effect he controls the Telecommunications Research Establishment at Worth Matravers.

It all couldn't have happened to a nicer chap—he must be the bounciest Air Marshal the RAF has yet appointed.

March   Wareham family has five sons in RAF.

Aspiring to some sort of record, Mr and Mrs R.J. Brennan of the bakery at Worgret, near Wareham, have written to a local newspaper saying that all their five sons have enlisted in the RAF. They are Samuel, Eric, Peter, Archibald and Edwin and their ages range from twenty to thirty-three.

The other two Brennan children are girls.

DORSET'S WAR

1 April **German bombers kill ten at Warmwell.**

Three Heinkel 111s slipped low across the Dorset coast from Lyme Bay and followed the railway east from Dorchester to the aerodrome at Warmwell. They had not been picked up by radar or spotted by the Observer Corps and the station had no warning of the attack. Ten were killed by the bombs, shortly after noon, and twenty injured.

Among the dead is Sergeant Fawcett, one of the Spitfire pilots of 152 Squadron. He was killed by a machine gun bullet as he sat eating lunch.

A bomb crashed through the room of Eric 'Boy' Marrs but the pilot was elsewhere—having the Distinguished Flying Cross, which was awarded last December, pinned on his uniform in Buckingham Palace by King George VI.

10 April **Poole buildings destroyed by fire.**

This evening's raid on Canford Cliffs and Parkstone has left incendiaries blazing in a number of buildings, including the Canford Cliffs Hotel, Tennyson Buildings and Pinewood Laundry. The Tennyson Buildings are in a main shopping street, Ashley Road, and the laundry stands beside the Pottery Junction. Paintings have been removed from the blazing hotel but otherwise the inferno will be left to itself as there is no longer any water coming out of the mains.

Footnote Canford Cliffs came out of it lightly as far as its residents were concerned; the Royal Engineers bomb disposal unit found and defused eight unexploded bombs in Haven Road the next morning.

11 April **Sleeping Bournemouth poet killed by German bomb.**

Cumberland Clark, a familiar figure in central Bournemouth with white hair and walrus moustache, was killed in his sleep last night when a German bomb destroyed his flat in St Stephen's Road at midnight. He was a prolific author with sixty-seven books to his credit, many of them poetry, and his *War Songs of the Allies* have proved a tonic for the town's morale:

> Down in our Air-Raid Shelter
> There's no cause for alarm,
> It is so sure and strongly built
> We cannot come to harm.
> Let the bombs bounce round above us,
> And the shells come whizzing by,
> Down in our Air-Raid Shelter
> We'll be cosy, you and I!

The same plane dropped an incendiary on Woolworths in the Square, which burnt fiercely for some time. It was brought under control at 2.20 hours and the all-clear sounded at 4.10 hours.

12 April **Bombs fall on Upton.**

Six high explosive bombs and a quantity of incendiaries fell on Upton shortly after midnight.

16 April **Poole flying boat 'Cordelia' is armed.**

Another Poole 'Empire' flying boat, *Cordelia*, has been armed with gun turrets and bomb-racks and provided with radar at a major overhaul in Belfast. From today she is AX 660 and will carry out depth charge trials with 119 Squadron.

Footnote She returned to BOAC's Poole fleet in September 1941 and survived the war, being scrapped at Hythe on 6 March 1947.

28 April Fairey Battle crashes off Hengistbury Head.

A twin-engined Fairey Battle fighter-bomber (K 9230) crashed into the sea off Hengistbury Head, Bournemouth, at 15.45 hours today. The pilot baled out and Second Lieutenant Andrew Page of the Lancashire Fusiliers swam to his aid but the airman was entangled in his sodden parachute. The soldier could not prevent the pilot from drowning and nearly lost his own life from exhaustion and the intense cold of the water. Two of his comrades dragged him back on to the beach.

Footnote In July Andrew Page would be awarded the George Medal for his heroism.

30 April Two Frenchmen fly to Christchurch in stolen Nazi plane.

Two young Frenchmen, former members of the Armée de l'Air, today landed at Christchurch Aerodrome in a German biplane, a Bücker Jungmann, they had stolen from an airfield near Caen.

They landed at 11.15 hours, after a flight of seventy-five minutes, and were spared some rounds of Bofors fire through the quick-thinking of Second Lieutenant H.G. Graham and Sergeant Gill of 229 Battery of the Royal Artillery who saw the swastikas on the plane but realised there was something unusual in a short-range aeroplane coming this distance. Monsieurs Boudard and Herbert will be debriefed by Free French Forces.

30 April 1941. Two young Frenchmen stole a Nazi Bücker biplane for their escape from Carpiquet aerodrome, near Caen, to Christchurch.

April Commando unit formed at Poole.

Under the command of Captain Gustavus March-Phillips, an operational guerrilla unit of commandos known as the Small Scale Raiding Force has been formed at Poole, with its headquarters in the High Street, in the Antelope Hotel.

Their rôle, in Winston Churchill's words, will be to create "a reign of terror down the enemy coasts".

7 May German bomber crashes at Oborne.

A German bomber crashed into the hillside below Oborne Wood, to the east of Sherborne, in the early hours of the morning. The pilot baled out and gave himself up but the remainder of the crew, Feldwebel E. Ebert, Feldwebel H. Ottlick, and Unteroffizier T. Kowallik, died in the wreckage.

Footnote Their bodies were buried the following day at 10 am in the north-west corner of Oborne churchyard. Prayers were given. In 1963 the Volksbund removed the remains to the German war cemetery, Cannock Chase, Stafford.

9 May All clear at Weymouth then six die.

After the all clear sounded at Weymouth earlier this morning, Mrs Lilian Adnam and her daughters Dorothy, Margaret, Mary, Violet and Vivian left their shelter and returned to bed. At 04.30 hours a single German bomber slipped over the town and dropped five bombs. The house received a direct hit and all six were killed. Two other daughters escaped with injuries.

10 May Christchurch Aerodrome bombed.

Christchurch Aerodrome and the buildings of Airspeed Limited, at Somerford, were bombed and machine gunned early this morning, between 00.40 and 01.09 hours. Several bombs failed to explode.

12 May Heinkel and flying boat sink in Poole Harbour.

A Heinkel 111 of the German 8th Staffel attacked the seaplanes on Poole Harbour in the moonlit early hours this morning and sank *Maia*, a BOAC 'Empire' flying boat, killing its watchman, off Salterns Pier.

12 May 1941. The flying boat 'Maia'—sunk in Poole Harbour. She was no longer in tandem with the smaller 'Mercury' float-plane but this is how she will be remembered.

The attacker was brought down with machine gun fire from the ships in the harbour and land-based light anti-aircraft fire from Bofors Mark II guns firing 40 mm shells. It plunged into the harbour off Patchin's Point, Arne.

Unteroffiziers Karl Scheuringer and Karl Rohl survived but the pilot, Willer Wimmer, and his other two crewmen were killed. Scheuringer, the flight engineer, received a punch in the mouth that sent him reeling back into the sea during the course of his rescue-cum-capture.

Maia, recently converted to a C-class flying boat, had been a pioneering composite aircraft as the mother craft, having a cradle between her wings, for a Mercury mail-carrying seaplane.

12 May Bomb blasts Ashley level crossing.

03.25 hours. The railway line from Ringwood to Wimborne has been blocked by a bomb crater at Ashley Heath level crossing. Twenty houses are damaged and the phone wires down.

12 May Kennels and cafe hit by Somerford bombs.

A raid on Christchurch Aerodrome at 02.18 hours hit nearby civilian buildings, wrecking the bungalow at Somerford Kennels and smashing Bert's Café. There are four craters opposite the café and the Somerford Road is strewn with debris for a hundred yards. The family at the kennels are safe and have returned to look after their horses.

14 May Swanage bomb hits Wesley's Cottage.

16.30 hours. Wesley's Cottage, a picturesque stone-roofed dwelling in the High Street at Swanage, where John Wesley stayed on a preaching trip, has been badly damaged by a German bomb. It has been the town's 315th air-raid alert.

Footnote The ruined cottage would be demolished.

22 May Christchurch loses war trophy to London's War Weapons Week.

The German Bücker Jungmann biplane in which two patriotic Frenchmen escaped from Caen to Christchurch on 30 April has been dismantled and taken to London for display in the War Weapons Week.

27 May 1941. HMS 'Dorsetshire'. She has finished off the 'Bismarck', in the South Western Approaches.

27 May 'Dorsetshire' sinks the 'Bismarck'.

The county of Dorset will take special pride in the fact that today the cruiser HMS *Dorsetshire* delivered the coup de grâce to the battleship *Bismarck* at 10.36 hours this morning.

The *Bismarck* had been pounded by Royal Naval gunfire and was ablaze from stem to stern, rolling in a heavy sea, as Captain Martin of the *Dorsetshire* received the order to finish her off—with two torpedoes into the starboard side from 2,400 yards. The cruiser then steamed around the battleship's bows to fire another torpedo into the port side, sending the great grey ship lurching and exposing her red-painted hull as she rolled over to sink within fifteen seconds.

For a time the *Dorsetshire* stopped amongst the clusters of some four hundred survivors but many were too weak to climb the rope ladders and a British midshipman jumped in fully clothed to help. He was nearly left behind when a hundred and ten of the Germans had been dragged aboard and a submarine alert was received. Many of the exhausted sailors fell from the ropes into the sea as the cruiser gathered speed and left the area.

So ended an epic of naval warfare in less than heroic fashion. This chase across the North Atlantic and into the South Western Approaches has been an expensive victory for the British—three days ago the Admiralty announced the loss of the battle cruiser HMS *Hood* without being able to offer any prospect of survivors.

May The wealthy hoard gold and butter.

Some of the best-heeled residents in the county have passed through the courts in the past few months to face accusations of ignoring wartime restrictions. Sir John Sherlock of West Wings, Clarence Road, Dorchester, was fined £4,000 with £100 costs for concealing 3,647 sovereigns, 4,590 half sovereigns and £499 in other gold. He was forced to sell his hoard to the Treasury.

Eyebrows were also raised when the county's premier political household, the Wimborne St Giles dynasty of Lord Shaftesbury, the Lord Lieutenant of Dorset, and his son Viscount Cranborne, MP for South Dorset, were charged with buying black-market butter.

At the other end of the social spectrum, Albert Bulley of the Bungalow at Owermoigne had the distinction of being the first in the county to be convicted for refusing to take in evacuee lodgers. He was fined £5.

May Bailey Bridge tested at Christchurch.

The Experimental Bridging Establishment of the Royal Engineers, formerly known as the Bridge Company, has spanned the River Stour at Christchurch with a prefabricated steel bridge. It took shape almost instantly, taking a total of thirty-six minutes from commencement to the first lorry driving across.

This seventy feet structure was designed in 1939 by Donald Coleman Bailey. The bridge-building sappers took over the former horse barracks beside the river at Barrack Road.

Footnote Bailey Bridges were taken to war in Tunisia and Italy and in the Normandy campaign of 18–21 July 1944 they enabled British armoured divisions to cross the River Orne at five points to the north of Caen.

The length of the bridges grew to meet the size of the obstacle, such as 1,200 feet to cross the Chindwin in Burma and a record 4,000 feet plus at Genneps in the Netherlands.

Donald Bailey would be knighted in 1946.

May Cunningham gets Langar over Shaftesbury.

One of the interceptions that has been brought about in the sky from the tented Operations Room beside the Type 15 radar unit in the field that is RAF Sopley has enabled Squadron Leader John Cunningham, flying a Beaufighter with 604 Squadron, from Middle Wallop, to claim the Luftwaffe ace Hauptmann Langar.

Trying to evade the Beaufighter in low cloud, Langar's Heinkel 111 bomber crashed into a hill near Shaftesbury. No shot was fired.

1941. Heathland tank training. The furze and heather of Purbeck and Bovington was to become increasingly churned as the war developed. This tank is an A13. It was a cruiser tank, a long-range vehicle, and the first British chassis to use Christie suspension. The idea for this was developed in the United States and smuggled to Britain in 1936 as tractor parts and in cases labelled 'grapefruit'.

May Minefield laid off Brownsea Island.

An electrically triggered anti E-boat minefield has been laid beside the passages between the scaffolding obstructions at the entrance to Poole Harbour. It is controlled from an observation post on Brownsea Island, manned by a unit who have taken over the derelict Rose Cottage.

9 June 'Dagmar' sinks off Swanage.

The steamship *Dagmar* was today sunk by a German bomber off Durlston Head, Swanage. One of the convoy escorts, the Free French Navy's gunboat *Chasseur* 43, picked up survivors and took them to Poole Quay. Many were admitted to hospital.

12 June Parkstone family wake up to a bomb in the kitchen.

A family in Bournemouth Road, Upper Parkstone, came downstairs to breakfast this morning to find an unexploded bomb in their kitchen. They had heard the explosions from a stick of bombs that were dropped across Layton Road but ignored their own lighter thud. A bomb disposal unit has pronounced it a dud.

June Dorset supports 'Dig for Victory'.

Helping to take the message of "Dig for Victory" to the people is the Dorset County Produce Association which has been sponsored by the Ministry of Agriculture to help promote the vital cause of restocking the nation's larder. Similar associations are being set up in other counties.

Each will in turn establish branch associations in the villages and towns to give technical advice and encouragement. More families must start keeping rabbits and hens in their gardens and be persuaded to turn over their lawns and flower beds to the growing of vegetables.

June **Lyme's £25 a head for a warship.**

Lyme Regis has contributed no less than £69,222 "towards sending another ship to fight in His Majesty's Navy for the freedom of mankind from the Nazi thrall". This is £25-10s per head from the 2,700 inhabitants.

Champion town crier Walter Abbott made the announcement of "this Empire's determination to guard our rightful place on the good earth".

1941. The newly introduced Churchill tank coming over a ridge on the Lulworth tank gunnery ranges.

June **Bere Regis boy, Fred, clambers into the first Churchill.**

Fred Pitfield, aged ten, of Bere Regis has enjoyed one of the privileges that extreme youth can sometimes bestow. He has been allowed by armed guards to momentarily ignore the security restrictions and climb into the brand new interior of one of the first three Churchill tanks that are en route to the Armoured Fighting Vehicles School at Bovington and Lulworth. The Driving and Maintenance Wing is at Bovington Camp and the Gunnery Wing is based at Lulworth Camp, with a coastal firing range on Bindon Hill and in the Arish Mell valley.

This tank is a winner; it has to be with a name like Churchill. Fred and his friends are used to all the tanks that Bovington can field but when these pulled on to the verge at Court Green they realised that here was the shape of things to come.

The thirty-nine ton Churchill has evolved from specification A20 into A22, the Mark IV Infantry Tank, and is produced by Vauxhall Motors with ten centimetre frontal armour and a two pounder gun.

Footnote Three would also get as far as El Alamein for their testing. They were then armed with six pounder guns, the Bovington crews having dismissed the two pounder as a peashooter.

17 July **Bomb dropped on boy saying his prayers.**

The funeral took place today in Melcombe Regis cemetery of a ten-year-old Weymouth boy, Kenneth Polden, who was killed when a German bomb dropped on his house. His mother had said to him a minute earlier: "Go to bed. Say your prayers and ask God to keep us safe."

The rescue squad found Kenneth beside his wrecked bed with his hands clasped in prayer.

25 July Warmwell's hero killed over Brest.

Pilot Officer Eric 'Boy' Marrs of 152 Squadron from Warmwell was shot down today over the French coast on one of the first offensive missions undertaken by the station, which was the backbone of Dorset's defences in last year's Battle of Britain. They flew to Brest.

Marrs's Spitfire was hit by chance flak, bringing true a station prophecy that no German fighter pilot was going to take the 'Boy'. In December he had been awarded the Distinguished Flying Cross.

Footnote His body was recovered and is in the military cemetery at Brest. He had celebrated his twentieth birthday on 10 July.

July Purbeck's howitzers withdrawn.

The 14th Super Heavy Battery, which has been stationed at Furzebrook in the heart of the Isle of Purbeck since 1 August 1940, is experiencing troubles with its two rail-mounted 12-inch howitzers. They are being taken to the Royal Artillery's main depot at Bulford on Salisbury Plain for trials. Though only fired a few times for practice shots the recoil system has failed and shattered the mountings.

Meanwhile, for their return, the Royal Engineers and Southern Railway are building two new sidings for railway-mounted guns: one half a mile on the Wareham side of Furzebrook and the other on Norden Heath, Corfe Castle.

Footnote The project was abandoned and no more rail guns were brought into Purbeck. The battery's locomotive, number 393, rejoined the Southern Railway on 9 August.

July Shirburnian hits back at American presumptions.

An ex-Sherborne schoolboy, A.N. Whitehead, has reminded Americans that "as a training in political imagination, the Harvard School of Politics and Government cannot hold a candle to the old-fashioned English classical education of half-a-century ago."

July Cinemas show selected US newsreels.

The *March of Time* is the most active United States newsreel propagandising for American aid and munitions for Britain. It is widely shown here, with the emphasis on Roosevelt's speeches—"We must be the great arsenal of democracy" is their theme—but never are there any clips from the speeches of his opponents. Neither is any mention made of the price exacted for United States aid; throughout the war nothing is going to be said about the realisation of British dollar assets as the price for lend-lease.

1 August Hurn Aerodrome opens for radar experiments.

RAF Hurn, a new aerodrome with hardened concrete runways, has been completed on the flat ground between the Stour meadows and the heathland to the north of Bournemouth. It has three runways.

Its first users will be the planes of 1425 Flight and Telecommunications Unit who provide aerial guinea pigs for the radar scientists of the Telecommunications Research Establishment at Worth Matravers.

18 August National Fire Service formed.

The local fire brigades which were organised by town councils are from today part of the National

Fire Service. Number 16 District covers Hampshire and Dorset, with the two Dorset divisions being based on Bournemouth and Weymouth.

9 September **Warmwell Pole is killed.**

T.W. Pytlak, serving at RAF Warmwell with 30 Squadron, has been killed. He was twenty-two.

13 September **Poole commandos killed in Normandy.**

A raid by No 62 Commando from Poole was last night foiled by the Germans as it attempted an attack on the defences of the Atlantic Wall West. Though the commandos had killed the seven-man German patrol that had come across them and retreated to their wooden boat it was then hit by a shell.

Three of the men were taken prisoner and one escaped; the others, including their commander, Major Guastavus March-Phillips, are dead.

25 September **Wavell's Dorset partridges for Teheran.**

The Daily Telegraph reports the following anecdote about General Sir Archibald Wavell. He had been shooting partridge in Dorset on a Friday and was departing on the Saturday with a couple of brace.

As he was leaving the country the following day his hosts asked the Commander-in-Chief India what he was going to do with the birds. "Eat them myself, of course," he replied, "in Teheran on Tuesday."

23 October **King and Queen visit Bournemouth.**

King George VI and Queen Elizabeth are in Bournemouth today to inspect Dominion airmen assembled at the Pavilion.

October **Leslie Howard in Christchurch to make 'The First of the Few'.**

Leslie Howard, the actor and film-maker, is staying at the King's Arms Hotel, Christchurch, to work on a motion picture, *The First of the Few*. This will dramatise the legend of the Spitfire from its creation by Reggie Mitchell whose inspired designs first took to the air from Eastleigh Aerodrome, Southampton, on 6 March 1936. The eight-gun Supermarine monoplane K 5054 was at the hands of Mutt Summers who was watched throughout by an already ailing and constantly stressful Mitchell.

A grass aerodrome is in keeping with the story and Warmwell was selected but Howard, who is also the director, has decided upon the new concrete runways at Ibsley, two miles north of Ringwood. Not only has this suddenly become the look of modern aviation but it has advantages for the film-makers in providing smoother footage, rather than having to track the fighters as they bounce up and down across the grass.

The film will also star Rosamund John and Major David Niven.

17 November **Buses and paper in short supply.**

There are further restrictions on the omnibus services which will mean even longer crowds for the last ones. In fact the Regional Transport Officer is trying to discourage any idea of having a night out using public transport because in future no bus may leave after 21.30 hours. Fuel shortages are to blame.

Paper controls are also being tightened. There will be no Christmas cards this year and it is

1941. Pilot Officer David Glaser's Spitfire of 234 Squadron at the edge of Warmwell Aerodrome and his co-pilot (below, left), Blackie. Right: actor Leslie Howard—in Christchurch to film the Spitfire's story, 'First of the Few'.

DORSET'S WAR 96

now illegal to use paper for advertising leaflets, posters, or the production of paper handkerchiefs. Efforts to recycle materials, particularly waste paper, scrap iron and pig-bin collections, are being intensified as the shortages become felt.

November **RAF Hurn fully operational.**

RAF Hurn, which has already been used by 1425 Flight and Telecommunications Unit and 170, 296 and 297 (Army Co-operation) Squadrons, is now a fully operational aerodrome for No. 10 Group of Fighter Command.

1941–42. RAF Sopley, the ground to air radar system near Christchurch which acted as an air traffic control to guide British fighters in their interceptions of enemy aeroplanes. The Type 15 antenna is seen above, and its tented Operations Room. Below is the original lorry-mounted mobile control room. The radar was turned by pedal power, using bicycle parts, by two airmen assigned to 'Aircraft Hand General Duties' who became known as 'Binders'. The unit's historian, Brian Jones who was the last commander of Operations Squadron of Southern Radar, suggests this complaining about pedalling to nowhere may have been the origin for 'Much Binding in the Marsh'.

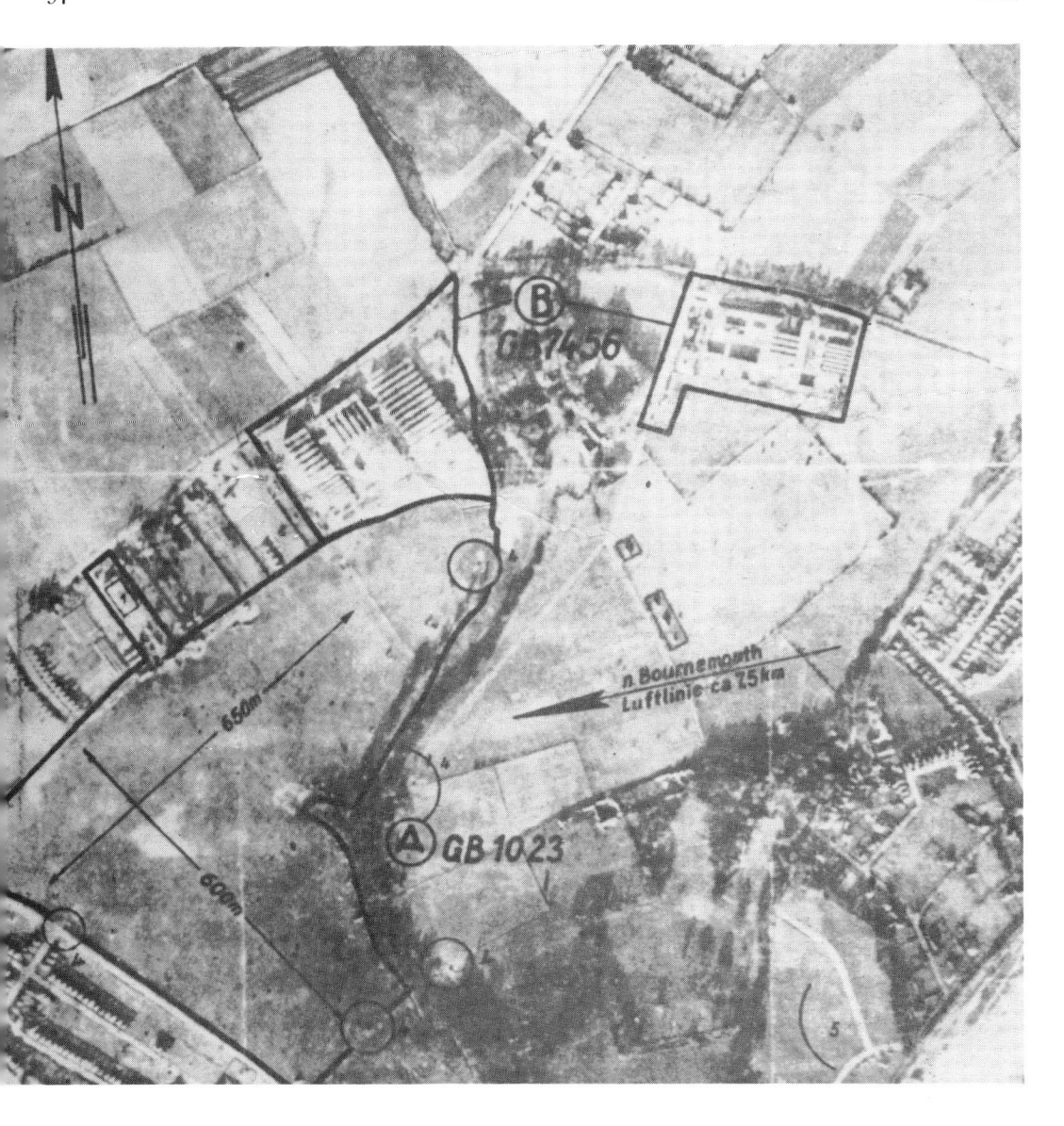

1941. German air reconnaissance photograph of Christchurch Aerodrome, taken before the building of the main runway. 'A' signifies 'Christchurch Flugplatz'—'Christchurch Flying landing-ground.' 'B' shows two 'Flugzeugzellen reparaturwerk'—'Aeroplane repair works'. Here the Germans underestimated the importance of the Somerford factories: for Airspeed was manufacturing aircraft and the Air Defence Research and Development Establishment of the Ministry of Supply (known in the town as the Air Defence Experimental Establishment) was one of the country's major producers of radar components. It made the apparatus pictured on the opposite page, working in conjunction with scientists of the Ministry of Aviation's Telecommunications Research Establishment at Worth Matravers. The arrowed 'Bournemouth Luftlinie' shows the flightline for Bournemouth. North is at the top, and the ringed positions show 'Kleinkampfanlagen' (light machine guns). '5' at the bottom right locates 'Scheinwerferstellung' (searchlight positions).

DORSET'S WAR 98

Short Sunderland:
landing on Poole Harbour.

18 February 1942. The Channel Dash: German battleships Scharnhorst (right), Gneisenau and Prinz Eugen escape from Brest to Kiel.

February 1942. 'C' Company of '2 Para', the Bruneval raiders, rehearsing their pick-up from the Cherbourg peninsula. The setting is Redcliff Point, Osmington, looking towards Ringstead Bay. Their 'rescue' is shown on pages 100 and 101.

January **The Yanks arrive, bringing good food.** **1942**

The first American contingents have arrived to the tune of *Lilli Burlero*, the Ulster Protestant march. The American soldiers have found it is a shilling a meal in the British Restaurants, but for what? They are much better fed in camp and for free.

The tendency to contrast the public menu with their own is being counteracted with a special US forces newsreel: "The best food in England is GI, but don't keep rubbing in how good your food is."

The commentator then added: "And don't say you've come over to win the war!" Which, of course, they have.

Footnote The Japanese attack on Pearl Harbor on the Hawaiian island of Oahu began at 07.50 hours Honolulu time, 7 December 1941—"a date that will live in infamy," in Roosevelt's words to Congress. There had been no declaration of war and isolationist sentiment in America ceased to exist; the Japanese had stung a sleeping tiger. The United States declared war on Japan on 8 December. The question of US neutrality in the European war was conveniently settled by the Axis powers themselves, when Germany and Italy declared war on the United States on 10 December.

18 February **The Channel Dash.**

Three of the capital ships of the German fleet escaped today up the Channel from Brest to Kiel. They were the battleships *Scharnhorst* and *Gneisenau* and the battle-cruiser *Prinz Eugen*. The Times is anguished: "Nothing more mortifying to the pride of sea-power has happened in home waters since the seventeenth century."

The Admiralty assumed that the break-out would start in daytime and pass southern England during darkness. In fact the reverse has happened. Admiral Ciliax left last night and sailed up the Channel in daylight, despite the efforts of Commander Esmonde and his Swordfish torpedo-dropping biplanes.

February 1942. Redcliff Point, Osmington. The rehearsal for the pick-up of '2 Para' at the end of the cross-Channel Bruneval raid—which is to bring home a German Würzburg radar for the Telecommunications Research Establishment to study at Worth Matravers. Things will go better on the night. Here, however, the men descend from Redcliff Point (above) to a landing craft that the tide leaves behind (below). Eventually (opposite) they are taken off and join the rescue flotilla.

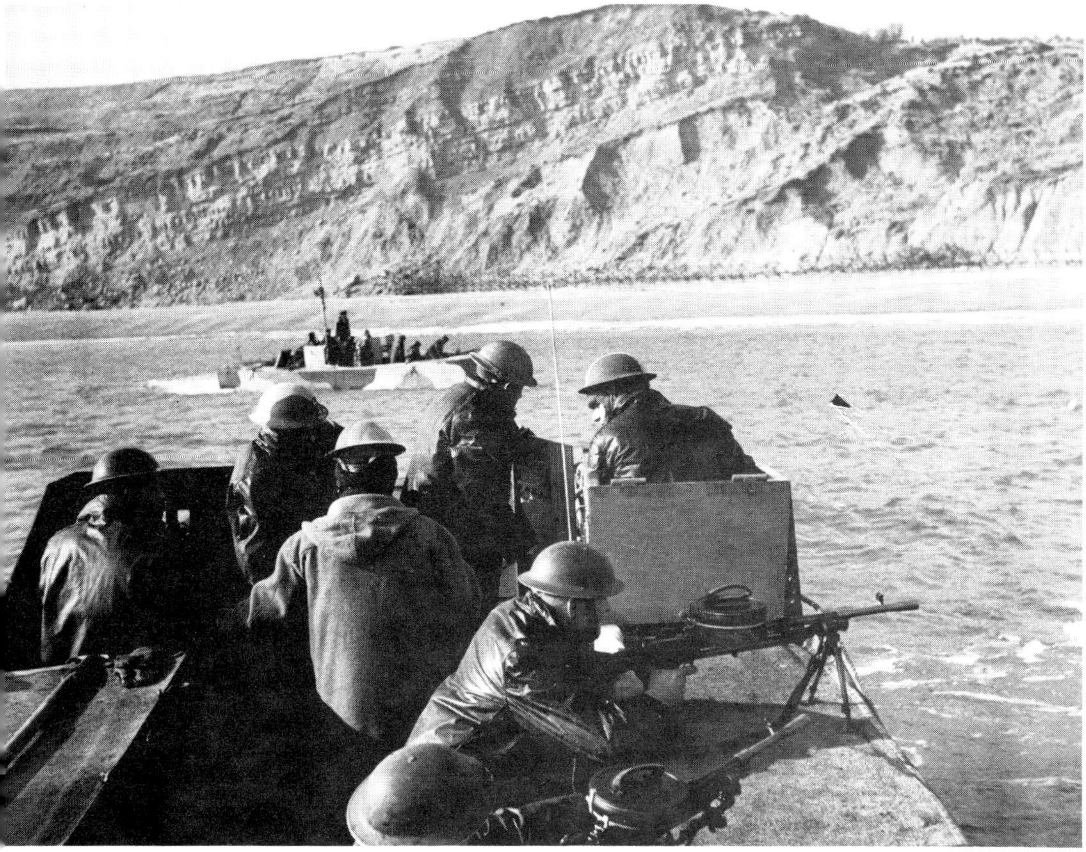

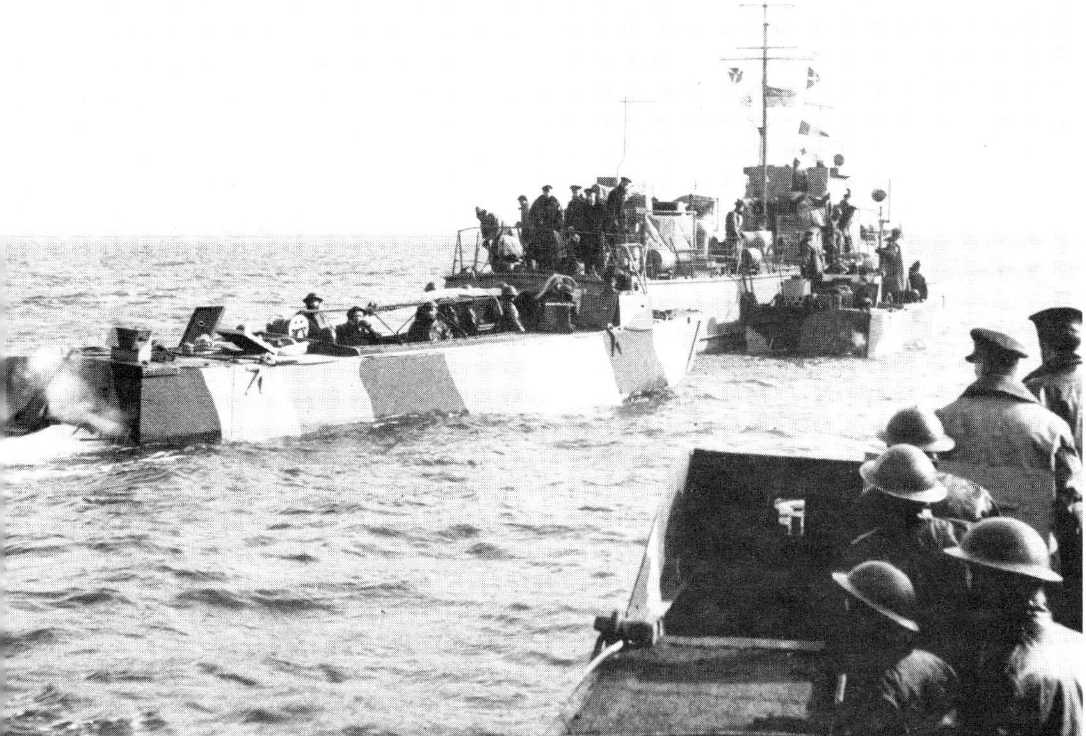

DORSET'S WAR

27 February **Bruneval raiders bring Worth a German radar.**

Having practised for the operation off Redcliff Point, Osmington, 'C' Company of the Second Battalion of the Parachute Regiment has sailed from Portland to Bruneval on the Cherbourg coast to bring back a German Würzburg radar apparatus. The raiding party is led by Major J.D. Frost with technical expertise being provided by Flight Sergeant C.H. Cox.

They jumped from twelve Whitley bombers and landed on top of the 400 feet cliff in deep snow to take their objective with complete surprise and dismantle the equipment for removal by landing craft from the beach below. Its components will be examined by the Telecommunications Research Establishment at Worth Matravers. Only one important piece had to be left behind, despite only ten minutes being available for the technical side of the operation.

Würzburg operates on 53 centimetres (between 558 and 560 mHz) and is a coast defence radar apparatus with a range of about forty kilometres. Its parabolic aerial had shown on air reconnaissance photographs of a clifftop at Cap d'Antifer. The Biting Plan for the seizure of its aerial, receiver and cathode-ray tube was organised by Combined Operations headquarters under Acting Admiral Louis Mountbatten.

8 March **Woman machine-gunned as she reads at Christchurch Quay.**

At 18.00 hours two Me109s machine gunned Christchurch Quay, hitting a woman who was sitting reading on a riverside bench. Josephine O'Reilly, of Iford Bridge Hotel, has been admitted to Fairmile House with a shoulder wound. Her condition is described as fair.

14 March **German raider escapes into Atlantic.**

There was naval activity off Dorset last night as the destroyer HMS *Walpole* and the New Zealand destroyer *Ferine* tried with twenty-one motor torpedo boats and four of the larger motor gun boats to block the passage of the Nazi raider Schiff 28 *Michel*. She slipped through, however, towards the Atlantic, with the aid of the 1,300 ton light destroyers of the 5th T-boat Flotilla, *Falke, Jaguar, Kondor, Iltis* and *Seeadler*, and nine minesweepers.

15 March **British destroyer sunk off Dorset.**

HMS *Vortigern*, a destroyer, was sunk last night in the English Channel by a Schnellboot, S104, though the Germans also suffered an own-goal when another E-boat, S53, was blown up by one of their own mines. S111 was also lost, following an attack by British motorgunboats (MGB87, MGB88, MGB91); she was captured but sank under tow.

HMS 'Vortigern' on a better day, in peacetime up the Avon Gorge.

March **Royal Fusiliers guard Christchurch radar establishment.**

The 12th Battalion of the Royal Fusiliers have been sent to Christchurch to guard the top-secret Air Defence Research and Development Establishment, at Somerford and Friars Cliff, against the possibility of the Germans staging a retaliatory Bruneval-style commando raid. The Establishment, known locally as the Air Defence Experimental Establishment, works in conjunction with the Telecommunications Research Establishment at Worth Matravers and specialises in radar and radio counter-measures.

1 April **King reviews 2nd Dorsets en route for Bombay.**

The 2nd Battalion of the Dorsetshire Regiment were today lined up along the Oxford Road at Banbury for an inspection by the King. 'A' Company then went through a jungle assault course high in the trees above the officers' mess. The battalion is under orders to move to Liverpool from where it will sail to Bombay.

1 April 1942. King George VI's farewell to the 2nd Battalion of the Dorsetshire Regiment, bound for India and the war against Japan. He is seen with Lieutenant Colonel G. N. Wood, inspecting 'A' Company.

2 April **Twenty killed and Weymouth's newspaper blitzed.**

21.00 hours. Twenty people are dead and fifty-six injured after Nazi dive-bombers indiscriminately swept across Weymouth. Only one of the bombs hit the central area of the town but it has devastated the Dorset Daily Echo's offices and works. A few hours earlier new foundry equipment was being installed and the current edition of the paper distributed for this Maundy Thursday.

The staff are gathering to salvage what's left. Just one item of standing type has been found and that, ironically, carries the headline: "Hitler's Nightmare!"

Footnote The eight-page paper could miss Good Friday but it appeared again on Saturday, 4 April, with 12,730 copies printed at Bournemouth. The Richmond Hill plant had already taken on the Southern Daily Echo, bombed out from its works in Southampton.

DORSET'S WAR

2 April 1942. Weymouth. The Dorset Daily Echo's offices and works were destroyed by the single German bomb that landed in the centre of the town.

12 April **Sinking of HMS 'Dorsetshire'.**

Japanese dive-bombers, coming out of the sun at 13.40 hours this Easter Sunday in waves of seven, sank the cruisers HMS *Dorsetshire* and HMS *Cornwall* in the Indian Ocean. The warships were hunting for surface raiders about three hundred miles west of Colombo.

Footnote The 1,100 survivors floated in clusters around two leaky whalers in which the worst of the wounded were tended. They were told by the *Dorsetshire's* captain, Commodore A.W.S. Agar VC, to conserve their strength by making as little noise as possible and cover their heads against the equitorial sun. Rescue did not come for thirty-three hours, after they were sighted by a Fleet Air Arm 'Stringbag', a Swordfish torpedo-reconnaissance biplane.

13 April 1942. Survivors from the cruiser HMS 'Dorsetshire'—yesterday the sinkers of the 'Bismarck' got the same treatment themselves. The myth of British naval supremacy went down off Ceylon as the Japanese showed once again what airpower can achieve. Some of these men will have been in the water 33 hours. The destroyer's rescue boats did not complete their task until after midnight.

April **Weymouth scholarship boys meet again in Libya.**

The war has brought about a surprise reunion for two of the brightest pupils of recent times from Weymouth Grammar School, A.E. Walkling and R.R. Head, who have had a brief encounter in the Western Desert. From 1928–37 they had competed at Weymouth for honours and both had gained scholarships and gone to Oxford.

   Lieutenant Alec Walkling has written to Norman Windust in Weymouth: "You will be amazed when I tell you who I ran into the other day. About a month after the campaign started, I was wandering the desert in a truck looking for Jerries.

   "I spotted a large column early one morning and crept up on it as stealthily as an army truck will allow. It was a friendly column, and out of the nearest vehicle popped a long thin figure with glasses. It was Head. I don't know which of us had the biggest surprise. It seems strange to me, but there was both of us, with more than our fair share of brains, yet we had nothing better to do than chase our fellow men around the desert."

Footnote It would be their last meeting; Head's parents, at Queen's Street, Weymouth, were to hear that their son had been reported missing. As for Walkling, he survived the war; to become Major General, and Colonel Commandant of the Royal Artillery in 1974.

14 May Charmouth radar station slips down cliff.

A radio location [radar] station on the Dorset coast was lost at 08.00 hours today through natural causes when three hundred feet of clifftop subsided in a landslip at Cain's Folly, to the east of Charmouth.

Footnote The concrete building lies partly submerged in the lias clays in the undercliff, 150 feet below the edge, and was half visible in 1985 with its seaward side tilting upwards.

19 May Germans lose two T-boats

Two of the 1,300 ton craft of the German 5th T-boat Flotilla, *Iltis* and *Seeadler*, have been sunk off Dorset in recent days. They were intercepted by Portsmouth-based motor torpedo boats. MTB220 was lost during the action.

25 May Brownsea decoy draws bombs from Poole.

The western end of Brownsea Island rocked to countless explosions in the early hours of this Whit Monday morning. Pathfinder bombers had dropped incendiaries nearly on target for the new Coastal Command base, RAF Hamworthy, and these landed with some high explosives in Rockley Road, Coles Avenue and Hinchcliffe Road. Many bungalows were destroyed and five civilians killed, including firewatcher Cecil Cowley, but fortunately for Poole the fires were extinguished in time for the newly completed 'Starfish' apparatus of the Major Strategic Night Decoy to come to light across the water on Brownsea Island.

The combination of wood, coal, paraffin and flushes of water produce white-hot flashes just like those of bursting bombs and lured the fifty-five enemy planes to unload 150 tons of high explosive harmlessly on to the island.

Only one bomb found a military target—a stray made a direct hit on Poole Home Guard's company headquarters in Lindsay Road, causing the unit's first death from enemy action with the loss of Private W.J. Griffiths.

The bombers had come from the Pas de Calais and been tracked by radar to St Catherine's Point, Isle of Wight, from where they turned north-westwards.

Footnote The Brownsea decoy was to save Poole and Bournemouth from a total of a thousand tons of German bombs.

May Worth radar establishment evacuated.

The Telecommunications Research Establishment is being evacuated from Worth Matravers to Malvern because of fears that the Germans might attempt a Bruneval-style raid on the Dorset coast. When they inspected the radar apparatus removed from Bruneval, Reginald Jones and Hugh Smith from Air Ministry Scientific Intelligence arrived on the Dorset coast with "revolvers ostentatiously strapped to our belts".

1 June Fleet Air Arm aerodrome for Charlton Horethorne.

An airstrip to the north of Sherborne, at Sigwells Farm, Charlton Horethorne, which has been used as an emergency landing ground, is to become a satellite aerodrome for the Fleet Air Arm station at Yeovilton. Flight Lieutenant H.C.V. Jolleff was today on the 600 feet high limestone plateau to the north of the farm to meet an advance party from Exeter.

4 June Arne decoy blaze saves Holton Heath.

The Royal Naval Cordite Factory on Holton Heath was saved from a potentially devastating major raid last night by the swift ignition of half a ton of waste shell propellant at its dummy factory on the other side of the Wareham Channel. Inspection of the Arne decoy site today revealed 206 craters and it is estimated that fifty or more bombs also fell into the harbour.

4 June **Germans nearly set Hamworthy ablaze.**

A German raid on Hamworthy and Poole, by fifty bombers in the early hours this morning, was partly thwarted by heath fires started by the incendiaries of the pathfinder bombers in the gorse and heather at Rocklea. This drew many of the bombers westwards from the urban area but it nearly created a disaster.

One of the bombs that exploded on Ham Common ruptured a giant tank of 100-octane aviation fuel concealed in the old claypits at Doulting's Pier. A million gallons flowed into lakes across the wasteland and fire teams could only pray that no one dropped a match let alone a bomb as the whole area began to reek with fumes.

Some of the bombs did find the urban areas of Hamworthy and the densely-packed Georgian buildings of the Old Town. A grocer's shop opposite the parish church was hit, as was Yeatman's Mill on Poole Quay. Bolson's store at their Wessex Wharf shipyard in Ferry Road, Hamworthy, was gutted. The yard manufactures twin-screw harbour defence motor launches, HDMLs, which are vessels of 72 feet. There a firewatcher, 55-year-old Louis Pittwood, was fatally injured. He died today in the Cornelia Hospital, Longfleet Road. Twenty-three others are having their injuries tended.

Mrs Florence Diffy of Green Road and a six-year-old boy who was staying at Hamworthy, Victor Park, have also died in the Cornelia Hospital from injuries received in the raid.

The Royal Navy's headquarters ship for the port, HMS *Sona* which is berthed beside Poole Quay, was sunk by a bomb which dropped through the funnel and buried itself in the mud beneath the hull. It did not explode and the sailors were able to scramble up the quayside.

7 June 1942. Poole. HMS 'Sona' is no longer the Royal Navy's headquarters ship.

7 June **Delayed bomb destroys Navy's Poole headquarters.**

00.52 hours. The bomb which sank the Royal Navy's headquarters ship at Poole Quay, HMS *Sona*, but failed to explode, has now detonated itself and completely destroyed what was left of the vessel and the frontages of several quayside buildings. The area had been roped off and there were no casualties.

18 June Royal Navy puts into Bournemouth for repairs.

The Royal Navy's coastal forces have anchored and tied up around the remnants of Bournemouth Pier—broken at the centre in 1940 to prevent it being used in a German invasion—for running repairs. They are leaving for Portland.

The damage to HMS *Albrighton* and SGB6 and SGB8 was sustained whilst trying to stop an Axis convoy of four German, Italian and Finnish ships that were being escorted by the 1st Schnellboot Flotilla. One of the four enemy transports was sunk but the Royal Navy lost SGB7.

June Campaign to replace the 'Dorsetshire'.

The HMS *Dorsetshire* Replacement Campaign, launched by the Earl of Shaftesbury, aims to double the level of war savings in the county and raise £2,750,000 in six months to the end of the year.

9 July The Battle of Lyme Bay.

This has been the battle of Lyme Bay, carried out by the German 1st Schnellboot Flotilla (S48, S50, S63, S67, S70, S104, S109) against Allied Coast Convoy E/P 91. 12,192 tons of shipping has gone down; the tanker SS *Pomella* and four freighters. One of the British escorts has also been lost, an armed trawler HMT *Manor*.

22 July Germans put more mines into the Channel.

The central part of the English Channel has been heavily mined by the Germans over the past three days through the efforts of Operation Rhein and Operation Stein. The 3rd T-boat Flotilla (T4, T10, T13, T14) have been depositing the mines through their torpedo tubes.

29 July HMS 'Poole' adopted by the town.

HMS *Poole*, a new Bangor-class minesweeper, has been adopted by the town, at a civic reception held on the edge of the harbour at Poole Park.

2 August And more German mines.

Once again the 3rd T-boat Flotilla (this time using T10, T13, T14) has been sowing German mines in the Channel sea-lanes, in Operation Masuren.

5 August Plane explodes off Bournemouth.

An aeroplane approached Bournemouth from the sea shortly before 03.00 hours with its navigation lights on. It then blew up with a tremendous flash.

6 August Portland radar test plays on German nerves.

A test off Portland today that amplified the enemy's radar echo from a formation of eight Defiant fighters caused the Luftwaffe to scramble thirty fighters from airfields in the Cherbourg peninsula to intercept the phantom force.

17 August First crash for Charlton Horethorne aerodrome.

The first squadron at the new Fleet Air Arm aerodrome at Charlton Horethorne, 887 Squadron, have left for St Merryn, Cornwall, and been replaced by 790 Squadron and the Sea Hurricanes of 891 Squadron.

A Hurricane of 891 Squadron crashed on landing. This was the first crash at this aerodrome. Only slight damage was done to the aircraft and the pilot was uninjured.

24 August **Poole and Weymouth boats at Dieppe.**

Boats from Poole and Weymouth have since 18 August been operating as support vessels for the Operation Jubilee reconnaissance to test the strength of the German West Wall at Dieppe. The Dieppe Raid returnees have brought back stories of amazing escapes and days of contrast which started with the Frenchmen uncorking wine in the belief that they had been liberated and ended with the Canadians setting up machine guns on parapets comprised of their own dead.

31 August **Australians fly into RAF Hamworthy.**

Nine Sunderland flyingboats of 461 Squadron of the Royal Australian Air Force today landed in Poole Harbour from Mount Batten, Plymouth. Squadron Leader R.C. Lovelock heads a complement of 132 men. The new base at Hamworthy was established as RAF Poole at the start of the month and renamed RAF Hamworthy a week later.

The Australians are flying anti-submarine patrols in the South Western Approaches and the Bay of Biscay, where U-boats have been caught napping by airborne radar and are now under orders to surface only for the recharging of their batteries.

August **Bovington's remaining Great War tanks rescued for a film.**

The old tanks from the Great War that were used as pill-boxes around Bovington in the anti-invasion defences of 1940 have come back to life for the making of a film, *Victory*. It has realistic scenes, shot on the Dorsetshire heaths at Turners Puddle and Gallows Hill, of British light tanks advancing under heavy enemy artillery bombardment in the war of 1914–18.

1942. Bovington. The Royal Tank Corps' historic collection of the world's first tanks was scrapped in 1940. Those machines that had not been broken up, and were merely lying around as pill-boxes near the Armoured Fighting Vehicles School, came back to life for an admiring audience in 1942: 'A realistic scene from the British film "Victory" which was filmed in Dorsetshire. British light tanks are seen advancing under heavy artillery bombardment from the enemy in the war of 1914-18.'

DORSET'S WAR

1942. Lulworth Camp. Tests at the Gunnery Wing of the Armoured Fighting Vehicles School for an American General Grant tank (below) and a British Valentine (above) which has been armed with a six pounder anti-tank gun, replacing its standard two pounder.

3 September **Poole Commandos raid the Channel Islands.**

No 62 Commando of Combined Operations, based at Anderson Manor near Bere Regis and operating out of Poole Harbour, last night raided a German U-boat signalling station in the Casquets Lighthouse in the Channel Islands. Code books have been captured and seven German wireless operators, who were taken completely by surprise, found themselves in Poole at 04.00 hours this morning and prisoners of war.

Footnote The leader of the Small Scale Raiding Force, Geoffrey Appleyard, was promoted to Major and awarded the Distinguished Service Order.

3 September **Prayers for the third anniversary.**

Today, the third anniversary of the outbreak of war, churches have been packed for the national day of prayer. Services have also been held at places of work, including the Bournemouth department stores of Allens and Beales.

9 September **Squadrons change at Charlton Horethorne.**

891 Squadron today left Charlton Horethorne for St Merryn, Cornwall, and are being replaced by 893 Squadron. The aerodrome is being used for working-up training, the Sea Hurricanes practising on target-towing Marinets.

11 September **Poole raider kills five.**

A single German bomber ignored the Bofors guns at Canford Cliffs today to come in from the bay and drop a single bomb that has killed five people in Poole. The dead are Rev William Russell and his son Frank at 11 Marlborough Road, Mrs Winifred Phillips and her 11-year-old daughter June at 'Woodgrove' in Bournemouth Road, and Mrs Annie Watts at 12 Earlham Drive.

14 September **Twenty-one killed on Poole flying boat.**

The Poole flying-boat *Clare*, outward bound for Bathurst, West Africa, with thirteen passengers and six crew has crashed in flames into the English Channel. She radioed soon after takeoff to report engine trouble and half an hour later to say she was on fire.

Footnote Nothing more was heard or found.

17 September **Piddletrenthide man found shot dead.**

In the early hours this morning the body of farm worker Louis Aubrey Stickland, aged 42, was found lying beside Chapel Lane, Piddletrenthide. He had a single gunshot wound in the chest.

Stickland enlisted with the Home Guard two months ago. Last evening he went to the Golden Grain Bakery for cigarettes but did not return. His wife was unconcerned because she thought he was having a long chat with the baker, Frederick Davis.

Mrs Stickland did not report her husband missing until 00.30 hours this morning. The body was found by the local magistrate, Henry Levi Green.

September **Coastal Command aerodrome at Holmsley.**

RAF Holmsley South, an aerodrome with concrete runways for Wellingtons of Coastal Command on anti-submarine patrols, has been constructed across the flat expanse of heather and gorse at Plain Heath on the south-western edge of the New Forest.

Footnote In 1943 they would be joined by four-engined Halifax bombers, the tugs for troop-carrying gliders.

DORSET'S WAR   112

September **Wimborne baker raises £3,600 for Russia.**

Joe Bright, the Mayor of Wimborne and the man voted "Best Baker in Britain", has raised £3,600 in aid of the other Uncle Joe. To help Stalin's heroic struggle and relieve some of the appalling suffering on the Eastern Front he has been working tirelessly for the Medical Aid to Russia and China Fund which he founded.

1 October **Sherborne postman loses his arm in a propeller.**

Levelling off runways and the rolling of relaid turf has led to some changes in the usual pattern of aircraft movements at the Fleet Air Arm station near Charlton Horethorne.

At 09.00 hours a Fulmar of 790 Squadron, being moved by Lieutenant Commander Hodgson, was involved in a taxying accident with a postman from Sherborne Post Office, Mr W.J. John. The latter was riding a combination motor cycle and hit the propeller of the Fulmar, severing his right arm at the shoulder. He was taken to the Royal Naval Hospital at Sherborne and is expected to recover.

7 October **Hamworthy becomes a landing craft base.**

The Admiralty today commissioned the Lake camp-site at Hamworthy, along with Hamworthy Common and the Round Island two miles away near the opposite side of Poole Harbour, as shore-based HMS *Turtle*. It will be concerned with training British, American and Canadian crews in the handling of landing craft at sea and their use in beach assaults.

14 October **Losses on both sides in major Channel battle.**

Last night a Coastal Command reconnaissance aircraft from Calshot spotted the German auxiliary cruiser Schiff 45 *Komet* attempting to break out from Le Harve, westwards into the Atlantic. She was being escorted by the 3rd Schnellboot Flotilla and German minesweepers.

In an attack by a Royal Navy flotilla of Hunt class destroyers (HMS *Cottesmore, Esdale, Glassdale, Quorn*) and motor torpedo boats (MTB55, MTB84, MTB95, MTB229, MTB236) plus the destroyer HMS *Albrighton* the *Komet* was sunk with the loss of all her crew by two torpedoes. They had been fired by MTB236.

From Portland a supporting force set sail comprising HMS *Brocklesby* and *Tynedale* with the Danish ship *Fernie* and the Polish *Krakowiak*. There were a large number of casualties aboard the *Brocklesby* though she survived the action.

In a separate incident the armed trawler HMT *Jasper*, making for Portland from Dover, was sunk by a German Schnellboot, S81.

17 October **Fuel shortages stop Royal Blue expresses.**

Royal Blue express services to London finally ceased operation today, after months of steadily slimmer timetables, as a result of the gravity of the national fuel shortages. Half of the familiar dark-blue fleet is anyway reserved for manoeuvres and other military uses.

A few of the coaches will still be seen with civilian passengers, however, as the following services have been licensed to run seven days a week. The Ministry of Transport concession has been granted because it is accepted that alternative ordinary bus services and rail facilities are less than adequate in many parts of Dorset:

Service 400, Bournemouth to Southampton. Four journeys each way of 88 minutes.

Service 402, Bournemouth to Dorchester, Bridport and Exeter. Two journeys each way of 250 minutes. Re-booking will be necessary at Dorchester as through tickets cannot be issued; the licence is for the run in two separate stages, Bournemouth to Dorchester and Dorchester to

Exeter.

Service 403, Bournemouth to Blandford, Sherborne and Yeovil. One journey each way of 136 minutes.

Service 404, Honiton along the A30 to Shaftesbury. One journey each way of 167 minutes.

Service 405, Bournemouth to Blandford, Shaftesbury and Trowbridge. Two journeys each way of 215 minutes.

Footnote The coach express service to London did not resume until 15 April 1946.

October **Weymouth's famous aviator killed in Middle East.**

The latest casualties in the Middle East include George Stainforth, an old boy of Weymouth College who rose to fame in 1929–31 when he took the world airspeed record in Schneider trophy flights. He pushed the speed to 246 miles per hour and then averaged 379 mph. Other records included flying upside down for a duration of eleven minutes seven seconds and the title of RAF revolver champion.

As a Wing Commander in the Middle East he was the oldest fighter pilot serving in that theatre. He was shot down in night fighting, his particular forte.

3 November **VIP Fortresses fly out of Hurn.**

General Dwight D. Eisenhower, the Commander of Allied Forces North-west Africa, has flown out from Hurn today with his staff officers and a British contingent for a conference in Gibraltar to discuss the break-out into the Western Desert from El Alamein and the advance towards Algiers. They are aboard five Flying Fortresses; a sixth had to abort its take-off when the undercarriage hydraulics failed.

The top-brass include General Kenneth Anderson, the Commander of the British 1st Army; Major General Mark Wayne Clark, the co-ordinator of the secret moves to see whether the Vichy French will defend French North Africa; and Brigadier Lyman Lemnitzer.

Footnote Eisenhower's pilot, Major Paul Tibbets, would fly the B29 *Enola Gay* to drop the first atomic bomb, on Hiroshima.

4 November **Sixth Fortress flies from Hurn.**

Major General Jimmy Doolittle, the aviator who set the world air-speed record in 1932, flew from Hurn today to Gibraltar aboard the Flying Fortress that experienced wheel-jamming yesterday. Doolittle is Commander of the United States air forces in North Africa.

The news today from General Bernard Montgomery, the desert Commander of the British 8th Army, is that everywhere Erwin Rommel's Afrika Korps is in full retreat. El Alamein is only seventy miles from Alexandria and Rommel had been poised to attack Egypt.

7 November **Churchill orders church bells to ring.**

Hearing that the 8th Army has taken 30,000 prisoners after the Battle of Alamein, Winston Churchill tells the nation to celebrate by ringing church bells—the first time they have been heard since the outbreak of war.

The prisoners include nine generals. Only the rains of the past two days have saved the enemy from utter annihilation.

Footnote There was still a psychological factor, that of Rommel's reputation, inhibiting what should have been a British stampede across the desert. For there was now literally nothing that could have stopped them; on 9 November 1942 the Afrika Korps was down to ten tanks and had insufficient petrol even to field those in combat.

8 November   **Eisenhower takes over French North Africa.**

A combined British and American force involving a total of 400,000 men has landed in French North Africa at Casablanca, Oran and Algiers. It is under the overall command of General Dwight D. Eisenhower and has five hundred transport craft being shepherded by three hundred and fifty naval vessels.

13 November   **Accused man's wife exhumed at Piddletrenthide.**

Following the charging of Frederick Davis with the murder of another Piddletrenthide villager, Louis Stickland, on the night of 16 September, police today exhumed the remains of the accused man's 32-year-old wife, Freda Davis. She died in August, with an illness described as ulcerative colitis.

The coffin was removed to the County Hospital for the body to be given an autopsy by Sir Bernard Spilsbury, the chief Home Office pathologist. At the graveside the accused man watched as soil samples were removed.

Footnote   No evidence of foul play was found.

3 December   **HMS 'Penylan' sunk off Bournemouth.**

The German 5th Schnellboot Flotilla (S81, S82, S115, S116) today attacked two British convoys in the Channel, in the area off Bournemouth and the Isle of Wight, sinking the escort destroyer HMS *Penylan* and a freighter.

10 December   **Poole, the port, gets Seamen's Mission.**

Admiral Sir Reginald Aylmer Ranfurly Plunkett-Ernle-Erle-Drax of Charborough Park, who fought in HMS *Lion* at the Battle of Jutland and headed the diplomatic mission to Moscow in 1939, has today opened the Mansion House in Thames Street, Poole, as a Mission to Seamen. It is a mark of Poole's restored status as a port that it should have a Seamen's Mission.

13 December   **The sea engulfs a hundred Portland houses.**

Shortly after 11.00 this Sunday morning the sea started to seep through the pebbles of the Chesil Beach at Portland. By noon the first waves were splashing over the top. Within a short time a shallow layer of water across Victoria Square surged to over five feet. It almost covered the letter box and the mail floated out on the tide.

More than a hundred houses in Chiswell were inundated and all road and rail communications between Portland and the mainland are dislocated. The stout stone wall beside the beach road is reduced to rubble at many points and the railway line breached for several yards; sleepers were swept away and rails buckled.

The water put the island's gasworks out of action and has left a trail of mud, clay, shingle and boulders across the low-lying part of Chiswell. Many are homeless and have been told that their ruined cottages will have to be demolished.

Portland Women's Voluntary Service was soon in action with hot dinners, bedding and clothes—at least help comes fast when there is a war on—and this evening the extensive damage caused by the chest-deep waters to the Cove House Inn had been cleared sufficiently for it to open punctually at seven o'clock.

England's motto is business as usual. In Portland that defiance has been extended to an older enemy—the sea.

16 December Lunchtime bombs kill four at Poole.

A Dornier 217 bomber swept low over Poole Quay at lunchtime today and dropped a stick of five bombs. They have fatally injured 14-year-old William Matthews and a Home Guard member, George Davis, who was working at Poole Iron Foundry, Thames Street.

There were casualties from other blasts, at the Gasworks, in Barbers Piles, and at Newman's Shipyard. A worker died as a result of the latter blast.

The other explosion sank a Royal Navy harbour patrol vessel, killing the only rating aboard.

17 December Airman's farewell to Came Woods.

Sergeant-Pilot Marcel Fussell of Monmouth Road, Dorchester, has been killed in action. Shortly before he died he wrote about Came Woods—autobiographically, though presented in the third person—appreciating it "for the last time, for tomorrow he was to leave his native life, his home, the fields and woods, where he had spent his life as a boy . . . to join the Air Force and serve his country."

At the top of the paper he had written one word:

"Farewell."

21 December French gunboat sinks off Swanage.

The sea was the villain today in its age-old war against those who take it for granted. The Free French Navy's gunboat *Chasseur* underestimated the tide-flow and rough waters off Durlston Head, Swanage, and sank after capsizing.

25 December Bells are enjoyed once again.

To celebrate El Alamein, and now this Christmas Day, we have enjoyed a rare sound. The bells of Christchurch Priory have echoed in joyful celebration. It is an unusual treat, not that their silence over the past three years has been in any way unwelcome; had they tolled it would have been to warn of invasion.

31 December Poole machine gunner brings down a Dornier.

New Year's Day at Poole will belong to Sergeant William Hanbury who was manning a Poole searchlight post. He illuminated a Dornier 217 bomber coming at low level across the sea and sprayed it with his Lewis machine gun. The pilot veered away but struck a gasometer and crashed into Poole Harbour.

Another raider was more successful and has destroyed Bradford's store on Poole Quay which had just been completely rebuilt after being hit on Whit Sunday.

December Piddletrenthide baker acquitted of murder.

Summing up after the trial for murder of Piddletrenthide baker Frederick Davis, Mr Justice MacNaughton said that in his opinion there was a matter of real doubt for the jury to consider: that the defendant's story might be true. He had said that he was examining a gun with Louis Stickland when it fired:

"When I found I had killed my best friend I was frightened. I was afraid of being found in the house with a dead man. On the impulse of the moment I moved the body."

After being out only forty-five minutes the jury returned to the Assize Court at Winchester with their verdict—not guilty.

DORSET'S WAR 116

December **No 5 Commando billeted in Boscombe.**

Back from Madagascar, which they helped recapture on behalf of Free French Forces, the men of No 5 Commando, Combined Operations, are being billeted in Boscombe and Bournemouth. Their base is at Boscombe, in the Broughty Ferry Hotel.

Footnote They were amalgamated with No 1 Commando and 42 and 44 Companies, Royal Marines, and became the 3rd Special Services Brigade.

December **Spies for France fly from Christchurch.**

Christchurch Aerodrome has been used by the Westland Lysanders of the Special Operations Executive for several cross-Channel missions to land and recover agents in occupied France.

1942. Lulworth Camp. Winston Churchill inspects the first formations of his tanks, the newly introduced Churchill, at the Gunnery Wing of the Armoured Fighting Vehicles School, at the western end of the Purbeck Hills.

Handley Page Halifax: tug-plane for glider troops, operating from Tarrant Rushton and Holmsley South.

1943

13 January   Dorchester anxiety at ploughing of public paths.

The Rights of Way Committee of Dorchester Rural District Council has expressed anxiety that public paths are being lost in the ploughing of grasslands for grain production. "With regard to the temporary ploughing up and diversion of rights of way consequent upon the service of directions under the Cultivation of Lands Order, the committee were extremely anxious that, during hositilities, the existence of rights of way should not be lost, and their chief anxiety was lest at the cessation of hostilities the formerly existing rights be not restored to the public."

15 January   HMS 'Dorsetshire' appeal reaches £3,057,703.

Dorset's savings campaign to raise the money, through the war loan scheme, to buy the Royal Navy a cruiser to replace HMS *Dorsetshire*, is well ahead of its original £2,750,000 target. This has been exceeded by £307,703.

January 1943. Warmwell Aerodrome. Four Burmese pilots flew with 257 Squadron. They had been training in India when the Japanese invaded Burma. Left to right are Pilot Officers M.H. Yi of Pegu, H.Y. Lau and S.J. Khin of Rangoon, and T. Clift from Shan States.

24 January   Halifax bomber crashes at Kingston Lacy.

A four-engined Halifax bomber from RAF Holmsley South [Plain Heath Airfield] at the south-west edge of the New Forest today faltered on take-off and smashed into parkland near Wimborne, fifteen miles to the west. It was fifteen minutes from take-off on a transit flight to Talbenny, Haverfordwest.

The bomber crashed to the north-west of the Kingston Lacy House, the seat of Ralph Bankes, and all the crew were killed. A terrified stag jumped through the ground floor dining room windows of the house. The aeroplane belonged to 58 Squadron.

The dead are Flying Officer M.A. Legg of the Royal New Zealand Air Force (aged 32), Flying Officer G.R. Pringle, a Royal Canadian Air Force air observer (29), and Warrant Officers L.E.

Gilpin (21) and S.J. Prince (25) of the Royal Canadian Air Force, who were wireless operators and gunners.

Footnote They are buried in Bransgore churchyard.

31 January H2S works—thanks to Worth, Christchurch, Hurn and West Howe.

Bomber Command last night operationally used H2S airborne radar sets for the first time, over Hamburg, and enabled the Pathfinder flares to be dropped on their target. The need for this apparatus has been apparent since the night of 9 March 1942 when Bomber Command, in its Chief's words, "attacked Hamborn by mistake for Essen". Sir Arthur Harris, Commander-in-Chief Bomber Command, has enthusiastically backed the development of H2S—promised for last autumn—which takes its name from the chemical formula for an obnoxious substance because Churchill's chief scientific adviser, Professor Frederick Lindemann, had commented about the excuses he heard from the Telecommunications Research Establishment at Worth Matravers: "It stinks!"

"TF" was its earlier code but that was reckoned to be a give-away [try for yourself, the answer is in the footnote] and it came into being after J.T. Randall and H.A.H. Boot invented the centimetric valve which was put into the new Beaufighter. Giving power on a low wavelength it provided an image of the ground below on a screen.

This was tested by a Blenheim bomber at eight thousand feet above the Air Defence Experimental Establishment beside Christchurch Aerodrome.

Six more flights were made and then a Halifax bomber was drafted to the new aerodrome at RAF Hurn for fitting with the first specially designed unit shielded in a protruding cupola from the belly which made the aeroplane seem ungainly and pregnant.

Then Air Commodore Donald 'Pathfinder' Bennett tried the apparatus with the result that Winston Churchill agreed it should be in production by the end of 1942. The Prototype Research Unit is making the sets—which have been perfected by Philip Dee and Bernard Lovell at Worth Matravers—in a factory beside the Northbourne Golf Links at West Howe, Bournemouth.

Footnote "TF", as you probably guessed, stood for "Town Finder".

The factory at West Howe that produced H2S now makes Max Factor cosmetics.

In practice, H2S was to create its own disaster. Not only could it be jammed but German technology advanced to exploit the signals and home in upon them. This again accelerated the rate of losses to the stage where on 30 March 1944 ninety-four bombers were shot down on a raid upon Nuremburg and seventy-one of those that made it home were damaged.

January Spitfire pilot rescued from Poole Bay.

The Poole Air-Sea Rescue launch *Commodore* has picked up a Spitfire pilot whose plane ditched in Poole Bay.

11 February Blandford Commandant dies in raid.

The Commandant of the Battle Training Camp at Blandford, Brigadier Harold Woodhouse of the local brewing family, has died from a heart attack caused by the exertion and excitement induced by a stick of German bombs. A single bomber attacked the camp and one of the cookhouses suffered blast damage.

29 February Germans sink four ships off Dorset.

In the past four days the 5th Schnellboot Flotilla has been harrying a Channel convoy in Lyme

Bay and between Portland and the Isle of Wight. Two of the escorts protecting Convoy CHA 172, the armed trawlers HMT *Harstad* and *Lord Hailsham* have been sunk. The freighter *Modavia* (4,858 tons) has also gone down, together with a new 658-ton tank landing craft, LCT381.

February **Evelyn Waugh oversees Special Services at Canford.**

Rifle-range shooting by the 2nd Special Services Brigade is being carried out at Canford Heath. It is being overseen by Evelyn Waugh, the author—who last year published *Put Out More Flags*. He is Staff Officer to Acting Admiral Louis Moutbatten, the Commander of Combined Operations.

The Brigade is also training with landing craft in assaults on Brownsea Island and at Shell Bay and Studland beach which have now been cleared of their anti-invasion scaffolding and mines.

February **Five rescued from bomber off Christchurch.**

The five-man crew of a RAF Whitley bomber were plucked from the eastern side of Poole Bay, five miles south of Christchurch, after they had crashed into the sea. The rescue was carried out by the Poole launch *Commodore*.

1 March **Cattistock man jumped out of a safe job.**

Sergeant-Navigator Robert Paull of Cattistock has been reported missing after a bombing raid. He previously had a safe reserved occupation as an inspector of 'Predictor' work in an aircraft factory but insisted upon volunteering for the RAF.

1 March **'The Advance Post' on the Wessex front-line.**

Such is the growing sophistication of this Second World War that the present major military game, Exercise Spartan, has been marked by the appearance of the "first daily newspaper of its kind to be printed specially for the purpose of a military exercise in this country".

The hypothetical cause had been the invasion of southern England by the British Expeditionary Force; but for southern England one should read northern France for the war is moving ahead. "On to Eastland," as the headline puts it. "We are not on the defensive; we are passing to attack, but if we carry the Spartan determination in defence into attack, then the battle will be won." This unusual newspaper is "Not to be published".

There is a reminder that those taking part in the exercise must leave RAF radar stations in peace so that they can carry on with the real war: "All vehicles, especially armoured fighting vehicles, should avoid operating, or coming to rest within 400 yards of RAF wireless stations. The RAF, you know, will probably be engaged with the real enemy and we want to avoid interfering with their functional efficiency."

8 March **Navy lands rescued Germans at Mudeford.**

E-boats failed to ambush a coastal convoy off Devon and escaped eastwards pursued by the Polish destroyer *Krakowiak*, until she pulled in to Poole to refuel. The six-inch coastal batteries then opened up from Brownsea Island, Hengistbury Head and Mudeford, aided by 3.7 inch dual anti-air and anti-ship emplacements and the 40 mm Bofors anti-aircraft guns on the Bournemouth cliffs. There were German losses in Poole Bay; two bodies and four survivors have been brought to Mudeford by the picket-boat *Robert T. Hillary* which is a former lifeboat crewed by the Royal Navy Volunteer Reserve.

30 March 1st Dorsets leave Malta.

The siege of Malta has been lifted and the 1st Battalion of the Dorsetshire Regiment today sailed for Egypt. It is part of the 1st Malta Brigade which is to be renamed the 231st Infantry Brigade.

Footnote They were welcomed to Fayid by Gerald Bernard Montgomery: "This morning I have seen some magnificent soldiers. These fine Regular battalions who have been shut up in Malta, and have now joined us, will be an asset to the 8th Army."

March Hurricane comes down off Green Island.

A Hurricane has crashed into Poole Harbour, off Green Island. Its pilot was picked-up by the Air-Sea Rescue launch *Commodore*.

21 April Mine damaged vessel puts into Christchurch.

The United States Coastguard Service vessel *Apache*, bound for Cowes from Boston, Massachusetts, has been forced to put into the River Avon at Christchurch for repairs after having hit a mine in the Channel.

Footnote Yesterday was Hitler's fifty-fifth birthday. His words of 23 August 1939 are being recalled: "I am now fifty years old. I prefer a war now to when I am fifty-five."

21 April Australian flying boats leave for Pembroke.

461 Squadron of the Royal Australian Air Force today left RAF Hamworthy and took their Sunderland flying boats to Pembroke in South Wales.

28 April German craft sunk off St Alban's Head.

Last night the German submarine chaser VJ 140Z was sunk by Hunt-class destroyers, the Royal Navy's main coast protection flotilla from Portsmouth, whilst it was trying to guard Axis Convoy code 37K/MS. It went down off St Alban's Head.

1 May American daylight raiders cross Dorset.

Elements of the first massed United States Air Force daytime bombing raid against Germany have crossed Dorset on their way to the Channel. The Royal Observer Corps log at Dorchester records: "09.30 hours. 20 Liberators spotted south-west. 10.45 hours. 47 Fortresses flying south." Planes returned individually through the afternoon. The Observer Corps, incidentally, was awarded the 'Royal' cachet on 11 April 1941.

9 May Exercise Demon in Sherborne's wrecked street.

Bomb-damaged Newland in Sherborne, one of the streets devastated by the air raid of 30 September 1940, has provided a realistic setting for Exercise Demon. Spectators watched from rows of seats on the rise that looks down towards the Black Horse Hotel as troops, firemen, ARP wardens and the Women's Voluntary Service practised their crafts—from street warfare to the arrival of tea urns.

16 May Halifax bomber crashes at Bransgore.

A four-engined Halifax bomber crashed today whilst on a flight from Hurn to the nearby RAF station at Holmsley South [Plain Heath Airfield] on the edge of the New Forest. A mile short of its destination, at Bransgore, it dived to starboard from twelve hundred feet and all but one of the

9 May 1943. Sherborne—Exercise Demon. Above it is make-believe, the detached eye being courtesy of the butcher. Below is reality, the arrival in Newland of the Women's Voluntary Service with urns of tea.

crew were killed on impact. A young Canadian was dragged out of the wreckage alive but died in Boscombe Hospital.

The dead are Royal Canadian Air Force pilots Flying Officers M.W. Collins and D.J. Smith, both aged 21, and Flying Officer P.S. Thomas, an RAF air gunner.

Footnote They are buried in Bransgore churchyard.

17 May Dambuster bombs were tested in Dorset.

The earliest version of the bouncing bombs that were dropped last night by Lancasters of 617 Squadron, to breach the Möhne and Eder dams in the Ruhr, were tested in Dorset. Prototypes of the weapon had been developed on a freelance basis by Barnes Wallis of Vickers Armstrong, working outside the official Ministry of Aircraft Production's armament programme. They were carried by a Wellington and dropped from sixty feet onto the flat waters of the Fleet lagoon, near Langton Herring.

This part of the Chesil Beach bombing range was used to ascertain that the bombs worked in principle, skimming across the water like a well-thrown stone, though the actual practice runs for Operation Chastise were carried out by the Lancasters over the Elan valley reservoir in the mountains of mid-Wales.

17 May 1943. The Ruhr floods—from an idea that first bounced across Dorset's Fleet lagoon.

Footnote Air Marshal Arthur Harris, Commander-in-Chief, Bomber Command, recalled that he "rang up Washington, where Churchill and Portal were at the time, to give them the news. The telephone personnel seemed never to have heard of the White House, and there was some little difficulty. When I did get through I was intercepted and asked for an assurance that the person I was calling was reliable. I don't know whether she was persuaded that Winston Churchill came into that category, but I got through to Portal in the end and told him that the two dams had gone." Eight of the nineteen Lancasters failed to return. The main aim had been to cause a shortage of water for industrial purposes in the Ruhr, rather than sweeping everything away in a flood which is how we tend to remember the exploit. Not that there were many happy farmers in Kassel when two hundred million tons of water spread across their fields.

23 May 1943. Bournemouth. The Punshon Memorial church and Central Hotel, Richmond Hill, devastated by lunchtime German bombs. The printing works of the Bournemouth Daily Echo, glimpsed to the left, had a near miss.

20 May **Another Holmsley Halifax crashes.**

Another Halifax bomber from RAF Holmsley South [Plain Heath Airfield] has failed on take-off and crashed with the loss of all crewmen. Its pilot, Flying Officer R.M. Reisner, was a Canadian. The aeroplane came down nine miles north-west of the airfield, near Fordingbridge, after it had cast-off a Horsa glider.

23 May **77 dead in Bournemouth's worst air raid.**

This has been Bournemouth's worst air raid. Beales department store was burnt out and West's Cinema, the Central Hotel, Metropole Hotel and Punshon Memorial Church shattered beyond repair as at lunchtime sixteen Focke-Wulf 190s bombed the central shopping areas of the Square and the Lansdowne.

Seventy-seven people are dead and 3,481 buildings damaged; it is estimated that about forty will have to be demolished.

Two hours later Sir Adrian Boult, the BBC Orchestra's conductor, took the Bournemouth

Municipal Orchestra through the 'Nimrod' passage from Edward Elgar's *Enigma Variations* in memory of those who had died. The bombs marred what had been intended as a celebration—it was the fiftieth anniversary concert of the Bournemouth Orchestra.

One bomb had exploded beside the omnibus standing area at the Bus Station in Exeter Road. Twenty-five Hants and Dorset buses lost all their glass and some are being sent back into service without any windows. Sacks have been tied across the fronts of the vehicles to reduce draughts.

Bombs also fell between Iford Bridge and Pokesdown. Five FW190s are reportedly shot down.

May **Catalinas take over RAF Hamworthy.**

Catalina flying boats of 210 Squadron of Coastal Command have moved into the seaplane base at RAF Hamworthy and are operating long-range flights into the Atlantic in the battle against the U-boats.

May **Hambro heir killed in Tripoli.**

It is reported that Major Robert Hambro, the only son of Captain Angus Hambro of Merley House, Wimborne, and his heir, was mortally wounded whilst serving in a reconnaissance regiment of the 8th Army. He died at Tripoli. Major Hambro was born in 1911.

12 June **321 more German mines laid off Dorset.**

A total of 321 German mines and 84 barrage protection floats have been laid off Dorset and the Isle of Wight in the past week by the combined efforts of the German 2nd, 4th, 5th and 6th

1943. Warmwell. 'Bellows' a Westland Whirlwind of 263 Squadron, was piloted by 22-year-old Flying Officer J.P. Coyne of Manitoba. Coyne had just won the Distinguished Flying Cross.

25 June 1943. Christchurch. Sub Lieutenant P. M. Lamb wears his hair long because of the scars he gained from landing his Royal Navy Seafire on a Stanpit bungalow. He had lost engine power at the end of a 500 mile delivery flight. Conversion work on the Seafire, the Navy's carrier-based version of the Spitfire, was carried out by Airspeed Limited at Somerford.

Schnellboot Flotillas. The Royal Naval Mine Sweeping Service has simply noted the areas concerned and is making arrangements to have them cleared as soon as resources and weather conditions allow.

23 June **Dutch vessel blown-up in Poole Bay.**

A Dutch craft, the *Leny*, was blown up today by a mine near the Swash Channel at the entrance to Poole Harbour. Only two of its crewmen have been rescued.

25 June **Bungalow landing for Christchurch pilot.**

19.54 hours. A Royal Navy Seafire, being flown into Christchurch Aerodrome from Donibristle, Scotland, has overshot the runway and crashed into a bungalow, 'Musoka' in Caroline Avenue at Stanpit. The aircraft is number MB315 RN, piloted by Sub-Lieutenant P.M. Lamb who has been taken to hospital with head injuries.

Footnote Lamb was stitched-up, though he had to grow his hair long to cover the scars. "Not my best landing," he wrote in his log, "engine tired of living, fortunately I didn't join it." Seafires were frequently seen over Christchurch as the Airspeed factory converted 160 of them, from standard Spitfires, for use by the Fleet Air Arm.

June **Thousand rockets pound Studland beach in thirty seconds.**

The RCL, a tank landing craft that has been modified at Poole to carry batteries of rocket launchers, has been tested in Studland Bay and at Kimmeridge. It fires more than a thousand explosive rockets in about thirty seconds, delivering them on to a small area of the beach; the aim is to annihilate enemy strongpoints with firepower that is devastatingly concentrated.

5 July **1st Dorsets sail for Sicily.**

The 1st Battalion of the Dorsetshire Regiment has sailed into the Mediterranean aboard the ex-P&O liner *Strathnaver* among the armada bound for the beaches of Sicily.

10 July **One German E-boat sunk and HMS 'Melbreak' damaged.**

An engagement last night off Dorset between the Hunt-class destroyers from Portsmouth and the German 2nd Schnellboot Flotilla on convoy-protection duty has resulted in Axis craft M135 being sunk. HMS *Melbreak* sustained serious damage.

10 July **1st Dorsets take Marzamemi.**

'C' Company of the 1st Battalion of the Dorsetshire Regiment, under Captain A.C.W. Martin, went over the side of the troopship *Strathnaver* at 03.00 hours to effect a scramble-landing on a rocky promontory at the right-flank of the projected bridgehead in Sicily. They took the village of Marzamemi and were also able to secure the proposed landing beach to the south.

Tracer shells fired vertically from a Bren gun was the dawn signal of success to the Commanding Officer offshore. The Battalion's 'A' and 'B' companies then landed to establish themselves inland.

Footnote The Royal Navy lost two submarines in the Sicilian invasion. One was HMS *Saracen*, commanded by Lieutenant M.G.R. Lumby of South Eggardon Farm, Askerswell, who was taken prisoner with his crew.

12 July **Poole's 'Apple' is killed in Sicily.**

One of the heroes who was able to thrill the nation with daring exploits in desperate times, Major Geoffrey Appleyard DSO of Poole commandos, is missing presumed killed in Sicily. He was known in Combined Operations as 'The Apple'. His men had been seconded to the North African Forces, where they were known as the 1st Small Scale Raiding Force, and Appleyard was the deputy commander of the 2nd Special Air Service Regiment. He was 26-years-old.

24 July **Worth's "Window" is opened at last.**

"Let us open the Window," Winston Churchill decided and last night it was done—this being the codename given by the Telecommunications Research Establishment's Superintendent, A.P. Rowe, to what was the parting shot of the Worth Matravers scientists to the war effort before their radar laboratories were moved to Malvern. It comprises thousands of metal strips that create a smoke-screen effect upon enemy radar sets at the onset of a mass bombing raid.

"Window" was perfected in Dorset over a year ago but opposition from Fighter Command and Robert Watson-Watt, radar's British pioneer, blocked its operational use. It had been feared that it might give the Germans the idea at a time when they were still liable to carry out major attacks against Britain.

The scientists and Bomber Command are elated with the results of "Window" in causing confusion and consternation to the German defences. Losses which statistically should have been about 6.1 per cent have been reduced to 1.5 per cent—"Window" last night saved seventy-five aeroplanes and their crews.

July **Advanced landing ground at Winkton.**

August 1943. Sopley. Extract from a Luftwaffe target map showing Winkton Advanced Landing Ground—though the Germans failed to notice the RAF's Sopley radar station (at spot-height '42' between Sopley village and Parsonage Farm).

Hedges and ditches have been removed across an area of flat farmland to the north-east of Sopley, beside the lane from Winkton to Ripley, for a temporary Advanced Landing Ground. This will enable additional fighter capacity to be brought into the Christchurch area for protection of the Channel convoys and the build-up of invasion shipping.

The runways of RAF Winkton have been laid as sheets of steel mesh directly on to the grass. There are two runways; one north-south from east of Parsonage Farm to west of Clockhouse Farm, and the other east-west from the Ripley lane to within a third of a mile of the cottages at Bransgore.

12 August **Christchurch bomb damage.**

There was an explosion near the railway, close to Christchurch Station, at 01.10 hours. A high explosive bomb caused widespread damage at Ringwood Road, Walkford, at 01.15. Many houses were shattered and one bed-ridden lady is homeless. Three people were injured. There are also reports of unexploded bombs.

28 August **'Second Front'—Eden, Brooke and Mountbatten fly into Poole.**

The Secretary of State for Foreign Affairs, Anthony Eden, together with General Sir Alan Brooke, Chief of the Imperial General Staff, and Admiral Louis Mountbatten, Chief of Combined Operations, landed at 14.00 hours today in Poole Harbour. They were aboard the BOAC Boeing Clipper *Bristol* and had returned across the Atlantic from the Quebec Conference which set the location and timetable for the launching of the Second Front.

The decision has been taken to go for the beaches of Normandy and forgo the need to capture a port by towing across pre-fabricated concrete caissons, codenamed Mulberries, to make two instant harbours. The provisional date for the invasion of Europe is 1 May 1944.

31 August **Echo of Sedgemoor.**

The Daily Telegraph reports that a Lyme Regis hotelier received a stamped addressed postcard from an anxious prospective visitor asking for "the date of the last enemy attack on your town".

The manager sent the card back with the date—"1685".

DORSET'S WAR   128

8 September 1943. The 1st Battalion of the Dorsetshire Regiment arrives at Pizzo in the Toe of Italy. Bryan de Grineau's sketch, for the Illustrated London News, shows Serjeant W. Evans winning a bar to his Military Medal.

8 September **Dorset mailbag leads the rearguard into Italy.**

Support landings at Pizzo, on the Toe of Italy, were carried out just before dawn to establish a rearguard to ease pressure on the Allied troops in the Reggio beachhead.

The commandos went astray, however, and the first craft to beach contained the headquarters unit of the 1st Battalion of the Dorsetshire Regiment. The landing was led—not that he realised it—by an NCO with a mailbag slung over his shoulder.

Later the Battalion's 'B' Company came under heavy counter-attack on the coast road. It knocked out a Mark IV tank but lost one of its two anti-tank guns. Sergeant W. Evans single-handedly immobilised an armoured car with a grenade, killing the crew, and shot a German officer who tried to climb out. The company's left-flank was under infantry attack. This was held off by Lieutenant L.G. Browne's platoon in fierce hand-to-hand fighting which left twenty enemy dead.

At one point the Brigade Commander called up air support and the Kittyhawk fighter-bombers arrived on time. They then confused the British positions for those of the enemy and proceeded to bomb and strafe them, destroying several vehicles. It has been that sort of day.

Footnote Some honour emerged from the chaos. Evans won a bar to his Military Medal and Lieutenant Browne was awarded the Military Cross.

September **Great Panjandrum tested at Clouds Hill.**

One of the more bizarre weapons of war, a Great Panjandrum rocket-fired assault wheel, has been tested by Combined Operations commandos from Poole on their explosives firing ground at Clouds Hill, near Bovington Camp. The cylinder at the centre of two ten feet high wheels contains 4,000lb of high explosive.

The rockets are intended to send the wheel out of an invasion landing craft and up the beach to blow a hole in ten feet of concrete of the German Atlantic Wall defences. The rocket propulsion was tried out on the sands of Westward Ho! and Instow, Devon, on 7 and 8 September with unpredictable results. Nevil Shute Norway, the aeronautical engineer and writer, figured out the size of the charges needed to breach the Atlantic Wall and is taking part in the experiments.

Footnote A final trial took place at Westward Ho! in January 1944. It was filmed by motor-racing photographer Luis Klemantaski who had to run for his life as the machine reached a hundred miles per hour and suddenly veered towards him. Onlookers tried to escape up the beach and became entangled in barbed wire. The Panjandrum, meanwhile, wobbled seaward again as rockets spiralled across the beach; one being chased by an Airedale hound, Ammanol. With this the project was abandoned.

One of the wheels of the Clouds Hill Great Panjandrum was discovered in 1946–47 by Bere Regis scouts who were camping nearby in Sare's Wood. Fred Pitfield, then aged fifteen, recalls the terrific fun they had rolling it up and down the hills adjacent to the camp, though even unpowered it still managed to demolish tents, bicycles and billie-cans.

9 October **Sandbanks Air Station closes.**

The Royal Navy's seaplane training school at Sandbanks was today disbanded.

10 October **P-o-Ws sent cigarettes.**

The following card, written in a camp at M. Stammlager, is typical of those being received by the Society of Dorset Men:

"Kriegsgefangenenlager. Dear Sir, Thank you very much for your letter of September. I have today received a parcel of 200 cigarettes, I believe they are from the Society. Cigarettes to us mean such a great deal. I am a Dorset man, born and bred, and to me it is still the finest little place in the world. Thanking you once again. Yours sincerely, G.W. Harris, 6848."

11 October **India's Viceroy flies out from Poole.**

Field Marshal Sir Archibald Wavell, Viceroy of India and Supreme Commander Allied Forces in India and Burma, today left Poole Quay by launch to board a BOAC flying-boat bound for Bombay.

October **Glider squadrons move to Tarrant Rushton.**

The newly formed 298 Squadron, flying four-engined Halifax bombers as tugs to tow troop-carrying gliders, has moved into Tarrant Rushton Aerodrome. They will be joined by the Stirlings of 196 Squadron.

1 November **Bournemouth air raid.**

17.45 hours. Bombs have been dropped on Bournemouth, though damage appears to be comparatively light.

6 November **First home leave for the 1st Dorsets since 1936.**

Dorset's Regular Army soldiers, the 1st Battalion of the Dorsetshire Regiment, disembarked on the Clyde at Gourock today from the troopship *Durban Castle*. The survivors of the Malta siege and assault landings in Sicily and Italy are looking forward to their first home leave since their transfer to the North West Frontier of India in 1936.

8 December **Americans arrive at Blandford.**

The 184th Auxiliary Anti-Aircraft Gun Battalion is the first unit of the United States Army to arrive at Blandford Camp. It has 716 enlisted men and twenty-five officers. Their task will be to provide protection around the proposed beach landing assault exercise area at Studland.

19 December **Tyneham villagers are evicted.**

Ralph Bond, the platoon commander of the Tyneham Home Guard and a Purbeck magistrate, has been evicted from his Elizabethan mansion along with his servants, farm labourers and the fishermen of Worbarrow Bay. The whole of the 3,003 acres of the parish of Tyneham plus other land beneath the Purbeck Hills have been depopulated by the order of the War Cabinet. The area will be occupied by the United States Army for invasion training exercises. No mention of this extension of the Lulworth tank gunnery ranges has been permitted in the press and there has been no consultation with the local councils.

Tenancies are, however, being maintained and each occupant has been assured: "This means that when the War Department has no further use for the property and it is handed back, you have every right to return to the property. It should not be assumed by you that, because that War Department has turned you out, you lose the right of occupying the premises again."

The prohibition of editorial mentions of the military take-over has not been extended to the advertising columns. On 2 December the Dorset County Chronicle published notices that the following farmers were quitting: S.G. Churchill (Tyneham Farm), A.E. Cranton (Lutton Farm), A.J. Longman (Baltington Farm), J.H. House (North Egliston Farm), R.J. Cake (West Creech Farm), T.W. Wrixon (Povington Farm), Arthur Cooper (Searley's Farm, Povington), J. Cooper (Jiggiting Corner, Povington), Mrs Vonham (Weld Arms Farm, East Lulworth), Mrs S.P. Damen (The Cat, East Lulworth), H.J. Sampson (Whiteway Farm, East Lulworth), H.C. George (Broadmoor Farm, West Creech), Frank Cranton (Rookery Farm, West Creech), A. E. Swain (Hurst Mill Farm, West Creech).

Appended is this note: "The Auctioneers wish to draw special attention to the before mentioned sales and sincerely trust that all farmers from over a wide area will endeavour to attend as many as possible, to assist in the dispersal of the stock on offer, all of which is thoroughly recommended by the Auctioneers."

25 December **Glider pilots posted to Tarrant Rushton.**

It is a Christmas present for the 1st Battalion of the Glider Pilot Regiment to arrive back in England today from Taranto, Italy. They are to be re-united with their Hamilcar gliders and the four-engined Halifax towing-craft of 298 and 644 Squadrons at Tarrant Rushton, on the edge of the Cranborne Chase chalklands between Wimborne and Blandford.

26 December **Puddletown farmer becomes international broadcaster.**

Ralph Wightman, known to the press as "the Dorset farmer" though he never actually farmed, has progressed from his career as Dorset's senior agricultural adviser to being the world voice of the English countryman. He talks into the microphone as if he were having a chat among friends in the village inn at Puddletown, where he lives in a sixteenth century stone-built house.

Last year he was heard on the wireless, in the *Country Magazine*, with established rural pundits such as A.G. Street and S.P.B. Mais. Wightman's dulcet tones, warm humour and

1943–44. Burton Bradstock. Off-duty GIs on the roof of a beach pillbox—Corporal Bert Markowitz of Queens, New York, serenades G. R. Miller of Louisville, Kentucky.

practical commonsense immediately appealed to listeners and he was invited back by the BBC to 'star' on the programme.

Tonight he has been given the honour of delivery the Sunday *Postscript* which will be relayed by the Forces broadcasting network to all theatres of the war, as well as across the British Empire and North America.

Footnote Ralph Wightman was to do 290 consecutive weekly broadcasts, describing the countryside at war, for listeners in the United States. He was to compère the bulk of the *Country Magazine* series as well as make regular appearances in *Country Questions, On the Land,* and *Any Questions*. For those who grew up with the wireless he was the best known Dorset man of his generation.

December **'In the Drink' Foss and other stories.**

Perhaps the kindest touch to a war story in the past few months has been that of RAF Sergeant Ronald Foss, from Bridport, who was on a Coastal Command flight over the Bay of Biscay. The first person to know he was missing happened to be his wife, whom he married in April 1942, as she was serving in the operations room of the same air station. Ronald, in fact, was still alive, and was picked up from the sea a week later with enough experience of war to fill a book.

On the other side of the coin, equally human but showing how war could have needlessly tragic consequences, some boys at Portland Royal Navy dockyard mocked a decent self-respecting soldier, of the Buffs, and told him he was no better than a Home Guard. Instantly, in pique, the sentry shot dead John Groves, a seventeen year old of Williams Avenue at Wyke Regis. It was all silly and unintentional, manslaughter rather than murder, and the situation rather than the participants were to blame. Give a man a gun and he may defend his pride as well as his country.

Footnote Regarding the first amazing story, Ronald Foss had in him not one book but three, *In the Drink, Three of us Live,* and *Famous War Stories*. He was to enjoy a long retirement with his wife in London, Ontario.

December **Eisenhower's deputy is an Old Dorset.**

Air Marshal Sir Arthur Tedder, who is General Eisenhower's Deputy Supreme Commander of Allied Forces Western Europe, began his military career with the Dorset Regiment in the Great War. He served in France in 1915 and transferred to the air service in 1916, rising to become Vice-Chief of the Air Staff in November 1942.

1943–44. Burton Bradstock. Village boy mans A. E. Cheney's pumps, the Red House Garage, as another cleans the windscreen of an American jeep. Either side it is still pastoral Dorset.

Lockheed P-38 Lightning: flown by the Americans from Warmwell.

1944

January Poole yards produce a landing craft a day.

Round the clock production in the three yards of shipbuilders J. Bolson and Son Limited at Hamworthy, Poole, brings about the completion of one assault landing craft a day. The LCAs are being tethered in Holes Bay. The yards, formerly the Skylark boat business which made yachts and other pleasure craft, also produce air-sea rescue speedboats and minesweepers, and carry out repairs on tank landing craft.

Work practices have been revolutionised. One squad is responsible for the complete production of a single vessel and this has helped Bolson's into their premier position—the largest assault landing craft manufacturers in Britain.

January US Army hospital built at St Leonards.

An extensive General Hospital of the United States Army is being built on twenty acres of heathland to the south of the main road between Ferndown and St Leonards, near Ringwood. It is being prepared for use as a major surgical centre for casualties brought out of France after the planned invasion of Europe.

5 February Germans lose M156.

Enemy boat M156 is effectively out of the war for some time to come having been seriously damaged last night in a lengthy engagement with British destroyers HMS *Brissenden*, *Tantside*, *Talybont* and *Wensleydale*. She has been towed by a Vichy French craft into L'Abervrach.

Footnote M156 was still not safe; at L'Abervrach she was further damaged by bombs from Coastal Command, Calshot.

23 February King visits the 1st Dorsets.

His Majesty the King today visited the 1st Battalion of the Dorsetshire Regiment who are undergoing training at Halstead, Essex. He watched a company attack on a strongpoint, supported by an assault pioneer platoon under Lieutenant W.F. Scott.

Early 1944. Poole. Rocket-firing landing craft RCL (B) 640 being completed in Bolson and Son's yard.

DORSET'S WAR 134

Early 1944. Above, Poole Harbour. A line of assault landing craft, built by Bolson's at Hamworthy and Poole, at anchor in Holes Bay. Production is running at one per day. Vast quantities of craft are accumulating in inlets and estuaries along the South Coast as central southern England prepares for the invasion of Europe.

Early 1944. Studland beach. Tanks and beaches don't go well together. Failure (top, left) as the Churchill tank fails to climb one of the steeper parts of the sand dunes. So enter one of Hobart's Funnies (top, right). Major General Percy Hobart of the 79th Armoured Division designed a series of ingenious machines that could ease the way for tanks, and however strange they looked, his vehicles were to save hundreds of lives in the Normandy campaign. Here, an AVRE lays a carpet from a bobbin, across the soft sand. Next, using the carpet that the AVRE has laid, the Churchill tank repeats its attempt at climbing the dune (above, left). This time it disappears over the top (above, right). On the lefthand side of this picture you can see the deep rut left by its first, unaided, failure.

April 1944. Opposite. Slapton Sands, Devon. In Exercise Fabious landing craft from Portland, Weymouth and Poole joined in the major dummy run for D-Day and the invasion of Normandy. Three tank landing craft are unloading in this sector, protected by barrage balloons from fighter attack.

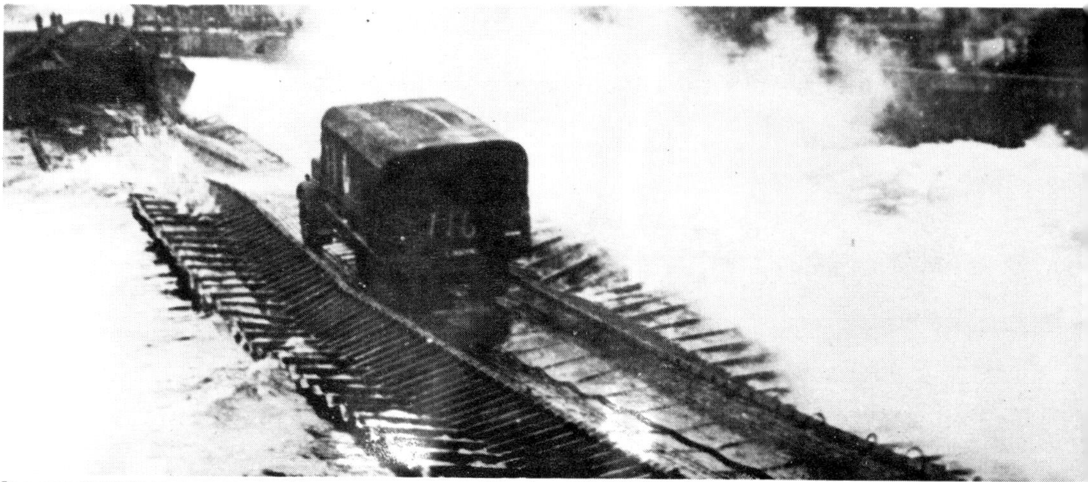

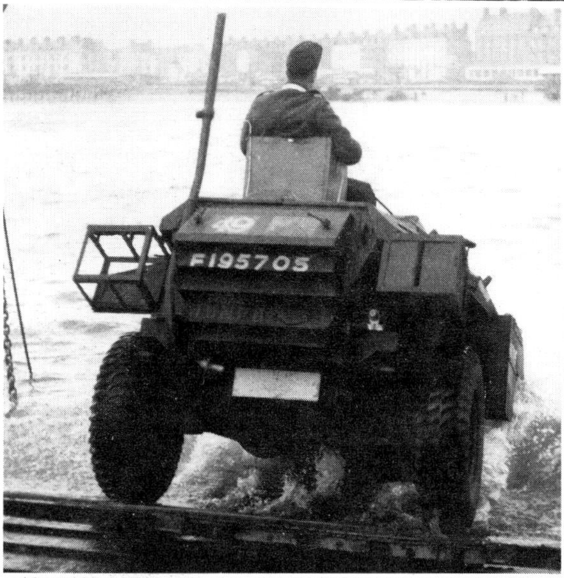
F195705

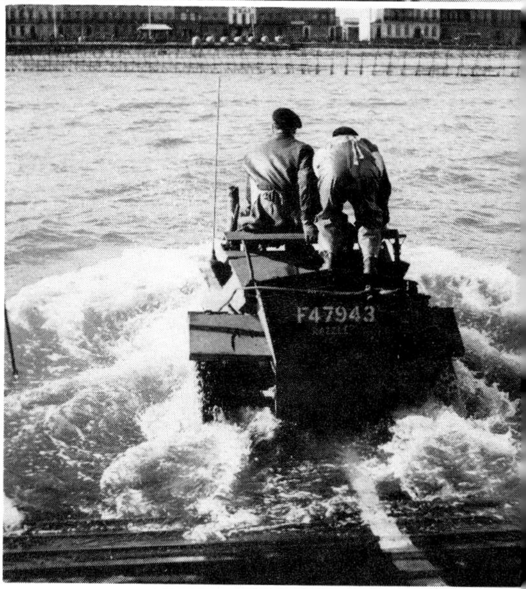
F47943

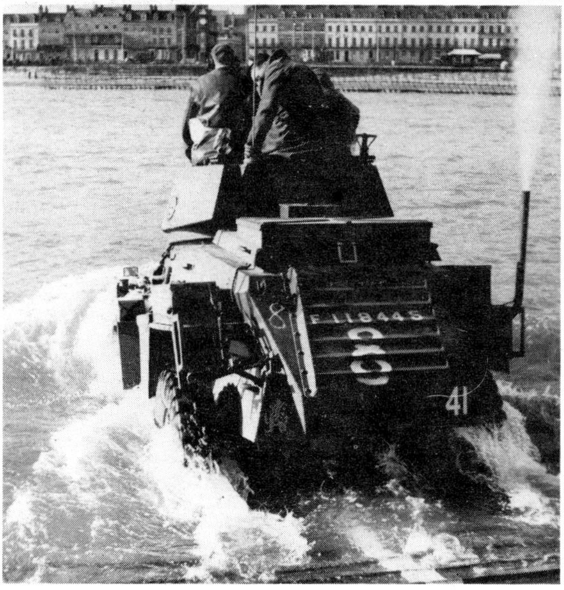
41

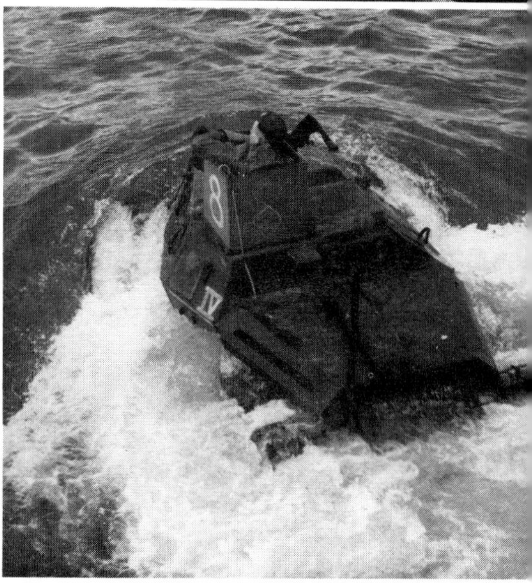

1944

Early 1944. Weymouth Harbour. Opposite, top, 'Scam' Project 'Swiss Roll' had a heavily laden Bedford lorry driving across the waves.

5 February 1944. Weymouth Bay. Opposite, four photographs. A Humber Scout car (bottom, left) drives into four feet of water off Weymouth promenade. It successfully drives through the sea (bottom, right). Next a Humber armoured car drives down the ramp of a tank landing craft (centre, left). And likewise a Daimler scout car.

5 February 1944. Weymouth Bay. The wading exercise continues. Weymouth's anti-invasion defences, dating from 1940, can be seen in the background of these shots. Perhaps the most amazing sight (top, right) was a Stuart tank travelling through six feet of water. Note the depth marker on its exhaust outlet. The other funnel carried air to the engine. Two other Stuarts pass in five feet of water (bottom, left). The timekeeper raises a flag to signal that the time limit of six minutes has expired (bottom, right).

Early 1944. Abbotsbury. Lighting up the night. Star shells fired from two-pounder Pom-poms illuminate the Channel in a 'Scam' project exercise. In that mass of light there are forty or more shells bursting. Silhouetted against the sea are the concrete anti-tank defences of the Chesil Beach, a reminder of the days when the invasion threat was in reverse.

Early 1944. Burton Bradstock. Rope ladders being fired by rockets from assault landing craft to the top of the 150 feet cliff. Grapnels are attached to the rockets. This is one of the better 'Scam' projects for invasion innovations.

February **Eisenhower and Monty at Bournemouth's Carlton Hotel.**

The Carlton Hotel on Bournemouth's East Cliff is one of the perquisites of the United States Army's occupation of this holiday coast—they would call it a perk. It is host to the American Forces Bureau of Investigation and some crews of self-propelled guns but still manages to rise to the occasional moments of style. General Dwight D. Eisenhower, Supreme Commander Allied Forces Western Europe, and General Bernard Montgomery, Commander-in-Chief Allied Land Forces, have used its facilities and the convenient clifftop view of rehearsals for invasion in the bay below.

These, sadly, have not been without their casualties including soldiers aboard several Valentine DD [Duplex-Drive] tanks which are both amphibious and land vehicles; failings in their 'skirts' whilst carrying out the former role being the cause of the sinkings. These swimming

February 1944. Bournemouth. General Dwight D. Eisenhower and General Bernard Montgomery at the Carlton Hotel, making plans for the invasion of Europe. They had been watching assault landing rehearsals in Poole Bay.

tanks have canvas screens and propeller shafts at the rear. Hundreds of Shermans are being converted into DD tanks for the invasion assault.

Landing craft are now everywhere around, including the bays of Poole Harbour, Christchurch Harbour, and the inlets of the Solent such as Beaulieu River which also conceals the sunken sections of Mulberry Harbours.

12 March Tragedy mars Warmwell's welcome for the Yanks.

15.00 hours. Tragedy has ended a flying display put on by four RAF Typhoons of 263 Squadron to welcome the 474th Fighter Group of the United States Army Air Force on their arrival at the former Battle of Britain aerodrome at Warmwell. One of the four RAF planes spun out of a low roll and crashed half a mile west of the field. The pilot of HHS MN 129, Pilot Officer Graham Smith, was killed.

12 March 1944. Warmwell Aerodrome. American Lockheed P-38 Lightning fighter-bombers of the 474th Fighter Group bring a new shape to the south Dorset's sky.

21 March Worbarrow radar foils an E-boat incursion.

An attempt last night by the German 9th Schnellboot Flotilla to carry out a raid in Weymouth Bay was foiled by the radar apparatus at Worbarrow Bay which with that on Portland Bill was able to correlate the movements of the enemy craft. As a result the gun-laying by the coastal batteries of the Royal Artillery, from Swanage and Upton Fort at Osmington into the sea off St Alban's Head, was so accurate that S84 collided with S139 as the attack was abandoned in disarray.

23 March Blandford AA gunners go to London.

The American 184th Auxiliary Anti-Aircraft Gun Battalion is on the move from Blandford Camp to London to supplement the capital's air defences. Its 'A' Battery has already left, having moved to Essex in January.

March Pluto is laid across Poole bay.

Pluto, the acronym of Pipe Line Under The Ocean, has been laid by the Tweedledrum, a great drum with cone-shaped ends, pulled by HMS *Conundrum* and a tug across twelve miles of Poole Bay to the Isle of Wight. This experiment by the Petroleum Warfare Department is to prove the feasibility of laying an underwater pipeline from a pumping station at Shanklin on the Isle of Wight across the English Channel to the proposed invasion beaches on the coast of Normandy.

March 1944. Weymouth Bay. One of the more bizarre 'Scam' projects was for a floating airfield, codenamed 'Lily'. It was tried out on a reassuringly flat sea, with a Swordfish biplane. The aircraft, loaded to 9,000 lb, is about to use rocket assisted take-off gear to become airborne.

March 'Scam' projects tested in Dorset.

The boffins are trying out their Scam Projects on the Dorset coast. A floating airfield, codenamed Lily, has been tested in Weymouth Bay by a Royal Navy Swordfish biplane carrying a bomb load and using rockets to enable the exceedingly short take-off.

For the Army there is a floating pier, the Swiss Roll, which has carried heavily laden Bedford lorries across Weymouth Harbour. More practical are the rockets being used to fire grapnels attacked to rope ladders for commandos to scale the 150 feet cliffs beten Bridport and Burton Bradstock.

March Swanage Great War VC passes on his experience.

Chief Petty Officer Ernest Pitcher of Swanage, who won the Victoria Cross in 1917 for staying at his gun in the classic action between an armed merchantman, a Q-boat, and a submarine, is back in uniform in this war at the age of fifty-seven. He rejoined in 1939 and is now training naval

1944. Warmwell. RAF Air Sea Rescue Spitfires operate (opposite) from the aerodrome.

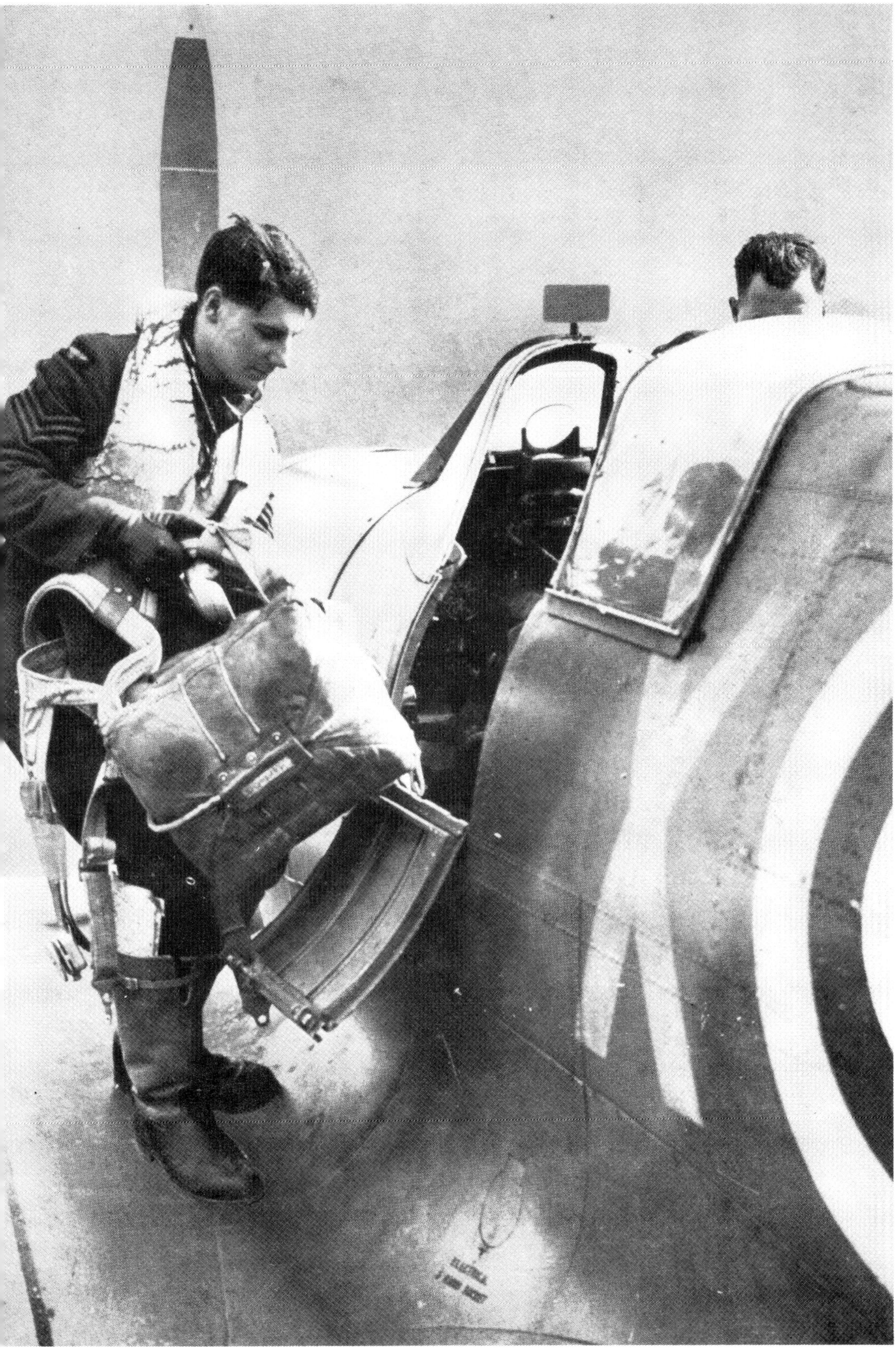

gunnery ratings.

Footnote Pitcher died in Gosport in 1946.

4 April **Warmwell airman's heroism in the water.**

Corporal Jerry Liroff, an off-duty American serviceman from the 474th Fighter Group at Warmwell, dived fully clothed into the sea off Plymouth today to rescue a drowning child.

14 April **Air-sea Rescue Squadron drafted to Warmwell.**

Another RAF squadron has returned to Warmwell Aerodrome, which is the base for forty-eight P-38J Lightnings of the American 474th Fighter Group. The 275 (Air-sea Rescue) Squadron flies Spitfires in coastal patrols, with an Anson to drop dinghies and a Walrus seaplane for pick-ups beyond the reach of a launch from Lyme Regis, Weymouth, Portland or Poole.

19 April 1944. Bovington Camp. General Bernard Montgomery strides through the Armoured Fighting Vehicles School, at home in his Royal Tank Corps beret.

19 April **Montgomery inspects units at Bovington Camp.**

Various defence and invasion assault units have assembled at Bovington Camp today for an inspection by General Bernard Montgomery, the Commander-in-Chief of Allied Land Forces in Europe.

19 April **Bournemouth coast guns in action.**

Royal Artillery coast defence batteries at Hengistbury Head, Mudeford and the Needles opened up last night on the German 5th Schnellboot Flotilla as they laid electro-magnetic mines in the eastern parts of Poole Bay and off the Isle of Wight.

S64 and S133 of the 8th Schnellboot Flotilla were damaged in a separate engagement last night where a Hunt-class destroyer, HMS *Whitshead*, caught up with them in foul weather.

22 April **Warmwell's Lightnings sweep Brittany.**

Forty-eight Lightnings of the 474th Fighter Group of the United States Army Air Force, from Warmwell, carried out a three-hour sweep across Brittany today in their first combat air patrol. All the planes returned safely.

24 April **Three killed in Poole incendiary attack.**

Houses were damaged last night in an incendiary attack on the northern parts of Poole and Broadstone. Three people were killed, including firewatcher Arthur Martin, aged 59. Many fires were started but almost all were brought swiftly under control, leaving only thirteen people without homes.

28 April **Six hundred Americans massacred off Portland.**

Last night a convoy of eight American landing craft, sailing west from the Solent for the big Exercise Fabius practice landings at Slapton Sands, Devon, were intercepted by E-boats as they rounded Portland Bill to enter Lyme Bay. Motor torpedo boats of the 5th and 9th Schnellboot Flotillas ran amock amongst the Americans off the Portland end of the Chesil Beach, which is known locally as Dead Man's Bay from the memory of earlier shipwreck calamities.

A total of 441 United States soldiers have been killed or drowned together with 197 seamen; LST507 and LST531 are sunk with the loss of twelve tanks; LST289 is damaged by a torpedo.

The coastal gun batteries at Blacknor, Portland, prepared to open fire but the American commander ordered them not to do so, in view of the number of his men who were in the water. The E-boats withdrew on the arrival of a corvette, HMS *Azalra*, and HMS *Saladin*, followed by HMS *Onslow*.

30 April **RAF Hamworthy closes.**

The short direct connection with military flying boats has ended at Poole with the closure of RAF Hamworthy. Service flying boats can, however, still be refuelled and oiled at Poole by BOAC.

April **Unexploded phosphorous bomb at Holton Heath.**

A five kilogram German bomb packed with phosphorous has failed to explode inside the Royal Naval Cordite Factory at Holton Heath. The contents have been steamed out and it is now on display as a trophy.

April **Exercise Smash assaults Studland.**

The 1st Battalion of the Dorsetshire Regiment has been back on its native heath, taking part in the repeated mock-invasion assaults of Exercise Smash across the sands of Studland Bay. Unlike normal exercises this one has been distinguished by the widespread use of live ammunition, from small-arms fire to bombs and rockets, and has been studied intently by high ranking officers and a succession of war lords.

From a massive concrete bunker, the Fort Henry observation post built by Canadian engineers on Redend Point, a row of field glasses has lined the slit that looks northward across Studland Bay and the whole of its beach. Users of the binoculars have included Winston Churchill, General Bernard Montgomery, and General Dwight D. Eisenhower.

DORSET'S WAR

April **Americans bring death to Dorset roads.**

The increase that the United States Army has brought to traffic on Dorset's roads is reflected in this month's accident fatalities, which have risen to seven from only two in April 1943. Colonel Frederick R. Lafferty, the Provost Marshall of 7-Base Section of the US Army is to instigate five military police patrol groups to control traffic flows at major junctions.

March–August 1944. Lockheed P-38 Lightnings of the American 474th Fighter Group, flying from Warmwell, are now the commonest aeroplane in the sky over south Dorset.

7 May **Warmwell loses two Lightnings in France.**

Two Lightnings from Warmwell, escorting B-26 bombers into France, have been shot down. Lieutenants Merkle and Thacker are missing. The returning planes claimed one probable kill, a Focke-Wulf 190.

Footnote Merkle was killed but Thacker was to surprise his colleagues by escaping into Spain and making it back to Warmwell in June.

13 May **2nd Dorsets lose 75 men to recapture a piece of Burma.**

Having cost seventy-five Dorset lives in fierce fighting against the Japanese that has dragged on for three weeks, the 2nd Battalion of the Dorsetshire Regiment today achieved its costly objective and ousted the enemy from the Kohima Ridge; a second-class hill station at 5,000 feet in central Burma. For the Japanese it is a major strategic disaster but for the West Countrymen it has been hell. Many of the Dorset dead have been left where they fell since 27 April.

The padre held a service on the tennis court near where 'C' Company had sustained the greatest losses in the initial attack. The men were joined by Richard Sharp of the BBC:

"We are still on the six hills in the centre of Kohima. We've mopped up nearly all the Japs on them, and we've taken the famous tennis court. A half-smashed bunker on one of the hills was giving us a good deal of trouble, but we took it at one [13.00 hours] today, and I've seen the hill myself. It's covered with dead Japs. I counted up to forty of them and then stopped. Our men have been sprinkling them with quicklime—a necessary precaution in this weather.

"The men who took it came from a battalion of a West Country regiment. They've been plugging away at that tennis court for sixteen days and they'd become personal enemies of the Japs there, who used to taunt them at dusk, calling across the tennis court:

'Have you stood-to yet?' Today they're on top and they walked on their toes, laughing, among the bulges in the earth of dug-out roofs; their muscles limber, ready to swivel this way or that in an instant.

"There was a company commander [Captain Clive Chettle], a robust man with a square, black jaw covered with stubble. The skin between his battle-dress trousers and his tunic was bloody, and he swayed as he stood with his legs straddled. But his brain was working at full speed, and he laughed and shouted to his men as they went eagerly from fox-hole to fox-hole with hand grenades and pole charges—that's twenty-five pounds of explosive at the end of a six-foot bamboo."

13 May **Eisenhower meets the 1st Dorsets.**

The Supreme Commander Allied Forces, General Dwight D. Eisenhower, today visited the 231st Infantry Brigade who are training in the New Forest at Cadlands Camp, Fawley. Representatives of the 1st Battalion of the Dorsetshire Regiment were among those whose confidence he gained.

15 May **Four hurt by Purewell bomb.**

Four casualties were rescued from Purewell Hill House, Christchurch, after it had been hit at 02.22 hours by a German bomb. Another fell at West View, Stanpit, about the same time and damaged houses over a wide area. Bombs also dropped behind the OK Garage, Somerford, and at Woolhayes, Highcliffe. The latter failed to explode.

21 May **American pilot killed at Cheselbourne.**

An American pilot from Warmwell, Lieutenant Kimball, was killed when his Lightning fighter crashed near Cheselbourne.

21 May **Acoustic mine defused in Lyme Bay.**

Lieutenant Commander Bryant and Petty Officer Clark of the Royal Navy have defused one of the new-type acoustic pressure mines that the Germans have laid in Lyme Bay. They were dropped from German Schnellboote S136, S138 and S140 on the night of 18 May.

Conventional mines have also been sown by Schnellboote S144, S130, S145, S146, S150 and S168 before three Royal Navy destroyers with three motor gun-boats, from Portland, forced their withdrawal to France.

22 May **Another Warmwell Lightning lost in France.**

Lieutenant Usas, an American Lightning pilot from Warmwell, was killed in France whilst on a mission to dive-bomb a strategic target.

25 May **Wellington crashes at Christchurch.**

13.00 hours. An RAF Wellington bomber has crashed near Christchurch Aerodrome, on the north side of the railway line.

28 May German mine-layers driven off.

An attempt last night by the German 5th Schnellboot Flotilla to lay mines off the Dorset coast was seen off by Beaufighters from RAF Holmsley South in the New Forest aided by the Poole Harbour coast defence batteries and Royal Navy destroyers from Portland and Portsmouth. The fleeing German boats used their speed to escape but all are taking home some damage.

29 May 1944. Weymouth. Melcombe Avenue, the morning after what would turn out to be the town's last major air raid of the war.

28 May Weymouth air raid damages 400 houses.

At 01.03 hours the air raid sirens warbled at Weymouth but two minutes earlier the bombs had started to drop and they were to damage four hundred houses. Some hundred of them are badly smashed and fire has also damaged Weymouth Hospital and the Christian Science Church. Three Civil Defence volunteers and a junior ATS commander have been killed and thirteen of the injured have been detained in hospital.

Patients from the Weymouth and District Hospital, hit by a bomb and with another still unexploded beneath it, have been evacuated by Colonel Knoblock and Medical Corps of the United States Army to the Emergency Hospital established in Weymouth College.

Footnote The hospital bomb had buried itself twenty-eight feet in the ground and could not be reached and deactivated for several days.

May Paddle-steamers lay hundreds of British mines.

Requisitioned paddle-steamers have joined the mine-layer HMS *Plover* in laying one thousand two hundred mines in defensive barriers to protect the concentrations of invasion craft in Dorset and Hampshire estuaries from enemy E-boats. The Auxiliary Paddle Minesweepers *Medway Queen, Ryde, Whipingham* and *Sandown* and the 10th, 51st and 52nd Mine-Laying Flotillas have been carrying out the task under the watchful eyes of an assortment of escort vessels from the 9th, 13th, 14th 21st and 64th Motor Torpedo Boat Flotillas.

Footnote These minefields were to claim the richest haul of Axis shipping in the Channel of the whole war; 102 enemy vessels would be accounted for.

May Seven hundred Americans invade Charborough Park.

A United States Army mechanised supply unit of seven hundred men with a hundred heavy six-wheeled vehicles has camped in Charborough Park and dug slit trenches against air attack. The only incident has been caused by a red stag that was nibbling grass and pushed its head into the side of a tent and a sleeping Yank.

The Americans, however, have swiftly developed a taste for young peafowl—not unlike turkey—and those from the Wild West are adept at throwing knives into the trunks of the cedar trees. Admiral Drax's staff have noticed that the Americans drive everywhere, even distances of a few yards, and there is hardly a lawn or patch of grass that isn't being worn bare.

4 June Montgomery: 'The time has come'.

Message to all ranks in 21st Army Group from its Commander-in-Chief, General Bernard Montgomery: "The time has come to deal the enemy a terrific blow in Western Europe . . ."

5 June The invasion—it's on.

04.00 hours. The Supreme Commander Allied Forces Western Europe, General Dwight D. Eisenhower, has given the order that the invasion of Europe is to take place tomorrow. It should have gone ahead today but has been postponed because of the heavy seas. A lull is expected in the winds tomorrow but they are forecast to gather strength again in the evening. This would rule out the 7th, the last day of the present favourable tide cycle, and it is therefore imperative that unless the entire operation is stood-down it must begin at midnight.

5 June Three Warmwell pilots killed on the Seine.

A cloud-base near ground level forced the Lightnings of the American 474th Fighter Group from Warmwell into the trees as they approached their target bridge over the River Seine. Major Bedford, Lieutenant Coddington and Lieutenant Temple were killed and several of the surviving planes brought back tree boughs in their tails.

5 June Hurn Wing Commander plucked from sea and returned to the sky.

Reg Jones, the chief of scientific intelligence at the Air Ministry, writes in his *Most Secret War* that today he flew over the Solent and realised the invasion was 'on' because the armada that had been in Spithead two days before was no longer there. He flew on to Hurn: "I was silently wishing them good luck when we had a head-on encounter with a whole wing of American Thunderbolts. It was like standing in a butt whilst a covey of enormous grouse is driven past you on all sides. What was more, the Thunderbolts with their big radial engines were climbing, and so none of their pilots could see us.

"We duly landed at Hurn, my main memory being of a Norwegian Wing Commander who had been taking part in the radar strikes. He had been shot down earlier that day, picked up out of the sea by one of the air-sea rescue launches, and had already flown another sortie."

Twenty-eight Typhoons had delivered ninety-six 60lb rockets and seven tons of bombs on German coastal radar stations—taking care to keep that at Fécamp intact so that it could report spoof activity aimed at convincing the enemy that the main thrust of the Allied invasion is further up-Channel, east of the Seine.

Five squadrons of Typhoons and two of Mosquitos are now operating from RAF Hurn.

DORSET'S WAR

1 June 1944. South Dorset. V Corps of the First United States Army is the county's army of occupation. It has gathered its tanks into vast fields of armour and the men file behind barbed wire for their briefings. From now on they are to have no conversations with civilians (the notice is at Puddletown; the lesser one reads—'In case of fire call N.F.S. [National Fire Service] Dorchester. Telephone Dorchester 766. You are at D3').
Weymouth Quay, above. The two black lads, Asa Jones and Furrell Browning from Dallas, man an anti-aircraft gun aboard USS 'Henrico'. The preparations for the D-Day embarkations were to go unmolested.

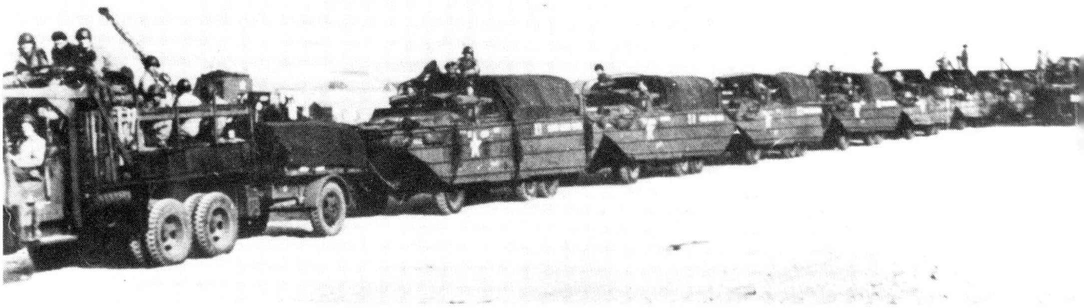

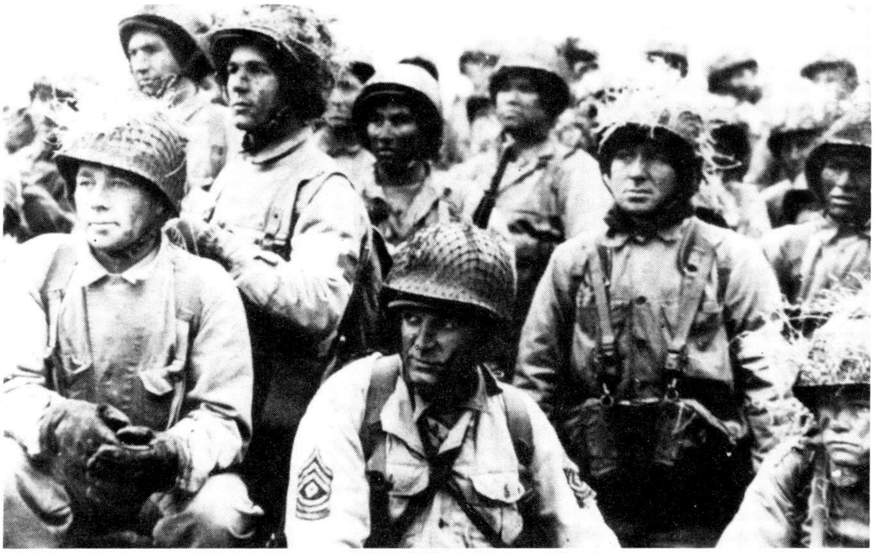

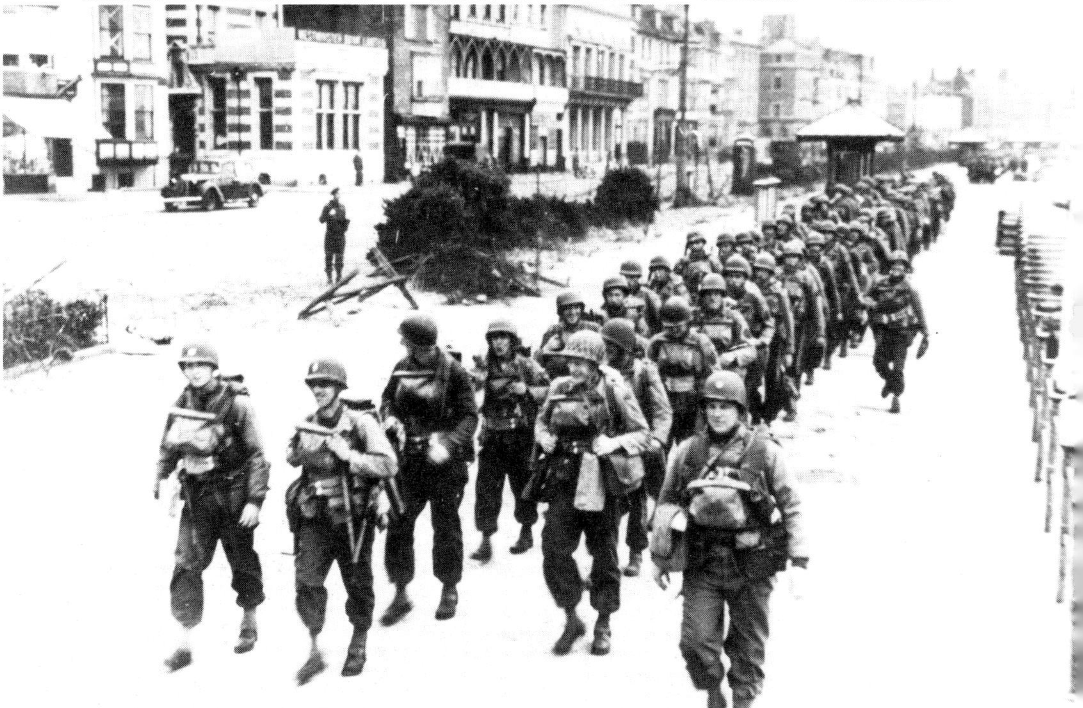

4–5 June 1944. Portland, opposite top, showing a line of American DUKWs beside the Chesil Beach, waiting their turn to go into landing craft at Castletown (above) and to join the armada that is being gathered (below) for the invasion of Normandy.
It is a time for final briefings (opposite, centre) and the march of the GIs southwards along Weymouth seafront (opposite, bottom) for embarkation at the Quay.

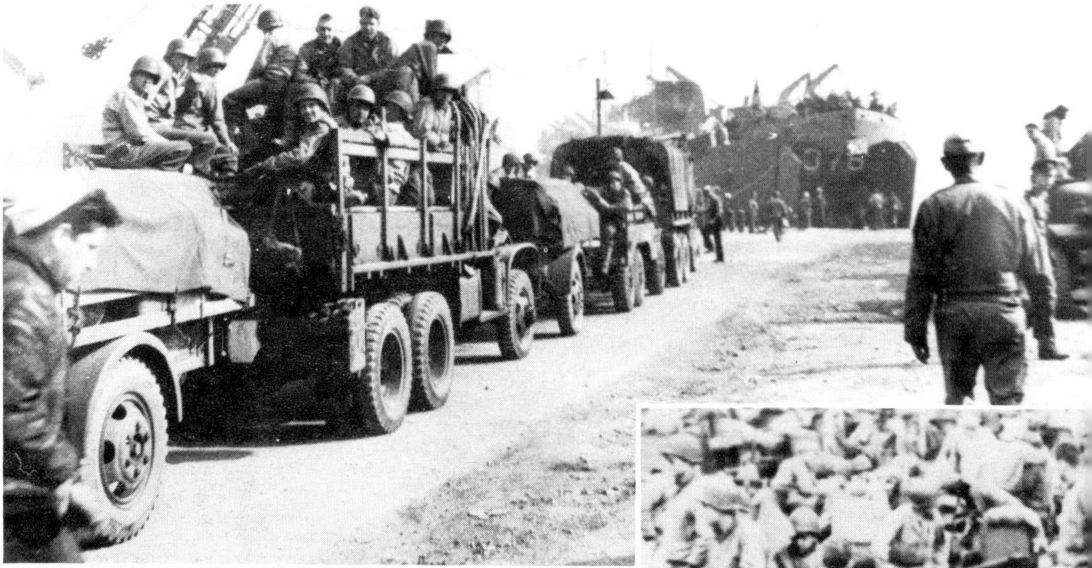

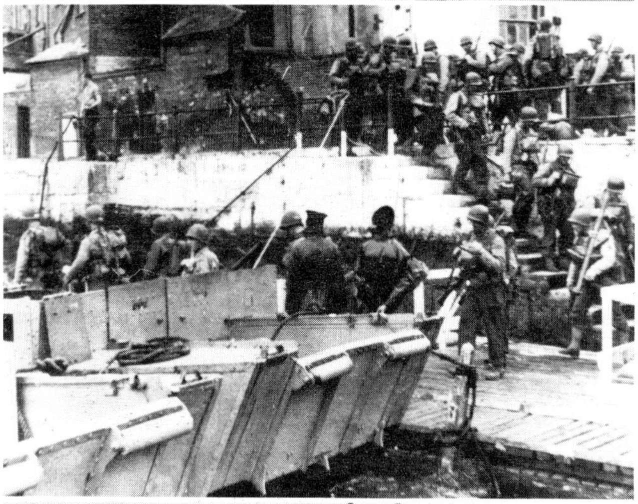

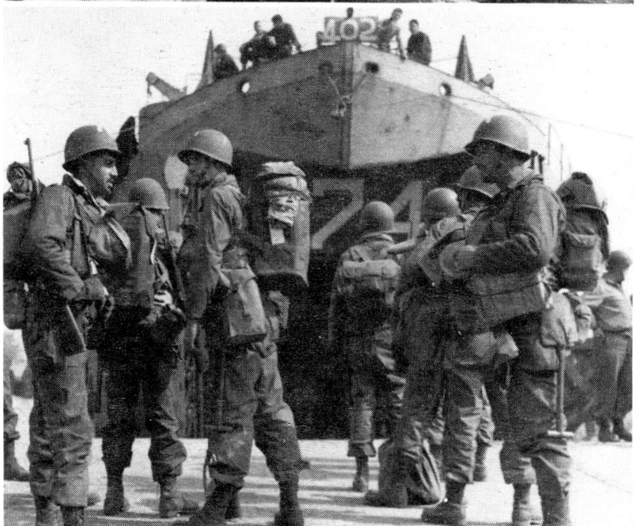

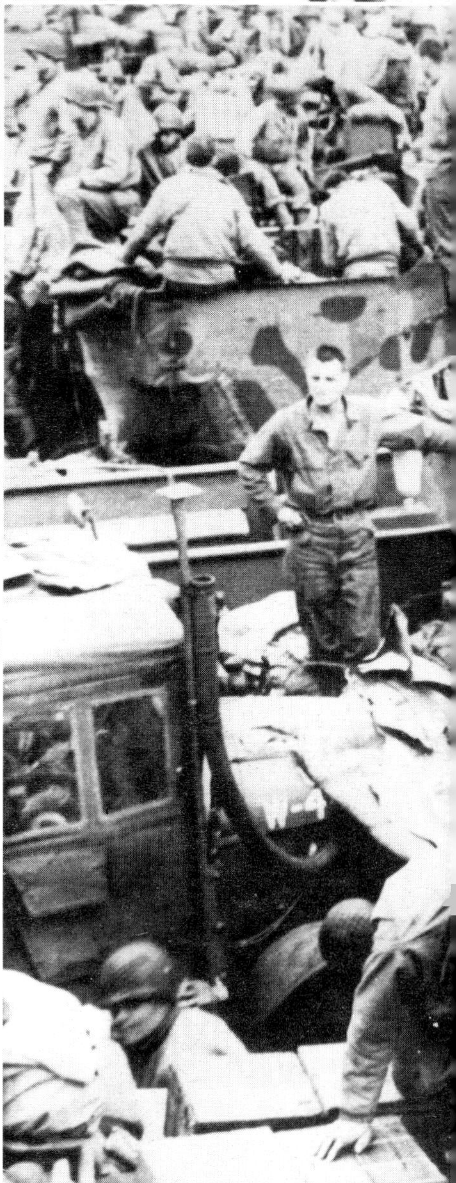

4–5 June 1944. Portland and Weymouth. V Corps of the United States First Army, setting off for Omaha Beach and the invasion of Europe. In the pictures opposite, the tank landing craft are at Castletown Dockyard, Portland, and the infantry are filing on to smaller assault craft at Weymouth Quay.
Everywhere in the two ports is a mass of men and equipment (below). For many of the GIs, June 6th would be the longest day of their lives. For the other thousand, however, it will be the shortest.

June 1944. Portland and Weymouth. The emblem that is everywhere around the two ports, and quite common at Poole as well: that of the 14th Major Port of the United States Army Transportation Corps.

4–5 June 1944. Portland and Weymouth. Above, top, an American DUKW reverses into a landing craft at Castletown Docks, Portland. Assault troops are packed like sardines at Weymouth Quay (above) and (right) GIs break into song as they wait to board the USS 'Henrico' at Weymouth.

4–5 June 1944. Weymouth Quay and the old Ritz Theatre (burnt down in the 1950s and replaced by the Pavilion), with lines of Negro 'static' troops passing stores on to the American assault landing craft which are to lead Force O on to Omaha Beach in Normandy.

5 June **Gliders ready at Tarrant Rushton.**

Painted with invasion-day stripes, trains of Horsa troop-carrying gliders are being prepared for take-off at Tarrant Rushton airfield. The men are part of the British 6th Airborne Division and will drop to the east of the Normandy beach-heads—at Bénouville, Merville, Randville, Varaville, Bures and Troarn—to hold the bridges on the River Orne and to break those across the River Dives.

The first three gliders to leave Tarrant Rushton are also being towed by twin-engined Albemarles and are destined for the coast at Merville. The following six gliders will be towed by four-engined Halifaxes and are also loaded with men from the Oxfordshire and Buckingham Light Infantry, bound for the Orne swing-bridge and canal bridge [codenamed Pegasus]. They are to leave shortly before midnight and are expected to be released about five miles short of their targets, at around 01.30 hours, to glide down on to French soil.

Once the infantry have secured the immediate dropping zones the two Halifax squadrons from Tarrant Rushton will return, at about 21.00 hours, with a convoy of thirty gliders of the British 6th Air Landing Brigade including the larger Hamilcars with the Division's heavier equipment including Tetrarch tanks, Bren-gun carriers, twenty-five pounder field guns, scout cars and Bailey bridge pontoons.

5 June **The gliders lift off from Tarrant Rushton for 'Pegasus' bridge.**

22.56 hours. The first Halifax has roared along the central runway at Tarrant Rushton Aerodrome and lifted off, towing a Horsa glider of the British 6th Airborne Division towards France. There are a mass of tug-planes and gliders to be cleared at minute intervals. Into the sky has gone the 1st Platoon of 'D' Company of the 2nd Battalion, Oxfordshire and Buckinghamshire Light Infantry. They are commanded by Major John Howard.

He arrived with his men at Tarrant Rushton on 26 May and they have been confined to camp, awaiting the codeword to 'go' which arrived at 09.00 hours on Friday 4 June. To everyone's disappointment this was cancelled because of the windy weather.

This morning Major Howard received the order again and it has been another day of loading and re-checking, leading up to a fat-less evening meal to calm the men's stomachs, and this moment when everyone's faith is in the renowned abilities of the Glider Pilot Regiment. Faces are blackened all have clambered aboard—for a promised gap in the German flak at Cabourg.

Howard's 'D' Company will be cast off at 5,000 feet to land beside the bridge over the Caen Canal which has been codenamed 'Pegasus'.

Footnote The *coup de main* party of the 6th Airborne dropped near Bénouville as planned with four of the six gliders only yards from their target spot. Both bridges were secured intact.

A total of 670 Horsa gliders for the Airborne Divisions were constructed at the Airspeed factory beside Christchurch Aerodrome.

5 June **Battleship 'Rodney' in Weymouth Bay.**

Weymouth Bay has its largest gathering of big warships since the Reserve Fleet was dispersed in 1939. The danger of air attack then prevented anything larger than a destroyer operating from Portland Harbour.

Operation Neptune has brought five American and two British cruisers to the bay, plus the strange cut-short silhouette of the 34,000 ton battleship HMS *Rodney*. The terrific destructive force of her broadsides is to be used tomorrow in French coastal bombardment—she is preparing to fire her full armament of nine 16-inch, twelve 6-inch and six 4.7-inch guns.

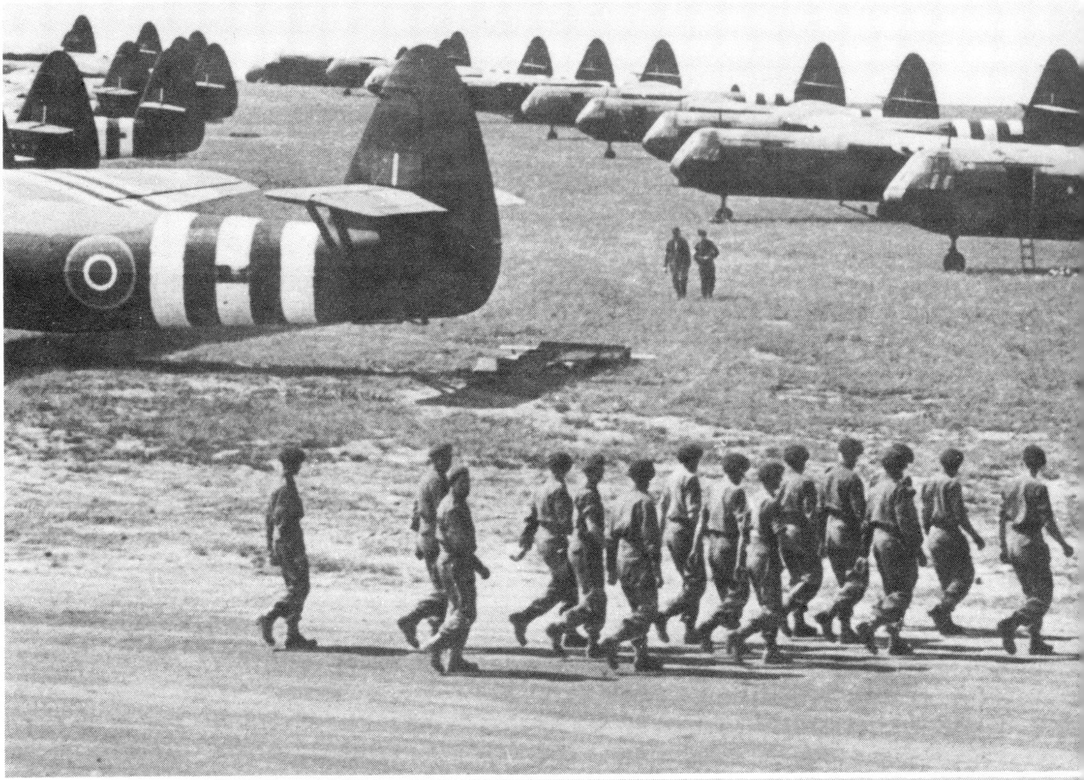

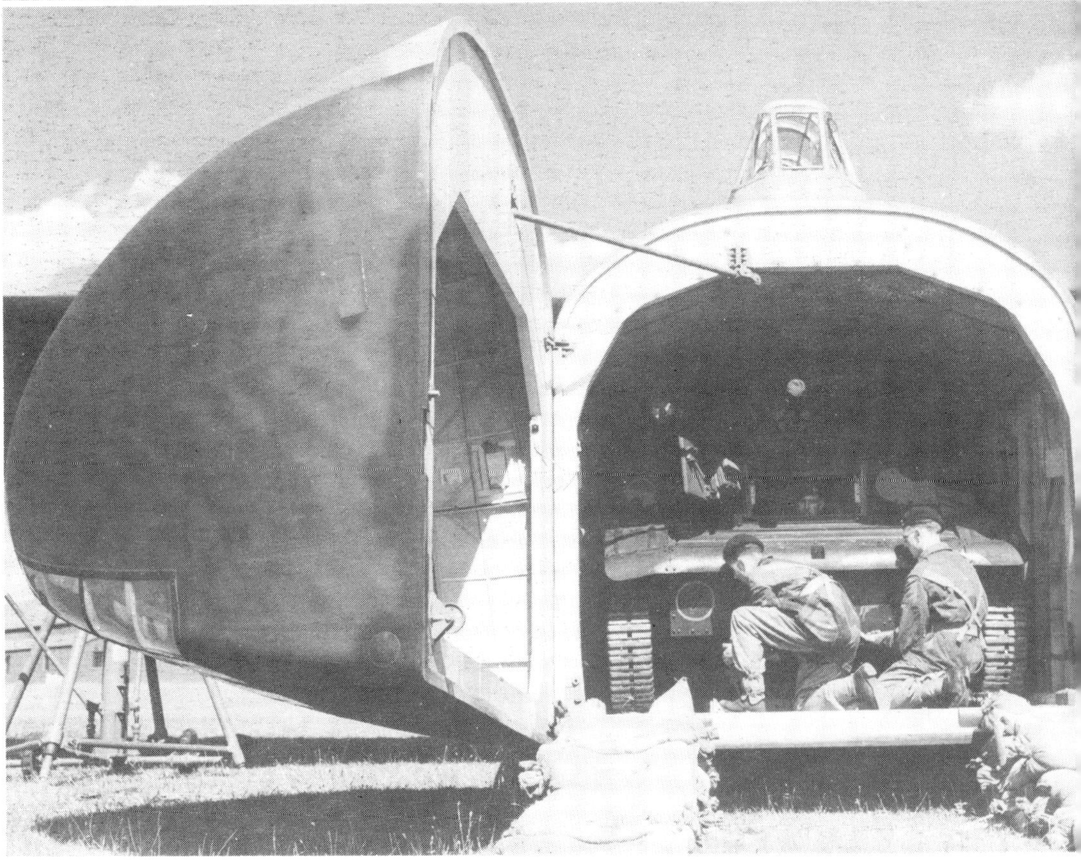

5 June 1944. The British 6th Airborne Division prepares at Tarrant Rushton, Hurn, Holmsley South and other aerodromes to drop in tomorrow on Normandy. Above the graffiti is defiant: 'The Channel stopped you, but not us. Remember Coventry, Plymouth, Bristol, London. Now it's our turn. You've had your time you German . . . swinhunds.' The original last words were rubbed out for the benefit of the photographer and eventual readers —but the men were allowed to have 'Swinhunds'.

Opposite. The men file towards lines of Horsa gliders painted with D-Day stripes, and a Tetrarch light tank is loaded into the belly of a Hamilcar. The Horsas were manufactured by Airspeed Limited at Christchurch.

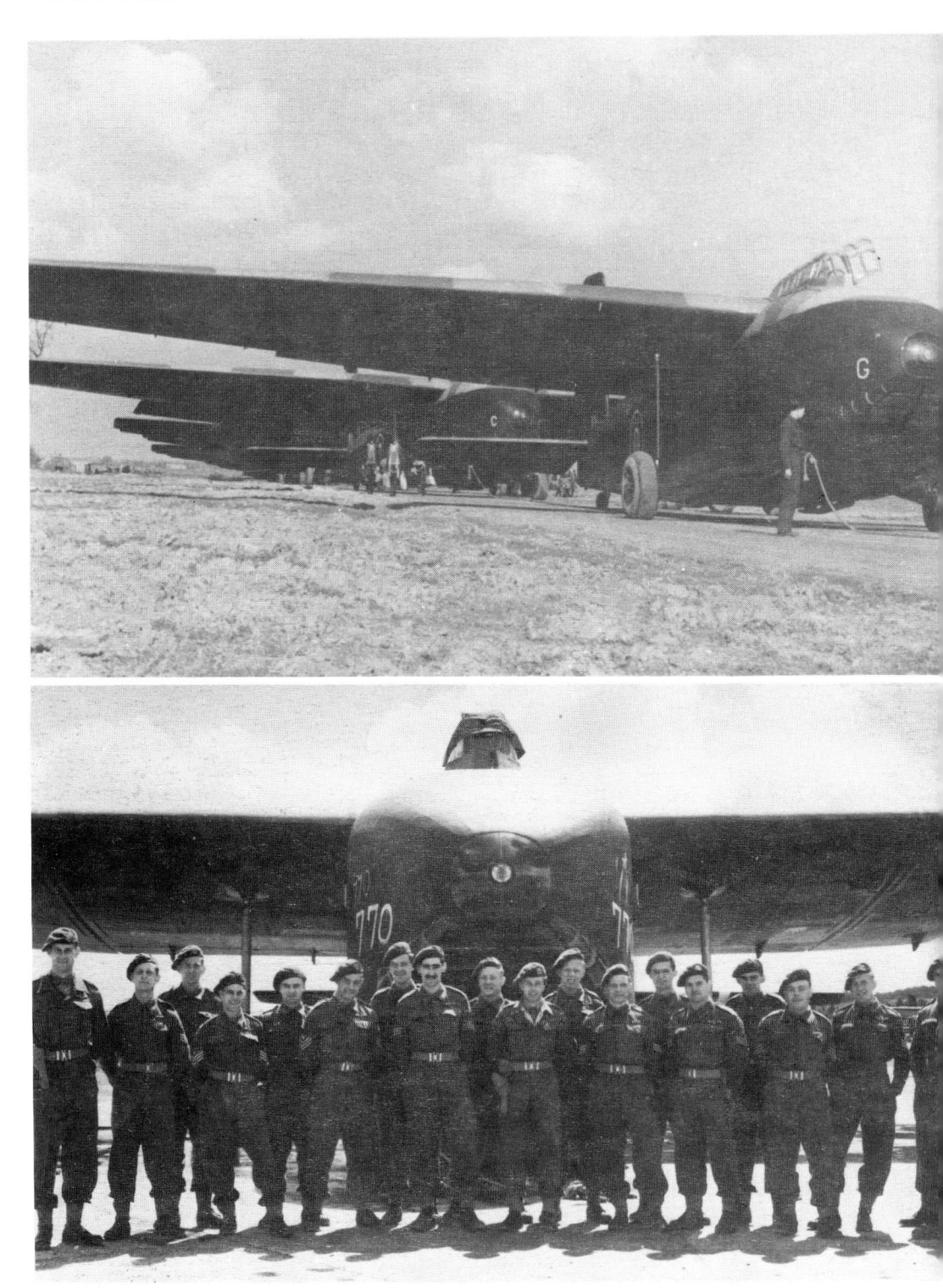

5 June 1944. Above. Hamilcars and in particular number 770, preparing to lift elements of the British 6th Airborne Division from Tarrant Rushton Aerodrome.
Opposite, line-up at Hurn Aerodrome of Horsa troop carrying gliders and their Albemarle tug aircraft of 570 Squadron.

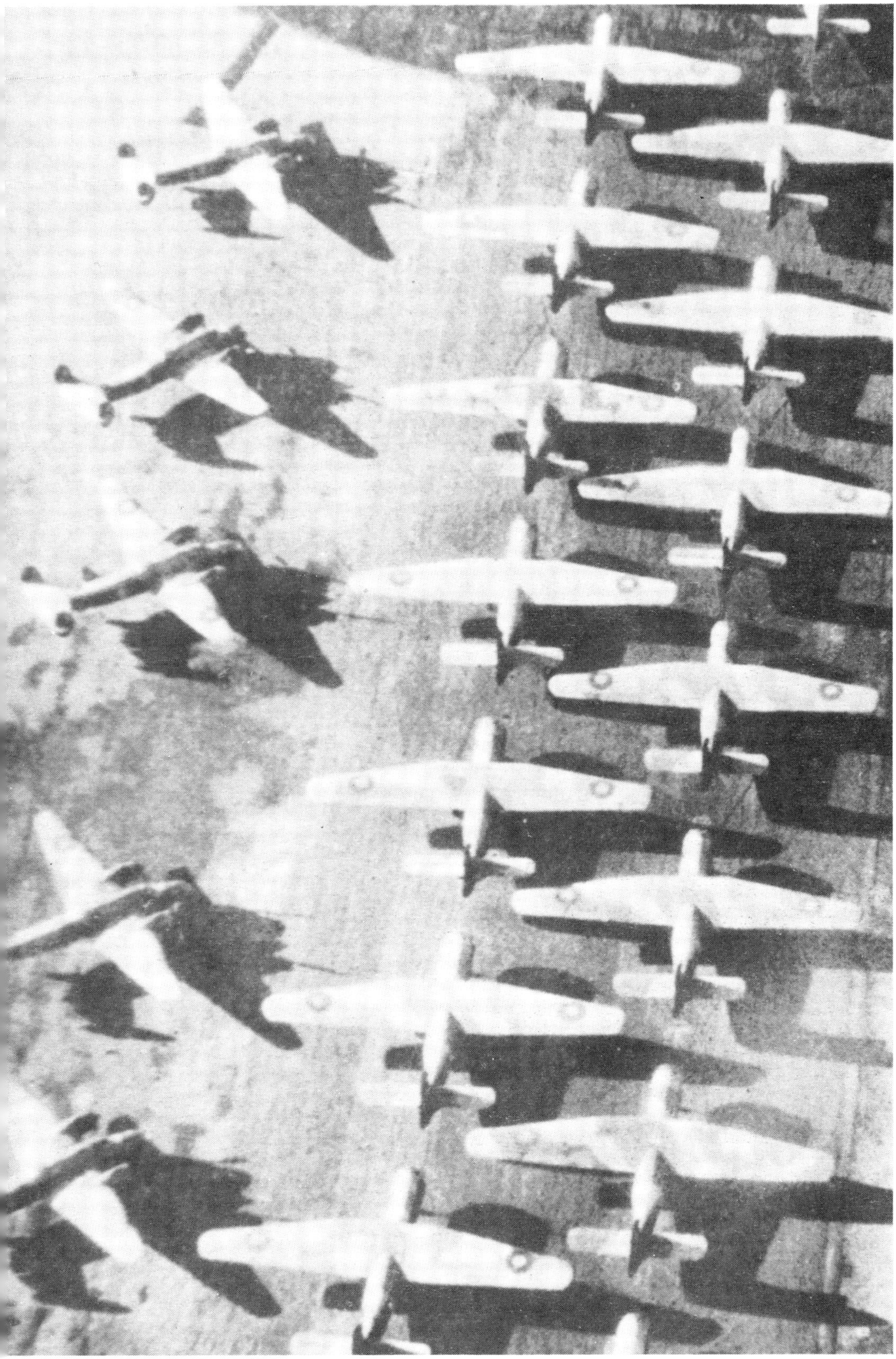

DORSET'S WAR

5 June 1944. Tarrant Rushton Aerodrome. British 6th Airborne Division preparations for D-Day.
Above. A Halifax tug-plane of 644 Squadron takes off with a Hamilcar glider.
Below. The Hamilcar (right) is towed by the Halifax over The Cliff escarpment and into the sky above Tarrant Monkton.
Opposite, top. A Hamilcar (right) and Halifax combination over the Crichel Estate woodlands with Badbury Rings (marked 'A') being just discernible. The planes have their D-Day stripes.
Opposite, below. A Hamilcar has its flaps down ready to land back at Tarrant Rushton. The skids on the belly were to help it survive more difficult terrain.

A

5 June 1944. Tarrant Rushton Aerodrome, D-Day minus one: the Halifax tugs and their Horsa gliders (along the runway) prepare for a midnight date with history. The photograph is from the north and as on the last page the Iron Age hill-fort of Badbury Rings has been marked with an 'A'. The planes are on the east-west runway (actually east-north-east/ west-south-west and the gliders are facing east-north-east; a south-westerly wind was still blowing but a lull was forecast, correctly).

Opposite. The British 6th Airborne Division—airborne in a practice for the drop on Pegasus Bridge and the other vital crossing points near Caen. The tugs in this instance are RAF Whitley bombers.

1944

DORSET'S WAR 166

7 June 1944. Major John Howard arrived yesterday with the Horsa gliders from Tarrant Rushton and today the 2nd Battalion of the Oxfordshire and Buckinghamshire Light Infantry control 'Pegasus' bridge over the Caen Canal. Their gliders can be seen on the east bank to the right of the bridge. Any German attack on the Normandy beach-head would had to have come along this road which lies between Bénouville and Ranville, about three miles from the coast.

6 June **Invasion Day—the sky fills.**

00.15 hours. Victor Swatridge of Dorchester Police was patrolling the town's Victoria Park with the intention of meeting his beat constable there at 00.30 hours. In 1971, Swatridge recalled what happened; he was witnessing the greatest mass movement of aircraft that has ever taken place:

"Britain was still suffering from its black-out and not a glimmer of light dared emit from any house or premises. It was a beautiful clear starlit night, when suddenly I became aware of the heavy drone of aircraft coming from inland. As it drew nearer, the sky lit up: thousands of coloured lights had burst forth and the whole atmosphere exploded into activity.

"It was an amazing transformation as hundreds of bombers towing gliders with their masses of human and vehicle cargo flew overhead and across the English Channel. This huge armada was a continuous procession for more than two hours. It was clearly evident that the invasion of Europe had commenced and I remember how excited I was. Yet still the civilian population were still quietly sleeping in their beds; everyone had become immune to the noise of aircraft travelling overhead, yet I venture to suggest if it had been enemy planes, the whole place would have been alive with activity, sirens would have wailed and woken them from their slumber.

"Invasion Day had been very secretively guarded; everyone had been warned that it would be treasonable to give the slightest indication to the enemy that it was about to take place, and the civil population kept that bargain. The police had been warned to expect heavy counter bombing and we were expecting frightening reprisals. We waited but no enemy air action occurred to our utter amazement."

6 June **D-Day.**

The sea forces deployed today are an armada unequalled in history—138 warships carrying out bombardments; 221 destroyers and other escort vessels; 287 minesweepers; 491 miscellaneous light craft; 441 auxiliaries—quite apart from the more than 4,000 landing craft that they are supporting and protecting. Merchant vessels are also involved in a myriad of support rôles, to a total of 6,488 vessels acting under Admiralty instructions.

6 June **'Fishpond' reveals the Dorset armada.**

The armada off Dorset of V Corps of the First United States Army on their way from Weymouth towards Omaha beach was such a concentration of steel that it showed on the Fishpond airborne fighter radar set in Roland Hammersley's aircraft. His first report of the blips sent the pilot, Ron Walker, looking for an enemy fighter force, but they saw to their astonishment the flotillas of landing craft heading towards Normandy. What Roland does not realise is that his brother, Walter, is down there on the sea.

Roland Hammersley was born at Swanage and lives at Bovington. He is a gunner with 57 Squadron, and took off this morning at 01.36 hours from East Kirkby, Lincolnshire, on a mission to attack coastal gun emplacements at La Pernelles.

6 June **1st Dorsets among first Britons ashore in France.**

Army Operation Overlord/Navy Operation Neptune/Air Force Operation Mallard. Supported by the cruiser HMS *Emerald* and the destroyers HMS *Cottesmore, Grenville, Jervis, Ulysses, Undine* and *Urania*, with the Polish destroyer *Krakowiak*, plus the softening-up efforts of four fighter bomber squadrons, the 1st Battalion of the Dorsetshire Regiment left LCH317 and touched down on the beach to the north-east of the village of Les Roquettes at 07.30 hours. 'A' Company is led by Major A.A.E. Jones and 'B' Company by Major P. Chilton.

They have landed in the Jig Green sector of the Gold Beach bridgehead and with the

Hampshires—a thousand yards to the east—can claim to be the first British troops to land in Normandy.

Captain C.R. Whittington, the Unit Landing Officer, wore a rainbow-coloured battle bowler. He was soon wounded but continued organising the clearing of corridors up the beach. Major Jones was withdrawn wounded and Major Chilton led the crossing of the minefields.

'C' Company [Major R.M. Nicholl] and 'D' Company [Major W.N. Hayes], helped the Hampshires take Asnelles-sur-Mer and proceeded to attack high ground at Point 54. 'C' Company had most of the fighting though the enemy eventually abandoned its four 155mm guns and by 18.00 the Dorsets had found convenient dugouts for Battalion Headquarters on the hillside north of Ryes.

'B' Company moved into Ryes, which had been captured by the Devons.

The Dorsets have achieved all the day's objectives but at the cost of heavy losses—three officers killed; thirty other ranks killed; eleven officers wounded; eighty-four other ranks wounded.

6 June 1944.

The invasion of Normandy gathers pace as the tide recedes.

6 June 1944. British Cromwell and Sherman tanks climb inland from the King (Red) sector of Gold Beach at La Riviere.

6 June **Dorset's Americans get the worst beach.**

Dorset's Americans, V Corps of the 1st United States Army—comprising the 29th Division, 1st Division and Ranger Battalions, who embarked from Weymouth and Portland—touched the shore of Normandy at 06.34 hours. These regimental combat teams are Force O for Omaha, as the beach is codenamed.

It lies between Point due Hoe and Colleville to the north-west of Bayeux. Unfortunately for the V Corps they have received the bloodiest reception of the day and for several hours it seemed they might well be thrown back into the sea.

Their misfortune was to find that the coast defences in the Omaha sector had recently been augmented by the German 352nd Infantry Division; a field formation which happened to be holding a stand-to exercise as the American assault began. Extreme sacrifice and gallantry—a thousand dead and twice that wounded—has by nightfall achieved a beachhead a mile in depth.

Footnote The Americans would have lost the beach if the German High Command had not held back their reserve units, thinking that the Normandy assaults were a feint and that the main invasion force would land between the Seine and Calais.

6 June **Warmwell sorties over the Cherbourg peninsula.**

Today and for the next nine days the American Lightnings of the 474th Fighter Group from Warmwell will dive-bomb strategic targets in the Cherbourg peninsula and cover convoys of Allied shipping.

Footnote The Americans lost two pilots on these combat air patrols, Lieutenant Doty and Lieutenant Robert Hanson. A second Robert Hanson also flew with the 474th and survived to organise an association of its ex-members.

DORSET'S WAR

March/June 1944. Poole Bay test for Pluto, and the end result—the Pipe Line Under The Ocean pumping petroleum into a beached tanker on the sands of Normandy.

8 June Surviving rocket-firing craft limp into Poole.

The first of the returnee vessels from the Normandy landings are a group of LCRs, American rocket-firing landing craft, which have limped into Poole Harbour peppered with shell-holes after their onslaught against the enemy beaches.

13 June HMS 'Boadicea' sinks off Portland.

HMS *Boadicea*, a Royal Navy destroyer, has been sunk off Portland. The past three days have seen other sinkings off the Dorset coast, as the German 2nd Schnellboot Flotilla evacuated Cherbourg and regrouped in Ostend from where it is concentrating on the supply convoys.

As Supply Convoy S-NS 08 assembled in Poole Bay it was seen by a German reconnaissance plane and intercepted by the Schnellboote in mid-Channel. S177 sank the *Brackenfield*, a 657-ton steamer, and the *Ashanti*, 534 tons. S178 claimed the *Dungrange*, 621 tons. A Norwegian destroyer, the *Stord*, sailed to the aid of the convoy with units of the Royal Navy but the Schnellboote outpaced them and escaped to Boulogne.

Some German losses have been sustained by the E-boat force in the past three days, however, as RAF Beaufighters of 143 Squadron and 236 Squadron, operating from the New Forest, have claimed to have damaged or sunk three Schnellboote, one Raumboot mine-layer, and an M-boat. Two of the fighters failed to return; one being brought down by anti-aircraft fire and the other credited to an Me163 Komet rocket-propelled fighter.

Footnote John Pitfield tells me that a Komet could not have brought down the Beaufighter as these German rocket-propelled planes had a short range and were operational only from German airfields. He says that it was a mistaken identification of one of the other remarkable new planes which the Germans deployed as the war drew to a close, either a Messerschmitt 262 or an Arado 234C. These jets had top speeds of 541 mph and 530 mph respectively. The poor Beaufighter could only do 320 mph.

13 June 500lb bomb removed from Highcliffe.

11.50 hours. A 500lb bomb that fell at Woolhayes, Highcliffe, on 15 May has been removed by a bomb disposal unit.

14 June Bomber Command soups up the defence of the Channel.

Bomber Command has supplied some four-engine aircraft to No 19 Group, RAF Coastal Command, who are now hard-pressed to keep the English Channel reasonably safe for the convoys supplying the Normandy forces.

Footnote By the end of June No 19 Group had sunk fourteen German U-boats in the Channel, three of them in the Dorset sector between Start Point and the Isle of Wight.

15 June British frigate torpedoed off Portland.

A frigate, HMS *Blackwood*, has sunk off Portland Bill after being torpedoed.

16 June An American bombs Warmwell.

As an engine cut-out on his aircraft at Warmwell, American pilot Lieutenant Cumbie of the 430th Squadron followed standard procedure and jettisoned his bombs, which—contrary to correct procedure—turned out to be armed. He scored a direct hit on the field's transformer station.

The pilot returned safely to the airfield, to congratulations from its RAF contingent: "Jerry's been trying to hit that for years!"

21 June War interrupts Warmwell's dress parade.

The American pilots of the 474th Fighter Group, dressed for inspection by General Kincaid at Warmwell when they were to receive medals, instead received an unexpected order to scramble and found themselves back over France. Two of the Lightnings were lost, killing Lieutenant Vinson. The other pilot, Captain Larson, parachuted to safety and lived to receive the medal.

Footnote Three other Warmwell pilots, Lieutenants Gee, Heuermann and Danish were killed in the last week of June as the Americans harried the railway system in northern France. Many of the attacks were on targets of opportunity—"boys, just go over and hit anything that moves" they had been told.

23 June US 3rd Armored Division embarked from Weymouth.

The 3rd Armored Division of the United States Army is now landing on Omaha White Beach, near Isigny, for the tank actions that will decide the Battle of Normandy. The craft had been kept in Portland Harbour for the past four days by a violent gale. Others have crossed from Southampton Water.

The arrivals include the 32nd and 33rd Armored Regiments, supported by the 486th Armored Anti-Aircraft Battalion and the 23rd Armored Engineer Battalion. Headquarters staff and the division's artillery, the 54th, 67th and 391st Armored Field Artillery Battalions, are following tomorrow.

Footnote The 36th Armored Infantry Regiment arrived on the 25th.

24 June Bridport officer killed in Normandy.

Lieutenant Colonel J.W. Atherton of Bridport was killed today in Normandy. He was blown up by a shell whilst fighting off a counter-attack by German tanks. Until recently Colonel Atherton was with the 5th Battalion of the Dorsetshire Regiment.

26 June St Alban's Head battle ends with Germans sent packing.

Last night there was short but fierce naval engagement off St Alban's Head which resulted in German Schnellboote S130 and S168 departing for Dieppe, and S145 sustaining damage and being forced to flee for repairs to the nearest bastion that the enemy still holds; the occupied Channel Island of Alderney.

29 June Sixteen killed as Thunderbolts crash on Mudeford.

Foxwood Avenue at Mudeford, Christchurch, was devastated today by three American P-47 Thunderbolt fighter-bombers in two separate mishaps on take-off from Christchurch Aerodrome. In the first, at 06.45 hours, the pilot survived and no one was hurt on the ground.

Then at 14.00 hours the same pilot tried again to take off. Once more he failed to gain proper height and over-shot the runway into a bungalow. His fuel tanks and bombs exploded, bringing down another Thunderbolt that was coming off the runway. The three planes belonged to the 405th Fighter Group.

As rescue workers pulled the wounded out of the debris another bomb exploded, killing a fireman and wounding others. Sixteen are dead and eighteen injured.

A mortally wounded pilot was comforted by nurse Irene Stevenson. He died in her arms in Boscombe Hospital.

Footnote Mrs Stevenson became a local councillor and Mayor of Christchurch. In 1975 the pilot's widow visited her husband's grave, at Bransgore churchyard, and found it was still being tended by Mrs Stevenson.

6 July Warmwell's two-all air battle over Brittany.

Clear weather saw the Warmwell's American Lightnings streaking across north-west France once again but they met with a flight of more than twenty Focke-Wulf 190s. Though they were able to claim two definite kills the Americans returned across the Channel without Lieutenants Rubal and Jacobs.

Footnote In another bombing run over France, against the rail network, Lieutenant Moore was killed when his plane ploughed into a bridge.

9 July Pigeon post from Normandy to Hurn in seven hours.

Pigeons supplied from Bournemouth lofts have been arriving at RAF Hurn today some seven hours after release from the battle grounds in Normandy. They are helping the front-line troops to keep contact with their air support units; in fact they are proving themselves as an air support unit.

18 July Warmwell Americans claim ten FW 190s.

The 474th Fighter Group from Warmwell routed a formation of twenty-five Focke-Wulf 190s over north-west France. They claimed ten, for the loss of three Lightnings. Two of the Americans baled out but the third, Lieutenant Goodrich, died in his plane.

27 July Warmwell pilot killed over Tours.

Lieutenant Patton, flying a Lightning from Warmwell on a reconnaissance mission over Tours, was killed in an attack by a number of Me 109s.

11 July 1944. The 1st Battalion of the Dorsetshire Regiment fighting in Normandy. Serjeant Turner and Privates Martin, Torrington (a Canadian 'Dorset'), and Smith, with Lance Corporal Wiltshire, are firing a three-inch mortar near Hottot. In the picture below the infantry and anti-tank guns are advancing along a tank track that has smashed through the hedgerows of the Bocage.

DORSET'S WAR 174

July **American Liberator crashes on Furzey Island.**

An American Liberator bomber has crashed in Poole Harbour, hitting Furzey Island, with the loss of all its crew.

July **Wounded American pilots rest at Shaftesbury.**

The American Red Cross are using Coombe House, near Shaftesbury, as a recuperation centre for wounded and exhausted bomber crews.

Footnote In 1945 the Institute of the Blessed Virgin Mary acquired the building and it became St Mary's Convent.

3 August **Another Warmwell pilot dies in France.**

Lieutenant Chamberlain, flying an American Lightning fighter from Warmwell on a combat air patrol over France, has been killed by enemy action.

4 August **Sea-shell lands in Christchurch.**

A shell fell this afternoon in the garden of 36 Seafield Road, Christchurch. Fortunately it failed to explode. It had been fired from the sea.

5 August **Warmwell's Americans move to French base.**

The 474th Fighter Group of the United States Army Air Force flew their final patrols from Warmwell today and landed on an airstrip in Normandy. This advance base on the other side of the Channel has been used for the past five days for refuelling and is now the Group's temporary home for the next stage of the war in Europe. Two Messerschmidt 109s were claimed as kills on their moving day.

28 August **Wessex troops first across the Seine.**

Eight separate battalion attacks were launched today by the 43rd (Wessex) Division to put the first British troops across the River Seine. Among them were the 5th Battalion of the Dorsetshire Regiment.

Footnote Lieutenant General Brian Horrocks, the commander of the 30th Corps, described it as "an epic operation". The logistical support behind the Allied advance was now stupendous and more than sufficient in everything except petrol. The Allies now had two million men and half a million vehicles in France. In tanks their numerical advantage over the Germans was twenty to one.

August **Poole blast kills three.**

Three naval ratings were killed and six hurt when ammunition detonated itself in one of the landing craft at HMS Turtle, the shore base at Poole Quay. The vessel was destroyed and nearby buildings damaged.

17 September **Tarrant Rushton Hamilcars join Arnhem airlift.**

Hamilcar gliders, towed by their Halifax tug-planes, have left Tarrant Rushton this Sunday morning to join the armada of three hundred Allied craft that are to land behind enemy lines in the Netherlands. Operation Market Garden is in the air and the Tarrant Rushton planes are towing the British 1st Airborne Division towards the farthest dropping zone, around Oosterbeek, four miles west of the great bridge over the Neder Rijn, the Lower Rhine at Arnhem.

Footnote This was the bridge too far. The Arnhem landings were a display of euphoric Allied over-confidence in the face of a mass of information that should have caused more than momentary reconsideration. Aerial photographs showed German tanks only a short distance from the drop-zone and Dutch resistance had reported "battered Panzer divisions" in Holland to refit. Furthermore there was an Enigma-coded intercept released two days before the operation was launched, stating that German Army Group B, under Field Marshal Walter Model who was a veteran of the great tank battles in the Ukraine, had moved his headquarters to Oosterbeek, the Tafelberg Hotel to be precise, which lay between the drop-zone and the target—the Arnhem bridge over the Rhine. These were no ordinary enemy troops, they were the 2nd SS Panzer Corps, comprising the crack 9th and 10th SS Panzer Divisions.

All this was known, but Montgomery—in the words of General Bedell Smith, Chief of Staff at SHAEF [Supreme Headquarters Allied Expeditionary Force]—"simply waved my objections airily aside". Eisenhowever, the Supreme Commander, admitted in 1966 that "I not only approved Market Garden, I insisted on it." He had on 5 September been so optimistic about the course of the war that he went as far as to declare the "defeat of the German armies is now complete". See the entry for 14 November, for their reaction.

22 September Ottawa conference VIPs fly into Poole.

British VIPs returning from the Ottawa Conference have flown back into Poole Harbour aboard a BOAC Boeing Clipper. The party includes the Chief of the Imperial General Staff, Sir Alan Brooke, the First Sea Lord, Admiral Sir Andrew Cunningham, and the Chief of Air Staff, Sir Charles Portal.

29 September Dorsetmen enter the Reich.

Infantrymen of the 1st Battalion of the Dorsetshire Regiment today formed the first infantry patrol to cross into Germany, though they are disappointed to have been forestalled by Sherman tanks of the Sherwood Rangers who have the distinction of being the first unit of the British Army to enter the Reich.

The Dorsets are operating in aid of the Guards Armoured Division in its breakout from the De Groote bridgehead. Trophies from the cross-border patrol include a German state flag and a black flag of the SS.

This evening, at the invitation of its supporting field battery, the CO of the Dorsets and his second in command fired token shells into Germany. One was painted with a message: "A present for Adolf Schickelgruber."

September Mudeford mine kills two sappers.

Two members of a Royal Engineers mine-clearance team have been blown up whilst trying to remove a device from the beach at Harbour Run Road, Mudeford.

4 October Dorset troops see the V2s go up.

The 1st Battalion of the Dorsetshire Regiment, holding what they call "The Island" at Bemmel, which is almost surrounded by Germans and linked only precariously with the main Allied advance, have seen several V2 rockets rise towards London from the enemy-occupied Hook of Holland. They are being launched skywards from positions to the east, north-east and south-east. The rockets go straight up to a height of about ten kilometres before tilting into a 45 degree trajectory. The first to land on London hit Chiswick on 8 September and another fell the same evening at Epping.

DORSET'S WAR   176

Footnote None of the German vengeance weapons fell on Dorset, as the opposite coast had been captured before they became operational. The closest stray was a V1 flying-bomb that dropped on Boldre churchyard in the New Forest.

The Daily Telegraph saw the shape of things to come, if not thankfully to pass: "V2 indicates the kind of weapons with which the Third World War will be fought if there is one."

14 October   Twelve drown in landing craft on Chesil Beach.

An American tank landing craft, LCT A2454, was washed on to the Chesil Beach at Wyke Regis last night in mountainous seas. The state of the sea prevented the Weymouth lifeboat and a Portland dockyard tug from coming round the Bill to its aid. Ten of the LCT's British crew were drowned despite the desperate efforts of the Fortuneswell Lifesaving Company who had run along the pebble bank from Portland and succeeded in firing a rocket-line into the stricken vessel. Two sailors were rescued by Coastguard Treadwell as a tremendous wave swept most of the crew and everything else that was moveable into the sea.

More lines were fired into the craft but as she shifted across the pebbles these fouled. Treadwell and Captain Pennington Legh were swept away, never to be seen again, as they struggled to free the lines.

The four surviving rescuers also risked their lives to save two more of the sailors. Cyril Brown, wearing a lifebelt, struggled through the waves to get the line to the crewmen, and then had to be hauled ashore himself and taken to hospital. The line broke before the last crewman could be brought ashore and this time it was Albert Oldfield, without any safety line of his own, who managed to wade out to throw another line. The fourth man leapt from the boat and was pulled from the water.

Footnote The four surviving rescuers were awarded the Lloyds' silver medal for lifesaving but one, V.F. Stephens of Wyke Regis, died in a car crash before he could receive it at the reception in Weymouth Guildhall. Cyril Brown, of Portland, also received the Stanhope Medal, for the bravest deed of the year.

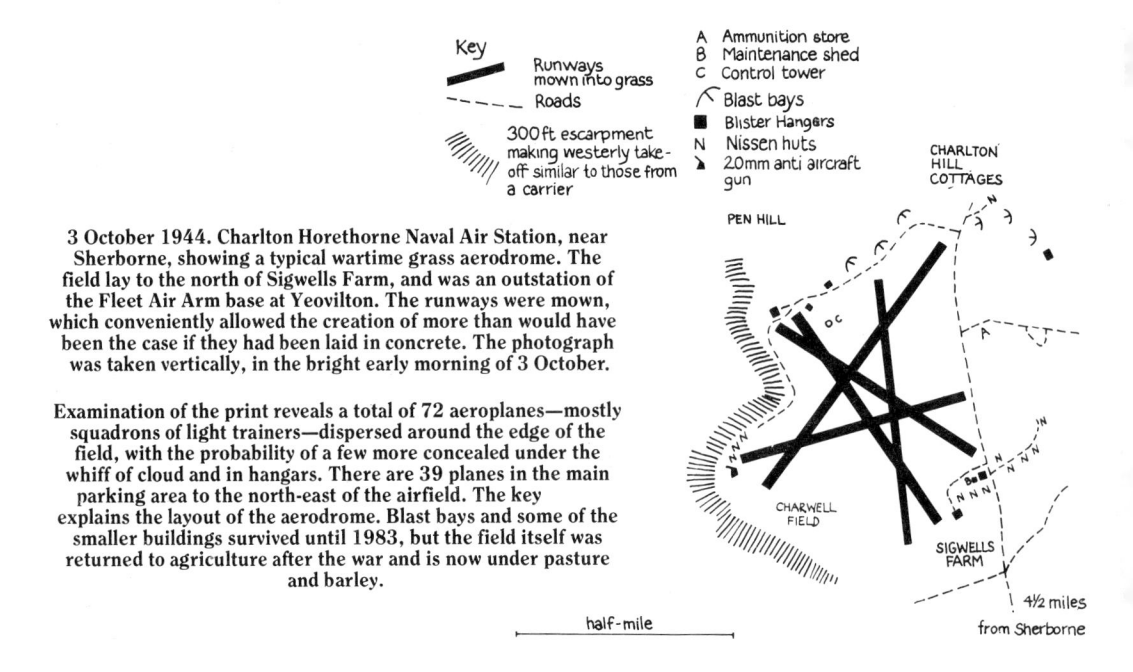

3 October 1944. Charlton Horethorne Naval Air Station, near Sherborne, showing a typical wartime grass aerodrome. The field lay to the north of Sigwells Farm, and was an outstation of the Fleet Air Arm base at Yeovilton. The runways were mown, which conveniently allowed the creation of more than would have been the case if they had been laid in concrete. The photograph was taken vertically, in the bright early morning of 3 October.

Examination of the print reveals a total of 72 aeroplanes—mostly squadrons of light trainers—dispersed around the edge of the field, with the probability of a few more concealed under the whiff of cloud and in hangars. There are 39 planes in the main parking area to the north-east of the airfield. The key explains the layout of the aerodrome. Blast bays and some of the smaller buildings survived until 1983, but the field itself was returned to agriculture after the war and is now under pasture and barley.

Key:
— Runways mown into grass
- - - Roads
/// 300ft escarpment making westerly take-off similar to those from a carrier
■ Blister Hangars
N Nissen huts
↘ 20mm anti aircraft gun
A Ammunition store
B Maintenance shed
C Control tower
⌒ Blast bays

PEN HILL
CHARWELL FIELD
CHARLTON HILL COTTAGES
SIGWELLS FARM
4½ miles from Sherborne

half-mile

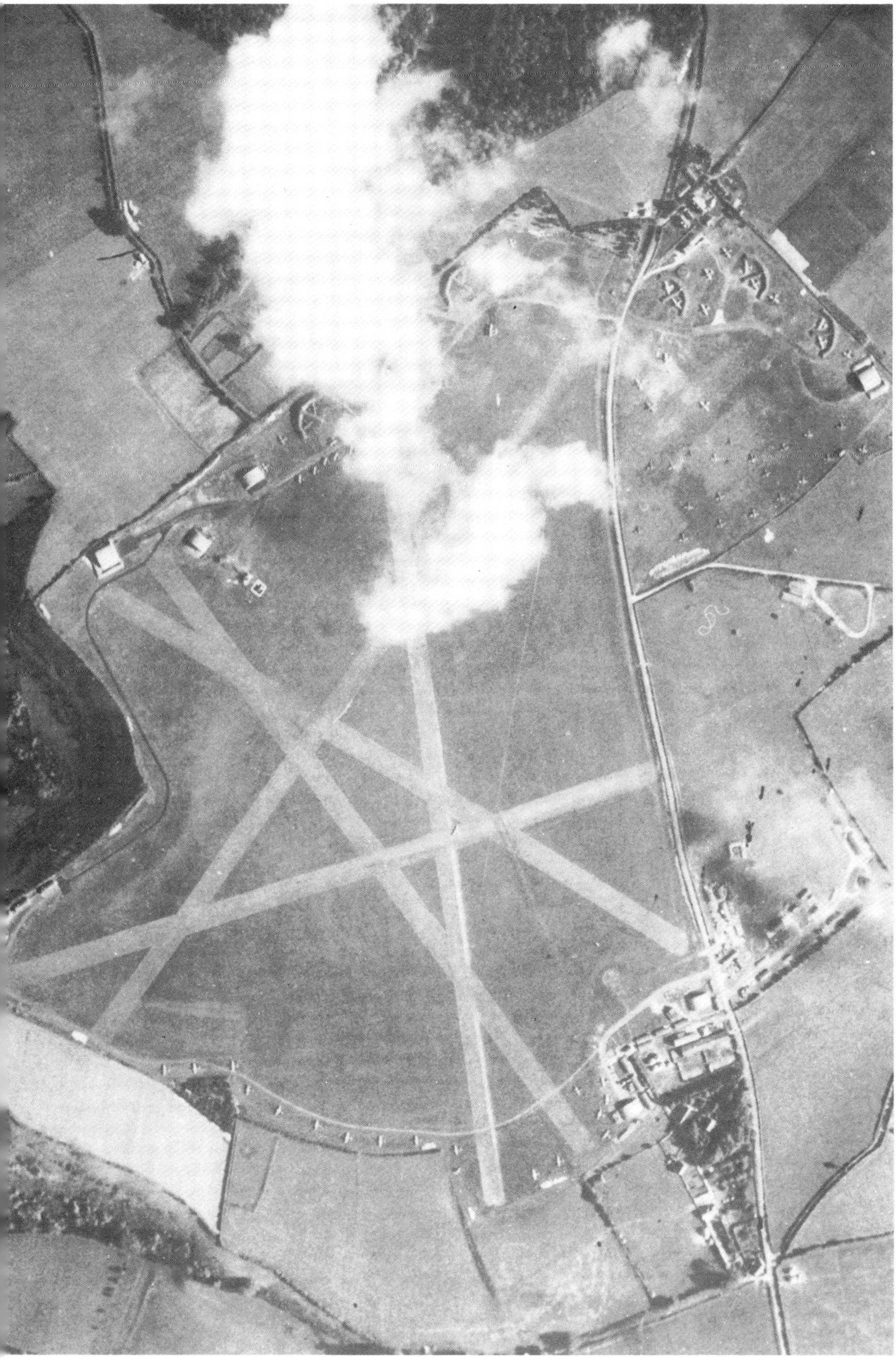

1 November Poole craft attack Walcheren to free Antwerp.

Twenty-five Poole landing craft manned by naval crews from the town's HMS Turtle base have landed commandos on Walcheren Island, the German-held strongpoint blocking the approaches to the Dutch port of Antwerp. Nine of the craft, the Support Squadron Eastern Flank, have been sunk and nine are immobilised.

Footnote The British commandos and Canadian ground forces took three days to capture the island. The channel to Antwerp was opened to Allied supply ships on 28 November.

11 November Dorsetmen are first gunners into Germany.

The 94th Field Regiment of the Royal Artillery, mainly recruited from Bournemouth and Dorset in 1939, has become the first field gun force to cross the German frontier. It is supporting the Anglo-American offensive in the Geilenkirchen sector.

14 November 4th Dorsets were heroes of Arnhem escapes.

It became known today that it was largely owing to the matchless heroism of 250 men of the 4th Battalion of the Dorsetshire Regiment, part of the 43rd Wessex Division, that 2,400 out of the original 8,000 airborne troops succeeded in withdrawing from the Arnhem bridgehead on the night of 25 September.

Few, however, of the Dorsets escaped—and some of those had to swim the Neder Rijn to do so.

In the salient of the British advance, "The Island" at Bemmel, three Battalions of the Dorsetshire Regiment, the 1st, 4th and 5th, found themselves fighting in adjacent fields for the same "thumb print" on the map—the first time events had brought them together. Other Dorsets were able to give covering fire to men of the 4th Battalion as they rescued the survivors of the 1st Airborne Division and the Polish Parachute Brigade with a shuttle service of assault boats across the Neder Rijn [Lower Rhine].

By dawn on 26 September, at 06.00 hours, the intensity of enemy fire made further rescue crossings impossible.

3 December The Home Guard stands down.

With the movement of the war into Europe throughout the second half of this year there have been the inevitable consequences on this side of the Channel and from today the Home Guard is stood down.

26 December Blandford sees the cost of the Ardennes.

The news today is that General George Patton has at last been able to lead the tanks of the 3rd United States Army in the relief of Bastogne. The tide of the great German counter-offensive in the snowy forests of Luxembourg and southern Belgium, the Battle of the Ardennes, has been turned.

It has, however, been an achievement of American grit. The staunch determination of the American soldier since 16 December has prevented the Germans from coming back across the River Meuse.

Casualties are streaming into Dorset. Up to five hundred wounded Americans have been flown into Tarrant Rushton by the Dakotas in a single night, en route for the 22nd General Hospital at Blandford Camp.

Footnote The Ardennes reverses for the Germans were to be worse; estimated losses of 120,000 men with 600 tanks and assault guns, plus dozens of aircraft. There was nothing in reserve for another counter-attack.

29 December American freighter sinks in Worbarrow Bay.

The *Black Hawk*, a United States steam-freighter, has sunk in Worbarrow Bay after being hit by a torpedo.

December Posthumous VC for Dorchester's Arnhem hero.

Captain Lionel Ernest Queripel of Dorchester has been posthumously awarded the Victoria Cross for his gallantry in the battle following the airborne landings at Arnhem. Born in 1920, he was fighting with the Royal Sussex Regiment; he died from his wounds.

December 1944. Bournemouth. The author's parents, Gladys and Ted Legg at 21 Easter Road, Moordown, Bournemouth, received their last Christmas card of the present hostilities from Ted's brother, Arthur Legg, who was having a good war as a dispatch rider in Italy. It gave him a bike and absolute freedom; he always boasted that as far as taxation was concerned he never returned from the Western Desert. Of the Yanks, his lasting memory was the sheer scale and excesses of everything they did—always bringing enough spares to rebuild every piece of equipment half a dozen times. Arthur had more of a sense of humour than the rest of the family put together, myself included. He was in his second childhood and had written: 'The welding went on my silencer at Taranto the other day and now she sounds just like the good old grass track days, and by the way I can't get my licence taken away out here or in Cairo yet. You want to see the speed and the noise we make, especially when on an Immediate Message. I have done 16,000 miles since coming to Italy in January [he wrote this on 14 June 1944, as 'typewriter and radio are tapping away'] and if old Deacon, Roe or Bryon [stuffy Bournemouth neighbours] was anywhere around in the busy streets of Bori, or when I was in Cairo, their hair would stand on end, and I guess I can't get the sack from the job till the Ruddy War is over. One-way streets mean nothing to us DRs [dispatch riders] and the 'Red Caps' [military police] just know we are on SDR [Special Dispatch Riding].' Arthur Legg lies in Talbot Village churchyard. If there is a life after death they will be enjoying something other than peace.

De Havilland Mosquito: made at Christchurch.

1945

January Warmwell joyrider takes a Spitfire to Cheselbourne.

Victor Swatridge of Dorchester Police wrote to me in 1971 with an account of an incident on a cold January night, apparently in 1945, when he was called by telephone at 2.45 am by the constable on the Broadmayne beat and told that a Spitfire had been stolen at 02.00 hours from Warmwell Aerodrome.

As there was a blizzard he thought this a little unlikely but the Observer Corps at Poundbury Camp confirmed they had heard a plane overhead at about 2.30 am. The missing plane had been said to have flown west and Poundbury reported the unmistakeable sound of a Rolls-Royce Merlin engine. They reported it disappearing about six or seven miles to the north-east.

Moonlight followed the snow and Swatridge went with another officer on to the Dorset Downs around Cheselbourne in the centre of the county:

At about 5 am on approaching Cheselbourne Water, to our amazement we saw a lighted hurricane lamp in the drive to a cottage. Naked lights were regarded as somewhat treasonable and very much frowned upon, as blackout regulations were strictly enforcible. Even the headlamps of cars were only allowed narrow slotted beams.

I immediately investigated the reason for this breach and a woman, on answering my call at the cottage, stated that she had heard a plane overhead about two hours previously which appeared to have landed nearby. She went on to say, that she had been expecting her husband home on leave from France and it was the sort of stupid thing he would do, come by any means possible. She had placed the lighted lamp as a guide to him. Amazing as it seemed, we trudged on and clambered on to a high bank overlooking an unploughed cornfield where to our utter surprise we came upon tyre marks. On following them we found the missing fighter plane with its nose embedded in the hedge and bank at the other end of the field, on Eastfield Farm a quarter of a mile north-east of Cheselbourne church.

Climbing on to the wing we found the cockpit lighting burning but the 'bird' had flown. There was no trace of blood inside and we found footmarks in the snow made by the culprit, when walking way from the scene, but they quickly became extinct owing to the drifting snow. To cut a long story short I returned to the divisional station, after leaving a constable to guard the plane and a search party was sent out in daylight and a Canadian airman of the ground staff was arrested, having celebrated too liberally the previous night and in a rash moment embarked on this venturesome journey. There was only slight damaged to the aircraft; the man was concussed and later dealt with by the authorities. So the escapade resolved itself.

25 February   **2nd Dorsets cross the Irrawaddy.**

The 2nd Battalion of the Dorsetshire Regiment today saw the "flying fishes play" as they crossed the Irrawaddy. Now, in Kipling's words, the British Army is "On the road to Mandalay." This has influenced the Dorsets' current battle cry: "There's a dirty white pagoda to the east of Payadu."

20 March   **2nd Dorsets help take Mandalay.**

Having left twenty-seven dead along the road to Mandalay, the 2nd Battalion of the Dorsetshire Regiment have arrived and are mopping up opposition as the Japanese withdraw. General Sir Oliver Leese, Commander-in-Chief Allied Land Forces South-East Asia, visited the men this afternoon and told them they would have to make the next four hundred miles to Rangoon before the monsoon broke—though this time, he promised, they would not have to walk all the way.

Hearing the news of the capture of the ancient Burmese capital, Winston Churchill remarked: "Thank God they've at last got to a place I can pronounce!"

21 March   **6th Airborne Division leaves Tarrant Rushton.**

The British 6th Airborne Division, with its Halifax tug-planes and Hamilcar and Horsa gliders, is today leaving Tarrant Rushton aerodrome for its new location, RAF Woodbridge. This Suffolk airfield is closer to the division's next objectives, in the Rhine valley.

March   **Duchess of Kent visits Blandford.**

HRH the Duchess of Kent has visited the 22nd General Hospital of the United States Army, which now works with the 125th, 131st and 140th General Hospitals in a major medical complex across the Anson-Craddock Lines at Blandford Camp. It has received 17,000 patients of the long-term type, many of whom are needing complicated surgery. The commander is Lieutenant Colonel Leonard D. Heaton.

March **Poles sink U-boat in Poole Bay.**

Polish pilots have claimed a U-boat in the Channel, sunk in the south-east extremity of Poole Bay, towards the Isle of Wight.

9 April **Warmwell ceases to be an operational airfield.**

152 Squadron, who have been operating at Warmwell since the dark days of 1940, have been withdrawn and the station is now only retained for training, by the Central Gunnery School.

17 April **Puddletown lad loses life for fame in the Argenta Gap.**

Trooper James Legg, aged 21, from Puddletown, serving with the Queen's Bays, has been killed in action in Italy. He drove the first tank to force its way through the enemy's main defensive line in the Argenta Gap.

4 May **Dorsets hear there is no longer a war in northern Europe.**

Cipher clerks to the units of the Dorsetshire Regiment in Germany received the signal at 20.50 hours today—"all offensive ops will cease from receipt of this signal." In other words, it's over. "Orders will be given to all troops to cease fire 08.00 hours tomorrow Saturday 5 May. Full terms of local German surrender arranged today for 21 Army Group front follow."

The times are stated in British Double Summer Time and the Instrument of Surrender was signed by General-Admiral von Friedeberg, the emissary of Grand Admiral Karl Döenitz who is exercising command in Schleswig-Holstein in place of Hitler, and General Kinzel, Busch's Chief of Staff. It unconditionally surrenders all enemy forces in northern Germany and was signed at 18.30 hours in the Tactical Headquarters of Field Marshal Bernard Montgomery on Luneberg Heath.

18.30 hours, 4 May 1945: Field Marshal Bernard Montgomery brings the European war to an end. In the next couple of hours the message will be with the troops in the field—that unless they are attacked there is to be no more fighting.

Footnote Though Hitler was dead, the Allies did not know it at the time.

8 May **VE Day.**

15.00 hours. The war in Europe is officially at an end. Street parties, bonfires and church services will mark VE Day this Thursday evening.

9 May U-boat 249 surrenders at Portland.

U-boat 249 today entered Portland Harbour to surrender.

10 May Two more U-boats surrender.

U-boat 825 put into Portland and U-boat 1023 came into Weymouth as the surrender of Grand Admiral Karl Döenitz's fleet continues.

12 May Dorsets in first victory parade.

The 5th Battalion of the Dorsetshire Regiment marched past Lieutenant General Brian Horrocks, the commander of the 30th Corps, at Bremerhaven today in the first victory parade to be held in Germany.

16 May Isle of Wight villagers send their prize to Portland.

Villagers at Freshwater on the Isle of Wight were amazed when a U-boat surfaced offshore and requested someone to take its surrender. Freshwater has a parish councillor or two but it has no mayor or any one of the kind of standing that a German naval officer might respect. Anyway it has no port facilities apart from a beach and the inhabitants considered they were in line for a rollicking from the Royal Navy.

So U-776 was asked to surrender somewhere else and it departed for Portland Harbour. Someone in the Isle of Wight has turned up a splendid opportunity. Think of how he might have answered that inevitable question: "Granddad, what did you do in the war?"

30 May 1945. Blandford Camp. American colour party at the opening of Roosevelt Park.

30 May Roosevelt Park opened at Blandford.

The first overseas memorial to the late President of the United States, Roosevelt Park inside the confines of Blandford Camp, was declared open today with an address by Colonel Daniel J. Fourrier of the US Army. A colour party fired ceremonial rounds.

The park is dedicated "to the everlasting memory of our fellow soldiers, at home and abroad, who gave their lives in this war, so that we who live may share in the future a free and better world". It has been provided through voluntary contributions of members of the Army Medical Department with the landscaping being designed by a patient, Private George H. Stuber.

Colonel Fourrier handed the park over to Colonel C. Topham of the Royal Engineers who received it on behalf of the British Army.

A six-foot high monument is under construction to enshrine the ideals behind the park permanently in stone.

6 June **Conservatives hold Dorset but lose Britain.**

The Conservative Party smarted today as the landslide of votes in yesterday's General Election is set to oust war-leader Winston Churchill and put a Labour administration in his place. Pre-war memories are blamed for the scale of the socialist success which has surprised the world in its rejection of the country's saviour. It is regarded as an unwarranted dismissal.

Even in Dorset, which must be quite blue, it has been a close-run thing for the Conservatives to hold their seats. The East Dorset constituency returned Lieutenant Colonel M. Wheatley with 26,561 votes against 25,093 to his Labour opponent Lieutenant Commander Cyril Fletcher-Cooke, with Liberal Colonel Mander having the remaining 8,975. Out of 80,816 on the registers there was a 60,629 poll, including 8,352 votes from men and women in the armed services.

Footnote Clement Attlee became Prime Minister on 25 July with Ernest Bevin as Foreign Secretary, Sir Stafford Cripps at the Board of Trade and Hugh Dalton as Chancellor of the Exchequer.

June **Gunnery School leaves and Warmwell closes.**

The RAF aerodrome at Warmwell closes this month with the departure of the Central Gunnery School for Sutton Bridge, Lincolnshire.

6 August 1945. Hiroshima's bomb—'brighter tnan the sun'—but another would be needed to bring about the surrender process.

15 August **Henstridge pilots celebrate VJ Day.**

It is Victory over Japan Day. Nowhere in Dorset has the celebration been more heart-felt than in Stalbridge and in particular the Wrens' Quarters on the Dorset side of the Royal Naval Air

DORSET'S WAR   184

Station at Henstridge which literally straddles the county boundary with Somerset.

Here a bonfire has been kept burning all night, despite a soaking at 05.00 hours when the rain intensified, having been started a few minutes after midnight when the station Tannoy had roused everyone from sleep: "Attention everybody. Attention. Japan has surrendered." The party began, and is still carrying on in the Swan at Stalbridge.

This was still an operational air station. VE Day had been only half the story. For the young New Zealand pilots and others under training the war was still a going concern and their lives under risk in what was becoming the "forgotten war".

The atomic bombs ended all that. Leaflets dropped on Hiroshima on the 4th warned: "Your city will be obliterated unless your Government surrenders." That blow was delivered from a single United States Army Air Force Boeing B-29 bomber, *Enola Gay* piloted by Paul Tibbets Junior, on the 6th. Then Nagasaki was threatened its "rain of ruin the like of which has never been seen on earth". That was from another B-29, *Bock's Car*, on the 9th.

The third atom bomb, standing-by and probably for Tokyo, did not have to be dispatched. Japan began the surrender process four days ago.

August   **Canford School counts 139 dead.**

Canford's School's roll of war dead has closed at a total of 139 lives, from this its first war. As the school was founded in 1923 it happened that all Old Candfordians were of an age to serve and indeed nearly a thousand of them held commissions.

22 August 1945. Portland. Depressing day in the rain for United States Ambassador Gil Winant, unveiling Portland's tribute to the Americans who fell on Omaha Beach. Winant's life was being destroyed for the love of Sarah Churchill.

22 August   **US Ambassador unveils Portland's memorial.**

Portland's memorial to the Americans of V Corps who passed through the harbour en route to D-Day and the fierce fighting on Omaha beach was unveiled today by the United States Ambassador, Gil Winant. He was welcomed by the chairman of Portland Urban District Council, A. N. Tattersall, after driving along the newly re-named Victory Road. The stone is in Victoria Gardens and the Stars and Stripes flies above beside the Union Jack. Disappointingly, it has been a very wet Wednesday.

Footnote "Fine, fine, perfectly fine," was Winant's famous remark of the war; which he kept repeating over the transatlantic telephone when Roosevelt told him of Pearl Harbor. By now, however, he was engulfed in personal problems and would shoot himself in 1947, after his return to the United States. He was said to have set his heart on Sarah Churchill, who was unable to reciprocate his love.

August British military back in Blandford Camp.

The British Army has returned to Blandford Camp—which saw out the war as a major American General Hospital—with the arrival of the 1st and 2nd Searchlight Regiments, Royal Artillery, in the huts of the Craddock and Benbow Lines. These units will train conscripts who have been called up to serve their national service with the Royal Artillery.

18 September First Jap prisoners arrive home at Poole.

The first BOAC flying-boat to bring repatriated prisoners-of-war home to Britain from Japan has touched down in Poole Harbour, amid sensational press interest in the men's stories of degrading and inhuman treatment.

3 October Christchurch colonel fires a V2.

Colonel Raby, the Director of Signals Research and Development Establishment at Christchurch Aerodrome and Steamer Point, Highcliffe, today test-fired a German V2 rocket which he had reconstructed from captured parts. It has been flown northwards, along the coast from Cuxhaven, near Bremerhaven, into the North Sea off Denmark.

This has been a secret test, codenamed Operation Backfire, and tomorrow another rocket will be fired. Raby's establishment is working on the first British guided weapons.

Footnote A third V2 was fired by the British team on 15 October, 1945; this time the world's press would be invited and bill it as "the first Allied test-firing of a V2 rocket".

October Blandford hospital staff leave on the 'Queen Mary'.

The 22nd General Hospital of the United States Army has finally pulled out of Blandford Camp. The last of its staff are now sailing back across the Atlantic from Southampton aboard the liner *Queen Mary*.

31 December Home Guard disbanded.

Today has seen the last rites for the Home Guard as it is finally disbanded by the War Office. "The spirit of comradeship and service which was brought to life by service to the Dorset Home Guard must never be allowed to die," says its last Commander, General Henry Jackson.

December 'Our man in Berlin'—Lindsay is dead.

Sir Ronald Lindsay, of Stepleton House near Blandford, died earlier this year. The retired diplomat was born in 1877. He rose through the ranks at the Foreign Office to become an under-secretary in 1920 and progressed to the highest postings in the service—being ambassador to Berlin (1926–28) and Washington (1930–39). When he bowed out the war, as they say, was an extension of diplomacy by other means.

The classical Stepleton House and its park, the home once of Peter Beckford, has passed to Sir Ronald's nephew, Lord Crawford.

December **Plaque at Portland commemorates the logistics.**

The 14th Major Port of the Transportation Corps of the United States Army has presented a bronze plaque to Portland dockyard commemorating the logistics of the invasion of Europe:

"1944–1945. The major part of the American assault force which landed on the shores of France 6 June 1944, was launched from the Weymouth and Portland Harbors. From 6 June 1944 to 7 May 1945, 517,816 troops and 144,093 vehicles embarked from these harbors. Many of these left Weymouth Pier. The remainder of the troops and all vehicles passed through Weymouth to Portland points of embarkation.

"Presented by the 14th Major Port, U.S. Army. Harold G. Miller, Major T.C. Sub Port Commander. Sherman L. Kiser, Colonel T.C. Port Commander."

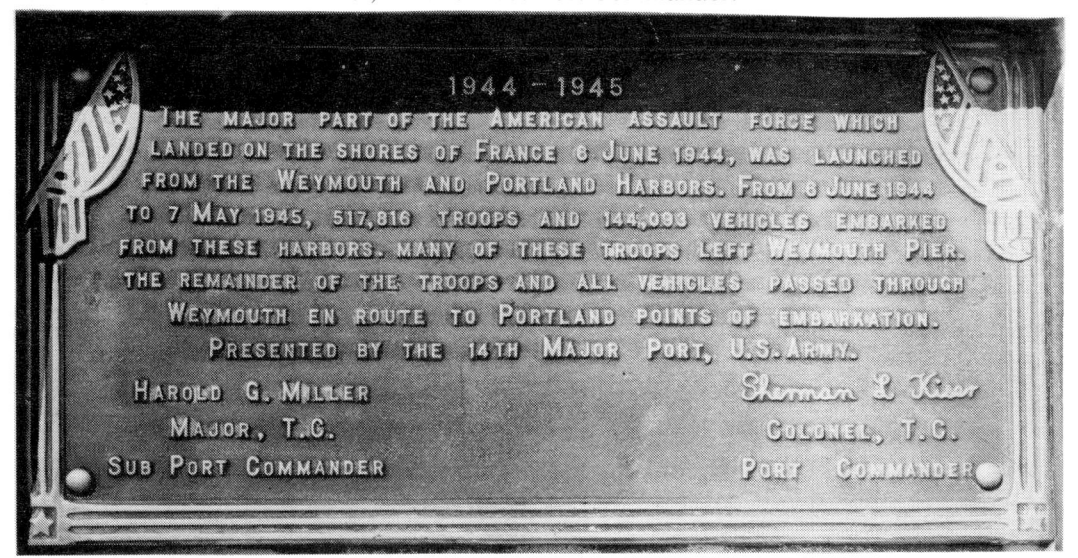

1946

February **War's upheavals bring Uplands School to Parkstone.**

Uplands School, which was founded in 1903 at St Leonards-on-Sea, Sussex, is on the move to Parkstone. It has come via Monmouthshire, where it was evacuated when invasion threatened in 1940, and it had been hoped to return to Sussex in 1944 but the flying bombs caused these plans to be abandoned. Instead it is coming to Parkstone, to the buildings of a sister church school for girls, Sandecotes, which was itself closed in 1940 when the buildings were requisitioned by the military.

1 July **2nd Dorsets on Tokyo's 'Buck House' guard.**

The 2nd Battalion of the Dorsetshire Regiment has been hastily consigned to Tokyo in Operation Primus, to relieve the New Zealanders on ceremonial guard duties in the Japanese capital. The Americans are its army of occupation on the streets. Dorset sentries are preparing for what they call "No 1, Buck House guard"—at the Imperial Palace.

The rosters assume that the battalion's eight hundred men will be able to maintain two hundred sentries at posts around the city.

Footnote Sharing the imperial guard with the Americans was not quite on Buckingham Palace lines, Lieutenant Colonel Geoffrey White recalled in *Straight on for Tokyo*: "It is not easy when your companion on the post allows himself rather a more relaxed form of stand-at-ease, and it is most disconcerting to have a doughnut offered you on the end of a bayonet."

1946. Off Brownsea Island, Poole Harbour. Hythe-class Short Sunderland Mark-3 flying boats, formerly RAF transports but now with gun turrets removed and in service with British Overseas Airways for the Empire route to India, Singapore and Australia. They still carry Transport command markings. The take-off above, heading westwards, is of G-AGES/OQZS for Bombay.

DORSET'S WAR

Index

... **of people, Dorset place-names, ships, aircraft types,** and **military units.** For the latter see 'British Army'/'German Forces'/'Royal Air Force'/'United States Army' for listings of specific regiments and squadrons. The Dorsetshire Regiment, however, has also been given its own entry. With the Royal Navy we have followed the usual practice of giving each ship a separate entry.

People's initials, where known, are given here — rather than their ranks, as with multiple references the individual's status tends to change with the progress of the book. Principal towns, events, military establishments and grouped listings are shown in **bold type**.

Abbott, Walter 92
Abbotsbury 5, 23, 41, 138
Abel Tasman 19
Adler Tag [Eagle Day] 38
Adnam family 88
Advance Post, newspaper 119
Agar, A.W.S. 105
Agazarian, Noel le C. 58
Airborne landings 111, 117, 129, 130, 157 to 166, 174, 175, 178, 180
Air claims, exaggerated 54, 66
Air Defence Research and Development Establishment [also known as Air Defence Experimental Establishment] 8, 58, 79, 96, 97, 102
Air Ministry 8, 14, 32, 33, 54, 72, 106, 147
Air Raid Precautions [ARP] 12, 13, 15, 18, 36, 64, 65, 120
Air–sea Rescue 18, 24, 118, 119, 120, 140, 142, 147
Airspeed (1934) Limited 81, 88, 97, 125, 157, 159
Akroyd, H.J. 67
Albrighton, HMS 108
Alex Andrea 10
Alex van Opstal 9
Allen, John Woodward 75
Alum Chine 29, 73
Americans – see 'United States Army'
Anderson, Kenneth 113
Anderson Manor 111
Anson, Avro 5, 8, 20, 142
Apache 120
Appleyard, Geoffrey 111, 126
Applin, Frank 36
Arado 234C 170
Arish Mell 92
Armoured Fighting Vehicles School 24, 29, 68, 92, 109, 110, 116, 142
Arne 89, 107
Arnhem landings 174, 175, 178, 179
Ashanti, HMS 170
Ashley Heath 89
Askerswell 126
Atherton, J.W. 171, 172
A13 tank 91
Attlee, Clement 5, 14, 183
Attrichter, Josef 55
Avro 504N 20
Ayles, Victor 30
Azalra, HMS 143

Backfire, Operation 185
Badbury Rings 162, 163, 164
Baldwin, Earl [Stanley] 16
Bailey Bridge 90
Bailey, Donald Coleman 90
Balfour, Harold 41
Ballard Down 72
Baltington Farm 130
Bankes, Ralph 117
Barnes, Leslie 36
Barnhill, SS 13
Barrett, W. 10
Barstow, Brigadier 20
Bartlett, Leonard 84
Bartlett, 'Nobby' 35
Battle, Fairey 87
Battle of Britain – see 'Warmwell Aerodrome', 1940 entries
Battle Training Camp 80, 118
Beales, store 111, 123
Beaminster 5
Beaufighter, Bristol 90, 146, 170
Beaumont, Roland 41, 43
Beckford, Peter 185
Bedford, lorry 136, 140
Bedford, Major 147
Beeling, Charles 10
Bellamy's Farm 57, 58
Bellows 124
Bennett, Donald 118
Bere Regis 2, 3, 11, 36, 92, 111, 129
Bevin, Ernest 183 *d*
Billinger, Margaret 62, 65
Bincleaves 14
Bindon Hill 92
Bimmendijk 89, 90, 105
Bismarck 89, 90, 105
Biting, Operation 102
Black Hawk, SS 179
Blackmore Vale 50
Blacknor 143
Blackwood, HMS 170
Blandford 6, 72, 75, 113, 130, 185
Blandford Camp 6, 8, 10, 50, 52, 70, 80, 118, 130, 140, 178, 180, 182, 185
Blenheim, Bristol 82, 83, 118
Boadicea, HMS 70
Bock's Car 184
Bolston, J. & Son Limited 18, 107, 133, 134
Boeing B-17 113, 120
Boeing B-26 144
Boeing B-29 184, 189
Boeing B-314 'Clipper' 40, 175
Bofors, gun 119
Boitel-Gill, Derek 38, 56
Bond, Ralph 130
Boot, H.A.H. 118
Boscombe 3, 13, 29, 116
Boudard, M. 87
Boult, Sir Adrian 123

Bournemouth 3, 5, 13, 14, 24, 26, 29, 38, 42, 43, 48, 49, 50, 53, 54, 67, 69, 73, 75, 77, 81, 82, 84, 85, 86, 87, 93, 94, 103, 104, 106, 108, 111, 113, 114, 123, 129, 138, 139, 178
Bournemouth Municipal Orchestra 123, 124
Bourne Valley 84
Bovington Camp 7, 20, 24, 29, 68, 91, 92, 109, 110, 129, 142, 167
Branksome 28, 29
Branksome Chine 29
Branksome Gas Works 84, 85
Branksome Park 10, 55
Brazen, HMS 16, 32

British Army – only specific references to numbered units are included. Note that they are given in numerical order [ie, by battalion numbers rather than regimental names].
1st Airborne Division 174, 178
1st Army 113
1st Commando 116
1st Battalion, Dorsetshire Regiment 6, 120, 126, 128, 129, 133, 145, 167, 168, 173, 175, 178
1st Division 77, 82
1st Glider Pilot Regiment 130, 157
1st Malta Brigade 120
1st Searchlight Regiment 185
1st Small Scale Raiding Force 87, 126
2nd Battalion, Dorsetshire Regiment 9, 14, 16, 103, 144, 145, 180, 186
2nd Battalion, Oxfordshire and Buckinghamshire Light Infantry 157, 166
2nd Battalion, Parachute Regiment 98 to 103
2nd Searchlight Regiment 185
2nd Special Air Service Regiment 126
2nd Special Services Brigade 119
3rd Special Services Brigade 116
4th Battalion, Dorsetshire Regiment 7, 178
4th Battalion, Royal Northumberland Fusiliers 29, 50, 51, 52, 70
5th Commando 116
5th Corps 77, 174, 182
5th Battalion, Dorsetshire Regiment 6, 172, 174, 178, 182
5th Battalion, Northants Regiment 47
6th Airborne Division 157 to 167, 178, 179, 180
6th Air Landing Brigade 157
6th Battalion, Green Howard 20
7th Battalion, Green Howards 20, 36
8th Army 113, 120, 124
8th Battalion, Royal Northumberland Fusiliers 50
12th Battalion, Hampshire Regiment 49
12th Battalion, Royal Fusiliers 103
14th Super Heavy Battery 70, 93
21st Army Group 147, 181
30th Corps 174, 182
42nd Royal Marines 116
43rd (Wessex) Division 6, 174, 178
44th Royal Marines 116
62nd Commando 94
66th Commando 111
69th Infantry Brigade 20
76th Heavy Field Regiment 35
94th (Dorset and Hants) Field Regiment 5, 178
102nd Battery, 522nd Coast Regiment 35
141st (Queen's Own Dorset Yeomanry) Field Regiment 5
141st (Queen's Own Dorset Yeomanry) Field Regiment 5
172nd Battery, 554th Coast Regiment 22
175th Battery, 554th Coast Regiment 22
218th (Hampshire) Field Battery 5
224th (Dorset) Field Battery 5
229th Battery 87
231st Infantry Brigade 120, 145
310th Anti-Aircraft Battery 5
347th Battery, 554th Coast Regiment 21, 22
375th Queen's Own Dorset Yeomanry Battery 5
386th Battery, 554th Coast Regiment 22
522nd (Dorset) Coast Regiment 34, 35
542nd (Dorset) Coast Regiment 34, 35
554th Coast Regiment 22

British Inventor 19
British Overseas Airways Corporation [BOAC] 8, 13, 24, 25, 28, 37, 86, 129, 143, 185, 187
British Resistance 33
British Restaurants 66, 99
British Union of Fascists 33
Bridport 70, 112, 131, 140, 171
Bright, Joe 112
Brissenden, HMS 133
Bristol 127
Broadmayne 179
Broadstone 10, 143
Broadway 10
Brocklesby, HMS 112
Brooke, Sir Alan 29, 127, 175
Brooke, Rupert 6
Broughty Ferry Hotel 116
Brown, Cyril 176
Brown, Dennis 10
Brown, George 18
Browne, I.G. 128
Brownsea Island 8, 14, 21, 22, 24, 91, 106, 119, 187
Browning, Furrell 149
Bruneval Raid 98 to 103, 106
Bryant, Lieut. 145
Bufton, H.E. 20

Bulley, Albert 90
Burgess, 37
Burrows, Hedley 24, 43
Burton Bradstock 10, 50, 131, 132, 134, 138, 140
Busch, Field Marshal von 181
Bussey Stool Farm 58
Butler, Harold 28
Butlin, John 61

Cabot 15
Cain's Folly 106
Cake, R.J. 130
Came Woods 115
Camouflage School 33
Capone, Al 12
Canford Cliffs 22, 33, 81, 85, 86, 111
Canford Heath 119
Canford School 184
Caribou 13
Carlton Hotel 69, 138, 139
Carretier, General 37
Carshel, Hans 58
Cartridge, Harold 19
Castletown Docks 151, 153
Catalina flying boat 124
Cattistock 16, 58, 129
Chacksfield, Bob and Merle 4
Chamberlain, Lieut. 174
Chamberlain, Neville 9, 14, 15
'Channel Dash' 98, 99
Chapman's Pool 14
Charborough Park 114, 147
Charles, Hughie 12
Charlton Horethorne Naval Air Station 106, 108, 111, 112, 176, 177
Charmouth 106
Chastise, Operation 122
Churchill, John 14
Churchill, Randolph 12, 14
Churchill, Sarah 184, 185
Churchill, S.G. 130
Churchill, tank 91, 116, 129
Churchill, Winston 4, 12, 14, 16, 29, 30, 31, 54, 113, 116, 118, 122, 126, 180, 183, 185
Chasseur-43 91, 115
Cheney, A.E. 132
Cherrett, Archibald 84
Cheselbourne 58, 145, 179, 180
Chesil Beach [or Bank] 42, 44, 138, 143, 151, 176
Chesil Beach Bombing Range 8, 42, 122
Chewton Common 53
Chilton, P. 167, 168
Chiswell 114
Christchurch [Aerodrome, harbour, town and bay] 7, 8, 19, 20, 24, 46, 47, 50, 53, 58, 73, 77, 79, 81, 82, 87, 88, 89, 90, 94, 97, 102, 115, 116, 118, 119, 120, 125, 127, 145, 171, 172, 174, 179, 185
Christian Contemplatives' Charity 10, 50
Christie, tank suspension 91
Ciliax, Admiral 99
Clare 37, 40, 111
Clark, Cumberland 86
Clark, Mark Wayne 113, 114
Cliff, The 162
Clio 84
Clipper, Boeing 40, 175
Clouds Hill 129
Coastal Command 24, 84, 106, 111, 112, 120, 124, 133, 171
Coddington, Lieut. 147
Codrington, HMS 32
Collins, M.W. 122
Combined Operations 85, 102, 119, 126, 127, 128
Commodore 118, 119, 120
Coombe House 174
Cooper, Arthur 130
Cooper, J. 130
Cordelia 86
Corfe Castle 11, 72, 93
Cornwall, HMS 105
Cottesmore, HMS 112
Cowley, Cecil 106
Cox, C.H. 102
Coyne, J.P. 124
Cranborne Chase 8, 50, 52, 130
Cranborne, Viscount 5, 90
Cranton, Frank 130
Crawford, Lord 185
Crichel Estate 8, 162, 163
Cripps, Sir Stafford 187
Crook, Pilot Officer 38
Cumbie, Lieut. 171
Cunningham, Sir Andrew 113
Cunningham, John 90
Curtis, Adela 9, 50

Dagmar 91
Daimler, armoured car 136, 137
Dakota, Douglas 178
Dalton, Hugh 183
'Dambusters' 122
Damen, Mrs S.P. 130
Danish, Lieut. 170
Darley, George 27
Davis, Charles 36
Davis, Freda 114
Davis, Frederick 111, 114, 115

Davis, George 115
Davis, Harry 12
Dawe, Leonard J. 61
Day, Ernest 75
Deanesley, 'Jumbo' 31
D-Day 147 to 170, 186
Dee, Philip 118
Defiant, Boulton Paul 108
Delight, HMS 32, 82
Demon, Exercise 120, 121
Deissen, Klaus 58
Delight, HMS 32, 82
Devitt, Peter 27, 28, 31
Dieppe Raid 109
Diffy, Florence 107
Digby, Hon. Pamela 12, 14
Dingwall, Louie 25
Dönitz, Karl 181
Doles Ash Farm 58
Domala 13
Dominey, Walt 13
Doolittle, Jimmy 113
Dorchester 5, 8, 9, 10, 18, 38, 40, 41, 53, 81, 86, 90, 112, 115, 117, 120, 149, 167, 179
Dorchester Evacuation Committee 5
Dorchester Rural District Council 8, 117
Dornier-217 31, 115
Dorset County Council 33
Dorset County Produce Association 91, 92
Dorset County School for Girls 9
Dorsetshire, HMS 89, 90, 105, 108, 117
Dorsetshire Regiment —
1st Battalion 6, 120, 126, 128, 129, 133, 143, 145, 167, 168, 173, 175, 178, 181
2nd Battalion 9, 14, 16, 103, 144, 145, 180, 186
4th Battalion 7, 178, 181
5th Battalion 6, 172, 174, 178, 181, 182
Doty, Lieut. 169
Doultings Pier 107
Dowding, Sir Hugh 54
Drax, Sir Reginald 114, 147
Drummond Hay, Pilot Officer 28
Druitt, Montagu James 53
Dungrange 170
DUKW amphibious vehicle 151, 155
Dunford, William [of Abbotsbury] 41
Dunford, William [of Winterbourne Abbas] 69
Durban Castle 110
Durlston Head 91
Durweston 74, 75

Eastfield Farm 180
East Man 72
Easton 36
East Weares 34, 35
Ebert, E. 58
Eden, Anthony 127
Einstein, Albert 12
Eisenhower, Dwight D. 113, 114, 115, 138, 139, 143, 145, 147
Eisold, Gefr. 38
Elgar, Sir Edward 124
Elmcrest, HMS 26
Emerald, HMS 167
Empire Sentinel 23
'Enigma' intercepts [of German radio traffic] 29, 32, 44, 50, 54, 68, 175
Enola Gay 184
Envoy, Airspeed 81
Esdale, HMS 112
Esmonde, Commander 99
Etrillita 23
Evacuees 5, 9, 18, 33, 65, 90
Evans, W. 128

Exercises —
Demon 120, 121
Fabius 134, 135, 143
Smash 143
Spartan 119

Experimental Bridging Establishment 90
Fabius, Exercise 134, 135, 143
Fairey Battle 87
Falke 102
Fairbrother, Pauline 45
Farley, Albert 81
Fawcett, Sergeant 86
Fay, Vernon 10
Feary, A.N. 67
Felicity 18
Ferine, HMNZS 102
Ferne Animal Sanctuary [since moved to Wambrook, Devon] 69
Fernie 112
Ferrybridge 44
Ferry Nymph 18
First of the Few, film 94, 95
Fishpond, radar 167
Fleet Air Arm 24, 105, 106, 108, 112, 125, 176, 184
Fleet, The [lagoon] 31, 41, 122
Fletcher-Cooke, Cyril 183
Flying Fortress, Boeing B-17 113, 120
Focke-Wulf-190 123, 124, 144, 172
Fort Henry 143
Fortuneswell 26, 176
Fortuneswell Life Saving Company 176
Foss, Ronald 131

Fougasse/'Sea Flame' 53, 76 to 79, 81, 82
Fourrier, Daniel J. 102
Foylebank, HMS 26
Frampton 38
Freeman, Edward J. 64
Freya, radar 32, 82
Friedeberg, von, General-Admiral 181
Friedrick Ihrs 68
Frost, J.D. 102
Fulmar, Fairey 112
Furzebrook 70, 71, 72, 93
Furzey Island 174
Fussell, Marcel 115

Gallows Hill 109, 130
Garrard, Derek 82
Gartell, Albertina 13
Gas-masks 7, 9
Gaulter Gap 58
Gee, Lieut. 171
General Election [1945] 183
General Hospitals [US Army] 133, 178, 180, 182, 185
George, H.C. 130
George VI [the King] 6, 86, 94, 133

German Forces [only specific references to numbered units have been included; they are in numerical order]
Army Group B 23, 53, 175
1st Schnellboot Flotilla 79, 108
2nd Schnellboot Flotilla 124, 126, 170
Stukageschwader-2 38
2nd SS Panzer Corps 175
3rd Minelaying Flotilla 37
Luftflotte-3 50
3rd Schnellboot Flotilla 112
3rd T-boot Flotilla 108
4th Schnellboot Flotilla 124
5th Schnellboot Flotilla 37, 114, 118, 124, 126, 170
5th T-boot Flotilla 108
6th Schnellboot Flotilla 124
8th Schnellboot Flotilla 143
8th Staffel 88
9th SS Panzer Division 175
9th Schnellboot Flotilla 139, 143
10th SS Panzer Division 175
Kampf Gruppe-26 13
Kampf Gruppe-100 70
Erprobungsgruppe-210 56
352nd Infantry Division 169

Gill, Sergeant 87
Gillard, T.E. 62, 63
Gilpin, L.E. 117
'Glamour Puffer' 84
Glanvilles Wootton 14
Glaser, David 95
Gneisenau 98, 99
Glassdale, HMS 112
Golden Cap 21
Goodrich, H. 172
Göring, Hermann 54
Gort, Lord 15
Goulter, Percy H.D. 61
Graham, Colin 23
Graham, H.G. 87
Grant, tank 110
'Great Panjandrum' 128, 129
Green, Henry Levi 111
Green Island 120
Greenwood, Arthur 14
Grenville, HMS 167
Griffiths, L.J. 106
Grimstone 38
Groves, John 131

Haack, Erich 38
Halifax, Handley Page 111, 117, 118, 120, 123, 129, 130, 157 to 163
Hambro family 124
Ham Common 107, 112
Hamilcar, glider 130, 157 to 163
Hamilton, Nina, Duchess of 69
Hammersley, Roland 167
Hamworthy 8, 84, 106, 107, 109, 112, 124, 143
Hamworthy Engineering Limited 73
Hamworthy, RAF [Coastal Command] 106, 109, 120, 124, 143
Hanbury, William 115
Hann, Henry 36
Hans Lody 53
Hants & Dorset Omnibus Co 124
Hardy, HMS 13
Hardy, Thomas 13, 16
Hardy, Vice-Admiral 13
Harris, Sir Arthur 3, 118, 122
Harris, G.W. 129
Harstad 119
Hartlepool, SS 26
Haven Hotel 26
Head, R.R. 105
Heinkel-111 55, 66, 67, 70, 81, 86, 88
Heinkel-178 12
Helmore, William 10
Hengistbury Head, 22, 26, 49, 67, 75, 82, 87, 119, 142
Henrico 149, 155
Henstridge Royal Naval Air Station 183
Herbert, M. 87
Hewitt, Edward 36
Highcliffe 19, 171
Hight, Cecil 42, 43
Hitler, Adolf 4, 109, 29, 30, 50, 103, 120
Hinks, C.O. 53
Hlavac, Jaroslav 68
Hoare, Mr and Mrs 43
Hobart, Percy 135
Hocking, John 10
Hohenseldt, Wilhelm 38
Holes Bay 133, 134
Holland, Ivor 18
Hollister, Tony 27
Holmsley South Aerodrome 111, 117, 120, 123, 146, 159
Holton Heath Royal Naval Cordite Factory 10, 13, 23, 84, 106, 143
Home Guard 16, 33, 36, 53, 54, 55, 58, 69, 106, 111, 106, 115, 130, 131, 185
H1 to H6, harbour patrol boats 23
Hood, HMS 90
Horrocks, Brian 174, 182
House, J.H. 130
Horsa, glider 123, 157 to 160, 166
Howard, John 157, 166
Howard, Leslie 94, 95
H2S, radar 3, 118
Hunt, Douglas 61

Hurn Aerodrome 77, 93, 113, 118, 120, 147, 159, 160, 161
Hurricane, Hawker 3, 8, 28, 41, 42, 55, 56, 64, 120

Ibsley Aerodrome 94
Iford 53, 124
Iltis 81, 102, 106
Imperial Airways 8
Inskip, Sir Thomas 6
Ireland, Henry 61
Island Queen 18
Iwerne Minster 58

Jackstedt, Gerog 57
Jacku, Theo 55
Jaguar 102
James, family 81
Jasper, HMT 112
Jennings, David 81
Jervis, HMS 167
Jiggiting Corner 130
John, Rosamund 94
Jones, A.A.E. 167
Jones, Asa 149
Jones, Brian 96
Jones, Reginald 32, 72, 106, 147
Joubert, Sir Philip 82, 85
Jowett, Rev. F. 26
Joyce, Louis 367
Jubilee, Operation 109
Jüngmann, Bucker 87, 89
Junior Leaders School 48
Junkers-87 ['Stuka'] 26, 27, 28, 31, 32, 38, 42, 43
Junkers-88 45, 54, 56, 72, 84

Karl Glaster 68
Kearsley, Bill 72
Kellaway, Charles 36
Kenny, Ronald 10
Kent, Duchess of 180
Ketele, Jules 20
Khin, S.J. 117
Kimball, Lieut. 145
Kimmeridge 58, 126
Kincaid, General 171
Kindred Star, HMS 19
Kingfisher, floatplane 24
Kingston Lacy 117
Kinson Potteries 72
Kinzel, General 181
Kipling, Rudyard 24, 180
Kiser, Sherman L. 186
Kitkat, Lillian 73
Kittyhawk, fighter 128
Klein, Sergeant 74
Klose, Unteroffizier 58
Knobbs, Horace G. 61
Knoblock, Colonel 146
'Komet', rocket-plane 170
Komet, Schiff-45 112
Kondor 102
Kowallik, T. 88
Krakowiak 112, 119, 167
Kugelgen, A. von 72

Lafferty, Frederick R. 144
Lamb, P.M. 125
Lancaster, Avro 122
Landrey, Frederick 45
Langar, Hauptmann 90
Langton Herring 122
Lansdowne 3, 5, 123
Larminat, Edgard de 37
Larson, Captain 171
Lau, H.Y. 117
Lee Motor Works 13
Lees, Sir John 6
Leese, Oliver 180
Le Gallais, Albert I.E. 61
Legg, Arthur 179
Legg, Gladys [author's mother] 3, 179
Legg, Horace G. 61
Legg, Jack 36
Legg, James 181
Legg, M.A. 117
Legg, Ted [author's father] 3, 179
Lemnitzer, Lyman 113
Leny 125
Lewis, gun 115
Liberator, Consolidated B-24 [RAF version] 120, 174
Lidtke, Emil 57
Lightning, Lockheed P-38 133, 139, 142, 143, 144, 145, 147, 169, 171, 172, 174
Lilliput 81
Lily, project 140
Lindemann, Frederick 118
Linderschmid, Feldwebel 38
Lindsay, Sir Ronald 185
Lintern, Arthur J. 61
Lion, HMS 114
Liroff, Jerry 142
Local Defence Volunteers [see also 'Home Guard'] 16, 19
Long Crichel 68
Longfleet 50
Longman, A.J. 30
Lord Hailsham, HMT 119
Lord Stamp, HMT 68
Lovell-Gregg, Terence 41, 42
Lovelock, R.C. 109
Lovell, Bernard 118

L27, HM Submarine 68
Lucking, Cecil 10
Lulworth Camp 92, 110, 116, 130
Lumby, M.G.R. 126
Lutz, Martin 56, 58
Lyme Bay 8, 28, 31, 33, 55, 58, 86, 108, 118, 119, 143, 145
Lyme Regis 42, 85, 92, 127, 142
Lys, family 36
Lysander, Westland 116

Maastricht 79
McAlpine, contractors 26
MacDonald, Ramsay 12
Mackie, Corporal 20
MacNaughten, Justice 115
McQueen, Ian 43
Magister, Miles 82
Maia 88, 89
Maiden Castle 40
Maiden Newton 5
Mais, S.P.B. 130
Major Strategic Night Decoy 106
Malmesbury Park 73
Manifould, W.K. 82
Manor, HMT 108
Manners, Lord 79

Mantle, Jack 26
March-Phillips, Gustavus 87, 94
Marden, Elizabeth A. 61
Marinet, biplane 111
Markowitz, Bert 131
Marlborough, Duke of 14
Marriot-Smith, Harry 16
Marrs, Eric 'Boy' 43, 54, 66, 67, 72, 86, 93
Martin, Arthur 143
Martin, Captain 90
Martinstown 10
Marx, Hans 58
Matthews, William 115
Medical Aid to Russia Fund 112
Medway Queen, PS 146
Meknes 31
Melbreak, HMS 126
Melcombe Regis 92, 146
Merkle, Lieut. 144
Merley House 124
Messerschmitt Bf-109 38, 41, 43, 74, 102, 172, 174
Messerschmitt Bf-110 56, 57, 58, 67
Messerschmitt-163 'Komet' 170
Messerschmitt-262 170
Michel, Schiff-28 102
Middlebere 58
Miller, Gertrude 36
Miller, Harold G. 186
Miller, G.R. 131
Miller, Michael 36
Miller, Mick 56, 57
Minterne Magna 12
Minimoa, glider 20
Mitchell, George 23
Mitchell, Reggie 94
Modavia 119
Model, Walter 175
Montgomery, Bernard 77, 113, 120, 138, 139, 142, 143, 181
Moore, Lieut. 172
Moore's Garage 72
Moreton 67
Morgan, William S. 61
Mosley, Sir Oswald 33
Mosquito, de Havilland 147, 179
Mountbatten, Louis 102, 119, 127
Mudeford 22, 119, 142, 172, 175
Mulberry Harbours 127, 139
Muller, F.H. 12
Muller, Paul 12
Murrow, Ed 12
Myers, Mrs 69

National Fire Service 93, 94, 149
Nechwatal, Karl 58
Neptune, Operation 157, 167
Neuralia 6
Newtown 73
Niebuhr, Arthur 58
Niven, David 94
Norden Heath 93
Norton, motorcycle 51, 52
Norman, John 38, 40
Normandy landings 147 to 170, 186
Nothe, The 44
Nowierski, Pilot Officer 38

Oakdale 50
Oborne 88
Observer Corps 16, 40, 41, 81, 86, 124, 179
Ohain, Hans von 12
Okeford Fitzpaine 75
Oldfield, Albert 176
Old Harry Rocks 77

Operations—
Adler Tag 38
Backfire 185
Biting 98 to 102
Cycle 18
Dynamo 18
Jubilee 109
Mallard (D-Day, air) 147, 167, 169
Masuren 108
Market Garden 174, 175
'Moonlight Sonata' 73
Neptune (D-Day, sea) 157, 167
Overlord (D-Day, land) 147 to 170
Pegasus (D-Day, airborne) 157 to 166
Primus 186
Rhein 108
Seelöwe/Sealion/Smith 23, 53
Stein 108

Osment, Harold 64
Osmington 99, 100, 101, 140
Ottlick, H. 88
Owermoigne 90
Oxford, Airspeed 81

Page, Andrew 87
Park, Victor 107
Parkstone 28, 50, 55, 74, 86, 91, 186
Parsons, Len 38
Patchin's Point 89
Pathfinders, flare aircraft 70, 106, 107, 118
Patton, George 4, 178
Patton, Lieut. 172
Paull, Robert 119
Pegasus, Operation 157 to 166
Pelton, HMT 79
Pennington Legh, Captain 176
Penylan, HMS 114
Peto, Sir Geoffrey 24
Petroleum Warfare Department 82, 140, 170
Pfannschmidt, Heinz 38
Phillips family 111
Piddlehinton 29
Piddletrenthide 10, 57, 111, 114, 115
Pitcher, Ernest 140, 142
Pitfield, Fred 2, 3, 92, 129
Pitfield, Harry 36
Pitfield, John 3, 170
Pitfield, Percival 36
Pitt-Rivers, George 33
Pittwood, Louis 107
Plover, HMS 146
Plush 10
Pluto, Project 140, 170
Pokesdown 13, 124
Polden, Kenneth 92
Poole [Port, town, flying-boat base, harbour, bay] 5, 8, 12, 13, 14, 18, 19, 20, 22, 23, 24, 25, 26, 27, 28, 33, 37, 38, 40, 45, 50, 55, 68, 72, 73, 74, 75, 81, 84, 86, 87, 91, 94, 106, 107, 108, 109, 111, 112, 115, 119, 120, 129, 133, 134, 139, 140, 142, 143, 145, 146, 154, 170, 174, 175, 186, 187
Portal, Sir Charles 122, 175

Portland [Dockyard, harbour, town, 'Bill' headland, sector of English Channel] 6, 9, 12, 13, 16, 18, 19, 26, 28, 31, 32, 34, 35, 38, 41, 42, 44, 45, 55, 58, 68, 79, 82, 102, 108, 112, 119, 131, 139, 142, 145, 151, 155, 171, 176, 182, 186
Portesham 13, 38
Portman, Gerald 74
Portesham 13, 38
Posner, Pilot Officer 31
Poundbury Camp 40, 41, 81, 179
Povington 130
Prien, Leutnant 10
Pride, E.W. 67
Prince, S.J. 117
Princess Juliana 18
Pringle, G.R. 117
Prinz Eugen 98, 99
Primus, Operation 186

Projects—
Fougasse 53, 76 to 79, 81, 82
Lily 140
Pluto 140, 170
Scam 128, 129, 136, 137, 138, 139, 140
Starfish 106

Prototype Research Unit 118
Puddletown 130, 149
Purewell 145
Puss Moth, de Havilland 82
Pytlak, T.W. 94

Queen Mary 185
Queripel, Lionel 179

Raby, Colonel 185
Radar/RDF [RDF=Radio Direction Finding, the original British term, but it has been usurped by the United States Navy's mnemonic, Radar=*Radio Direction And Range*] 13, 14, 20, 32, 43, 54, 58, 72, 79, 82, 84, 85, 86, 90, 93, 96, 89, 102, 103, 106, 108, 118, 119, 126, 139, 167
Randall, J.T. 118
Read, E.G. 38
Reason, A.H. 61
Recoil, HMT 58
Redend Point 77, 79, 143
Red House Garage 134
Reisner, R.M. 123
Reith, Lord 8
Renscombe 14, 20
Reserve Fleet 6, 157
Richard Britzen 81
Richeter, Gerhard 58
Ricketts, Stanley 68
Ringstead Bay 100
Ripper, Jack the 53
Ringwood 68, 89, 94, 133
Ritz Theatre 156, 157
Robert T. Hillary 119
Rockets 3, 4, 126, 128, 129, 138, 140, 147, 170, 175, 176, 185
Rocklea 84, 107
Rodney, HMS 157
Roger Robert 23
Rogers, J.C. Kelly 37
Rohl, Karl 89
Rommel, Erwin 113
Rosa Arthur 23
Roosevelt, Franklin D. 12, 93, 99, 185
Rössiger, Wilhelm 58
Rotherham, —37
Round Island 112
Rowe, A.P. 126

Royal Air Force—Groups:
10 Group, Fighter Command [see also 'Warmwell' and 'Spitfire' entries] 19, 54, 72, 96, 126, 192
19 Group, Coastal Command 24, 84, 106, 111, 112, 120, 124, 133, 171
Squadrons:
30 94
57 167
58 117
87 41
109 20
119 13, 86
143 170
170 96
152 27, 28, 31, 38, 42, 43, 50, 52, 56, 58, 66, 67, 72, 74, 75, 84, 86, 93, 181
196 129
201 84
210 124
217 8
234 42, 82, 95
236 170
238 55
257 117
263 124, 139
275 142
296 96
297 96
298 129, 130
461 109, 120
504 56
604 82, 90
609 27, 28, 31, 38, 54, 56, 57, 66, 67, 77, 82
617 122
644 130
765 24
790 108, 112
887 108
891 108, 109, 111
893 111
1425 93, 96

Royal Artillery [see 'British Army' for Battery listings] 5, 21, 22, 29, 34, 35, 70, 84, 87, 93, 178, 185
Royal Blue Coaches 84, 112
Royal Engineers 33, 86, 90, 175

Royal Navy [Ships are listed individually: HMS=His Majesty's Ship. HMT=His Majesty's Trawler. Mine Laying and Motor Torpedo Boat flotillas are listed on page 146. Most of the 'Portland' entries concern naval activity, as do many of those for 'Lyme Bay' and 'St Alban's Head', and some for 'Poole'. The Royal Naval Cordite Factory has its own entry, see 'Holton Heath'. So too do the Royal Naval Air Stations—Charlton Horethorne, Henstridge and Sandbanks—and shore-base HMS Turtle. There is also an entry for the 'Reserve Fleet'.]

Royal Oak, HMS 10
Royal Observer Corps [see also 'Observer Corps'—their original name] 120

Rubel, Lieut. 172
Russell family 111
Ryde, PS 146

St Alban's Head 19, 20, 82, 120, 140, 172
St Bride's Farm 10, 50
St Catherine's Hill 50
St Leonards General Hospital 133
St Mary's Convent 174
Salterns Pier 8, 88
Salter's Wood 58
Sandbanks 24, 25, 26, 29, 45, 129
Sandbanks Royal Naval Air Station [Royal Navy Seaplane School] 24, 129
Sandecotes School 186
Sandown, PS 146
San Remo Towers 13
Saracen, HMS 126
Sare's Wood 129
Savage, Billy 10
Scam Projects 128, 129, 136, 137, 138, 140
Scharnhorst 98, 99
Scheuringer, Karl 89
Schmidt, Gerhard 58
Schön, Anton 58
Schupp, Fritz 58
Scott, W.F. 133
Seeadler 81, 102, 106
Sea Hurricane 108, 109, 111
Seafox, floatplane 24
Sealion, Operation 23, 53
Seatown 21
Shaftesbury 6, 58, 69, 90, 113, 174
Shaftesbury, Earl of 90, 108
Sharp, Richard 144
Shell Bay 26, 119
Sherborne 6, 58 to 66, 69, 88, 93, 106, 113, 120, 121
Sherlock, Sir John 90
Sherman, tank 139, 167, 175
Sherwood family 73
Shute Norway, Nevil 129
Sikorsky, Igor 12
Signals Research and Development Establishment 185
Sigwells Farm 106, 176
Singapore, Short 8
Skinner, Denis 36
Skylarks 18
Small Mouth 44
Small Scale Raiding Force 87, 126
Smiling Through 19
Smith, Bedell 174
Smith, D.J. 122
Smith, Graham 139
Smith, Hugh 106
Smith, Private 173
Sneaton, 10
Society of Dorset Men 129
Somerford 8, 58, 79, 88, 89, 97, 145
Sona, HMS 107
Sopley RAF Radar 79, 82, 90, 96, 127
South E,gardon Farm 126
Southern Command 29, 33, 68
Southern Queen 18
Special Countermeasures Unit 20

Special Operations Executive 116
Spilsbury, Sir Bernard 114
Spitfire, Supermarine 2, 3, 27, 28, 29, 31, 38, 40, 41, 42, 43, 53, 54, 56, 57, 58, 66, 67, 72, 74, 75, 82, 84, 86, 93, 94, 95, 118, 125, 140, 179
Stainforth, George 113
Stalbridge 183
Stanpit 125, 145
'Starshells' 138
Steamer Point 19, 185
Steele, Maud 61
Steinbrinck, Erich 68
Stephens, V.F. 176
Stepleton House 185
Stevenson, Irene 172
Stevenson, R.L. 73
Stewart, Wing Commander 16
Stickland, Louis Aubrey 111, 114, 115
Stirling, Short 129
Stainer Family 72
Strang, Jock 36
Strathnaver 126
Stratton 38
Street, A.G. 130
Stuart, tank 137
Stuber, George H. 182
Studland [1940–41, anti-invasion efforts/1943–44, Assault Training Beach] 19, 26, 33, 55, 76, 77, 78, 79, 82, 119, 130, 135, 143
'Stukas' 26, 27, 28, 31, 32, 38, 42, 43
Summers, Mutt 94
Sunderland, Short ['Empire' flying boats] 8, 13, 15, 24, 28, 37, 40, 84, 88, 89, 98, 111, 187
Support Squadron Eastern Flank 178
Swain, A.E. 130
Swash Channel 18, 19, 23, 125
Swanage 22, 27, 72, 89, 91, 115, 140, 167
Swatridge, Victor 167, 179, 180
Swordfish, Fairey ['Stringbag'] 24, 99, 105, 140

Tarrant Gunville 58
Tarrant Monkton 162
Tarrant Rushton Aerodrome 117, 129, 130, 157 to 166, 174, 178, 180
Tedder, Sir Arthur 131
Telecommunications Research Establishment 14, 20, 79, 82, 85, 93, 97, 99, 102, 103, 106, 118, 126
Temple, Lieut. 144
Tetrarch, tank 157, 159
Thacker, Lieut. 144
Thomas, P.S. 122
Thornicombe 75
Thrifty, HMS19
Thunderbolt, Republic P-47 147, 172
Tibbets, Paul 113, 184
Topham, C. 183
Torrington, Private 184
Training Bank 18
Trask, Barry A. 61
Treadwell, Coastguard 176
Trito, SS 55
Turner, Serjeant 173
Turners Puddle 109
Turtle, HMS, shore base 112, 174, 178
Tynedale, HMS 112

Tyneham 58, 130
Tyneham Cap 72
Type-15, radar 79, 82, 90, 96
Typhoon, Hawker-Siddeley 147

U-boat surrenderings 182
Uplands School 186
Upton [Poole] 24, 86
Upton Fort [Osmington] 35, 140
Urania, HMS 167
Urdine, HMS 167

United States Army [only specific references to numbered units have been included; they are in numerical order]
1st Army 148 to 156, 167, 169, 171
1st Division
3rd Army 178
3rd Armored Division 171
Vth Corps 148 to 156, 167, 169, 171, 184
7th Base Section 144
14th Major Port, Transportation Corps 154, 186
22nd General Hospital 178, 180, 185
29th Division 169
23rd Armored Engineer Battalion 171
32nd Armored Regiment 171
33rd Armored Regiment 171
36th Armored Infantry Regiment 171
54th Armored Field Artillery Battery 171
67th Armored Field Artillery Battery 171
125th General Hospital 180
131st General Hospital 180
140th General Hospital 180
184th Auxiliary Anti-Aircraft Gun Battery 130, 140
391st Armored Field Artillery Regiment 171
430th Squadron, US Army Air Force 171
405th Fighter Group, US Army Air Force 172
474th Fighter Group, US Army Air Force 139, 140, 143, 147, 169, 171, 172, 174
486th Armored Anti-Aircraft Battalion

Usas, Lieut. 145

Valentine, tank 110, 138, 139
VE Day 4, 181, 184
Victory, film 130
Vinson, Lieut. 171
Virac Lart, Edward Collis de 85
VJ Day 183
Vonham, Mrs 130
V1, rocket 176
Vortigern, HMS 102
V2, rocket 4, 175, 176, 185

Wakefield, Kenneth 56, 58
Wakeling, S.R.E. 31
Walker, Ron 167
Walkford 127
Walkling, A.E. 105
Waller, General 66
Wallis, Barnes 122
Walpole, HMS 102
Walrus, Supermarine 24, 142
Warburton-Lee, Captain 13
Wareham 8, 10, 16, 74, 85, 107

Wareham and Purbeck Civil Defence Corps 36
Warmwell Aerodrome 2, 3, 8, 27, 28, 29, 31, 38, 40, 41, 42, 43, 44, 50, 53, 54, 56, 57, 58, 66, 72, 74, 75, 82, 93, 95, 117, 124, 133, 139, 140, 141, 412, 143, 144, 145, 169, 171, 172, 174, 179, 181, 183
Warren family 61, 64
Warrior II 28
Waters, Elsie and Doris 6
Watson, A.R. 74
Watson-Watt, Robert 126
Watts, Annie 111
Waugh, Evelyn 119
Wavell, Sir Archibald 94, 129
Wellington, Vickers-Armstrongs 111, 122
Wensleydale, HMS 133
Wesley, John 89
West Bay 70
West Howe 3, 118
Westland Aircraft Co 66, 67
Weymouth [Port, town, harbour and bay] 6, 7, 9, 10, 16, 18, 19, 26, 31, 35, 38, 44, 73, 88, 93, 100, 103, 104, 105, 109, 113, 136, 137, 139, 140, 146, 148 to 157, 176, 182, 186
Weymouth College 113
Weymouth Grammar School 105
Wheatley, M. 183
Whipingham, PS 146
Whirlwind, Westland 66, 124
Wilcockson, G.R.B. 37
Wightman, Ralph 57
Williams, Herbert 84
Wills, Philip 20
Wilson, Eric 4, 68, 69
Wiltshire, Lance Corp. 173
Wimborne 89, 112, 117, 124, 130
Wimborne St. Giles 90
Winant, Gil 184, 185
'Window', radar counter-measure 126, 127
Winkton Advance Landing Ground 127
Windust, Norman 105
Winton 82, 85
Whistler, Laurence 67
Whitehead Torpedo Works 44
White, Geoffrey 186
Whitley, Armstrong Whitworth 102, 119, 164, 165
White, — 37
Whitehead, A.N. 93
Whitshead, HMS 143
Whittington, C.R. 168
Wolton, Ralph 'Bob' 31, 42, 53, 56
Women's Voluntary Service 114, 120, 121
Wool 29
Worbarrow 130, 139, 179
Worgret 85
Worth Matravers 14, 20, 79, 82, 93, 97, 99, 102, 103, 106, 118, 126
Wren, HMS 32
Würzburg, radar 98, 102
Wyke Regis 5, 131, 176

X-Gerät, radio beam 72

Y-beams, radio 68
Yi, M.H. 117

Zwick, Werner 58

Dorset military books consulted.

Derek Beamish, Harold Bennett and John Hillier, *Poole and World War II*, 1980.

Lieutenant Colonel A.E.C. Bredin, *Three Assault Landings: the story of the 1st Battalion the Dorsetshire Regiment in Sicily, Italy, and N.W. Europe.* 1946.

Leslie Dawson, *Wings Over Dorset: Aviation's story in the South*, 1983, 9 pages of which were by the present author and copyrighted by him on its credit page, along with the captions — a fresh look at the original shows that pages 92–93 were also mine and some material from them is also incorporated here.

HMS Dorsetshire Replacement Committee. *Action Stations!* 1942.

Alan Harfield, *Blandford and the Military*. 1985.

Michael A. Hodges, *Prepared for Battle: some details of forts in and near Christchurch over the past millenia.* 1982.

Garry Johnson and Christopher Dunphie, *Brightly Shone the Dawn: Some Experiences of the Invasion of Normandy.* 1980.

Ivan Mason, *The Spitfires of Warmwell* (Dorset County Magazine issue 71) 1979, and *The Yanks at Warmwell* (in issue 112) 1985.

John Murphy, *Dorset at War,* 1979, which incorporated additional material and picture research by the present author; some of this is reused here.

Major G.R. Pack and Major M.A. Edwards, *The Story of the 5th Battalion the Dorsetshire Regiment in North-West Europe.* 1945.

Kenneth Wakefield, *Luftwaffe Encore*, 1979.

Lieutenant Colonel O.G.W. White DSO, *Straight on for Tokyo: the War History of the 2nd Battalion the Dorsetshire Regiment, 1939–48,* 1948.

April 1944. Opposite.
Exercise Fabious,
the major dummy run for D-Day.

The Union Jack would be taken across the Channel, but first it was raised on Slapton Sands.

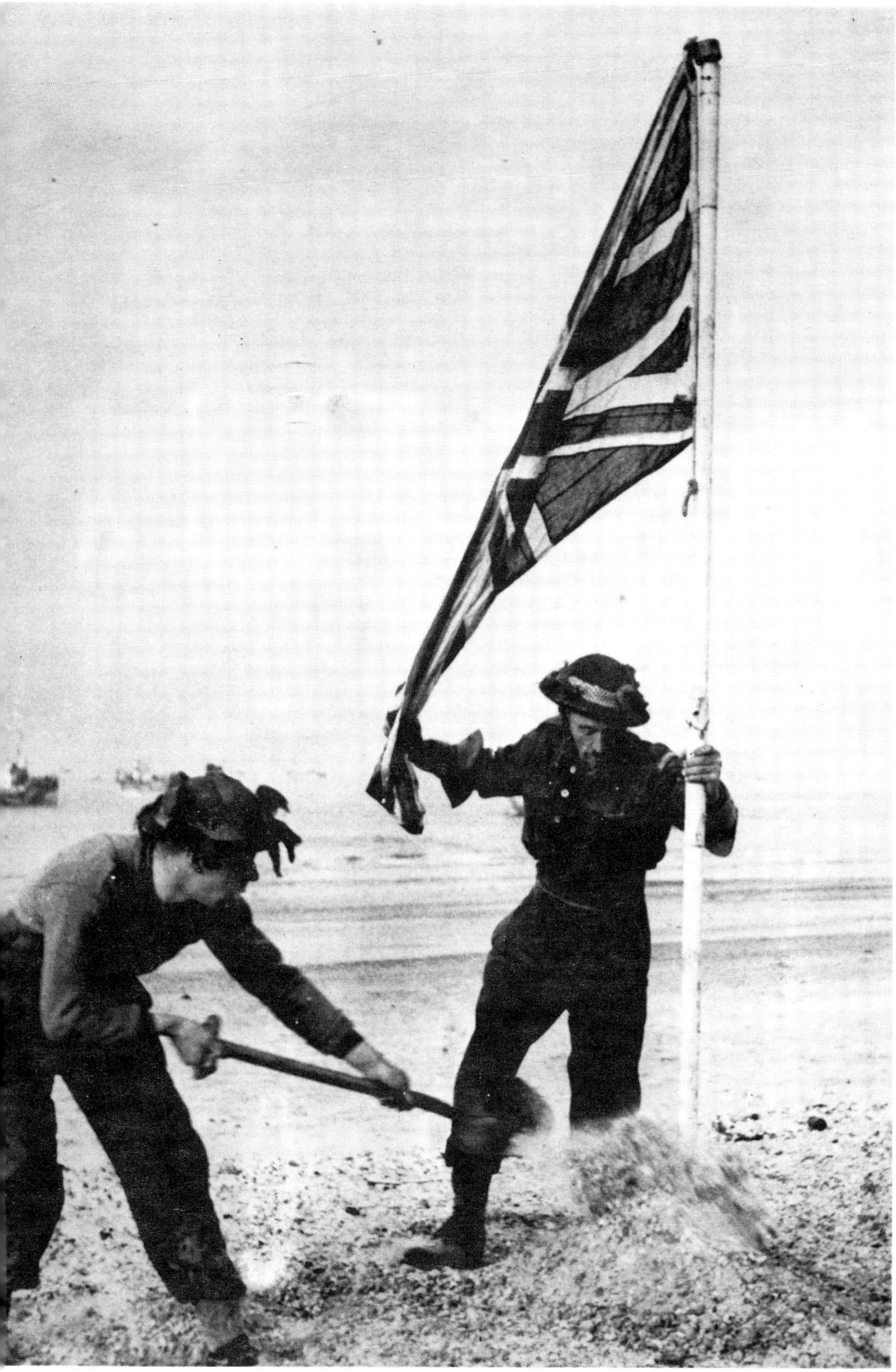

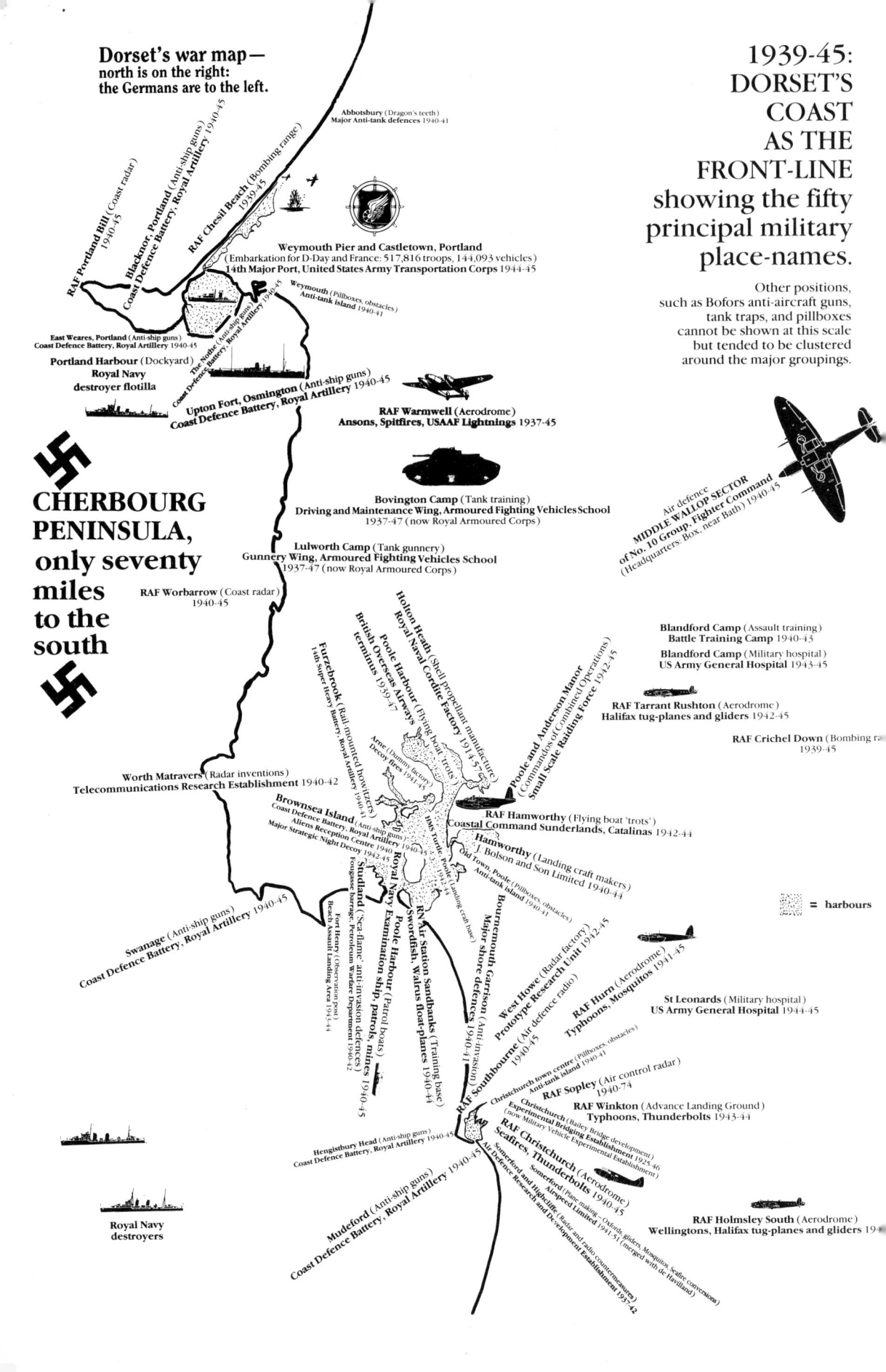

Dorset's war map—
north is on the right:
the Germans are to the left.

1939-45: DORSET'S COAST AS THE FRONT-LINE
showing the fifty principal military place-names.

Other positions, such as Bofors anti-aircraft guns, tank traps, and pillboxes cannot be shown at this scale but tended to be clustered around the major groupings.

Abbotsbury (Dragon's teeth)
Major Anti-tank defences 1940-41

RAF Portland Bill (Coast radar) 1940-45

Blacknor, Portland (Anti-ship guns)
Coast Defence Battery, Royal Artillery 1940-45

RAF Chesil Beach (Bombing range) 1939-45

Weymouth Pier and Castletown, Portland
(Embarkation for D-Day and France: 517,816 troops, 144,093 vehicles)
14th Major Port, United States Army Transportation Corps 1944-45

Weymouth (Pillboxes, obstacles)
Anti-tank island 1940-41

The Nothe (Anti-ship guns)
Coast Defence Battery, Royal Artillery 1940-45

East Weares, Portland (Anti-ship guns)
Coast Defence Battery, Royal Artillery 1940-45

Portland Harbour (Dockyard)
Royal Navy destroyer flotilla

Upton Fort, Osmington (Anti-ship guns)
Coast Defence Battery, Royal Artillery 1940-45

RAF Warmwell (Aerodrome)
Ansons, Spitfires, USAAF Lightnings 1937-45

CHERBOURG PENINSULA, only seventy miles to the south

Bovington Camp (Tank training)
Driving and Maintenance Wing, Armoured Fighting Vehicles School
1937-47 (now Royal Armoured Corps)

Lulworth Camp (Tank gunnery)
Gunnery Wing, Armoured Fighting Vehicles School
1937-47 (now Royal Armoured Corps)

RAF Worbarrow (Coast radar) 1940-45

Air defence **MIDDLE WALLOP SECTOR**
of No. 10 Group, Fighter Command
(Headquarters: Box, near Bath) 1940-45

Holton Heath (Shell propellant manufacture)
Royal Naval Cordite Factory 1914-57

Poole Harbour (Flying boat 'trots')
British Overseas Airways terminus 1939-47

Furzebrook (Rail mounted howitzers)
14th Super Heavy Battery, Royal Artillery 1940-4

Arne (Dummy factory) Decoy fires 1941-44

Poole and Anderson Manor
(Commandos of Combined Operations)
Small Scale Raiding Force 1942-45

Blandford Camp (Assault training)
Battle Training Camp 1940-43

Blandford Camp (Military hospital)
US Army General Hospital 1943-45

RAF Tarrant Rushton (Aerodrome)
Halifax tug-planes and gliders 1942-45

RAF Crichel Down (Bombing ra 1939-45

Worth Matravers (Radar inventions)
Telecommunications Research Establishment 1940-42

Brownsea Island (Anti-ship guns)
Coast Defence Battery, Royal Artillery 1940-4
Aliens Reception Centre 1940
Major Strategic Night Decoy 1942-45

HMS Turtle, Poole (Landing craft base)

RAF Hamworthy (Flying boat 'trots')
Coastal Command Sunderlands, Catalinas 1942-44

Hamworthy (Landing craft makers)
Old Town, Poole
J. Bolson and Son Limited 1940-44
Anti-tank Island 1940-41

= harbours

Studland ('Sea-flame' anti-invasion defences)
Fort Henry (Observation post)
Fougasse barrage, Petroleum Warfare Department 1940-42
Beach Assault Landing Area 1943-44

Swanage (Anti-ship guns)
Coast Defence Battery, Royal Artillery 1940-45

RN Air Station Sandbanks (Training base)
Swordfish, Walrus float-planes 1940-44

Poole Harbour (Patrol boats) 1940-45

West Howe (Radar factory)
Prototype Research Unit 1942-45

Southbourne (Air defence radio) 1940-45

Bournemouth Garrison (Anti-invasion)
Major shore defences 1940-45

RAF Hurn (Aerodrome)
Typhoons, Mosquitos 1941-45

St Leonards (Military hospital)
US Army General Hospital 1944-45

Christchurch town centre (Pillboxes, obstacles)
Anti-tank island 1940-41

RAF Sopley (Air control radar) 1940-74

Christchurch (Bailey Bridge development)
Experimental Bridging Establishment 1925-46
(now Military Vehicle Experimental Establishment)

RAF Winkton (Advance Landing Ground)
Typhoons, Thunderbolts 1943-44

Hengistbury Head (Anti-ship guns)
Coast Defence Battery, Royal Artillery 1940-45

RAF Christchurch (Aerodrome)
Seafires, Thunderbolts 1940-45

Somerford and Highcliffe (Plane making – Oxfords, gliders, Mosquitos, Seafire conversions)
Airspeed Limited 1941-51 (merged with de Havilland)

Mudeford (Anti-ship guns)
Coast Defence Battery, Royal Artillery 1940-45

Somerford (Radar and radio countermeasures)
Radar Research and Development Establishment 1937-42

RAF Holmsley South (Aerodrome)
Wellingtons, Halifax tug-planes and gliders 194

Royal Navy destroyers